Other books by
Dorothy H. Jenkins

Fortune in the Junkpile

with Edith Gaines
The Woman's Day Dictionary of Antique Furniture

The Woman's Day
Book of Antique Collectibles

by Dorothy H. Jenkins

The Main Street Press

The Main Street Press

Distributed by St. Martin's Press, Inc.

First Edition, 1981

Produced by The Main Street Press
William Case House
Pittstown, New Jersey 08867

Distributed by St. Martin's Press
175 Fifth Avenue
New York, New York 10010

Library of Congress Cataloging in Publication Data

Jenkins, Dorothy Helen.

The Woman's Day Book of Antique Collectibles
   1. Antiques. I. Title. II. Title: Book of antique collectibles.

NK1125.J43   745.1   80-28068
ISBN 0-312-88647-0

Printed in the United States of America

Contents

Introduction

Collecting today is a highly competitive business. Many collectors and dealers find themselves locked in an ever-escalating battle of prices and availability. As recently as ten years ago lacy Sandwich cup plates could be purchased for as little as $1. Produced in enormous quantities in the first half of the 19th century, these pieces of pressed glass cannot be found quite so easily today, and when located may bring anywhere from $15 to $50, depending on the pattern. What is true of these once-common Sandwich objects holds true for hundreds of other kinds of antiques or collectibles. As inflation has eaten away more and more of the value of the dollar, wise investors have turned to the security of the fine and decorative arts.

The collector, beginning or advanced, has every good reason to explore the antiques market with considerable care. While the pleasure of collecting beautiful objects should serve to guide one's progress, the collector must be armed against fakes and artificially inflated prices with the best possible advance information. Price guides are often useful indicators of value but quite uninformative when it comes to such essential facts as condition or rarity. Frequently the prices are based only on auction figures which reflect nothing more than the presence or mood of an assorted group of buyers on a particular day. A sensible range of prices for an antique object is not hard to come by. A few conversations with different dealers will produce this basic information.

Equally as important to the collector is learning how to identify an object and to determine its intrinsic value. Who made it and how? Where was it made and when? How many of such pieces were produced? *The Woman's Day Book of Antique Collectibles* is designed to answer these questions as well as others in thirty-seven chapters devoted to a wide variety of decorative and useful objects. Some are classic "antiques," that is they were made before the beginning of the Industrial Revolution in America in the 1840s; other pieces were produced in mid- to late-19th-century factories in England and America and are commonly thought of as being "antique" today; a few categories of objects such as carnival glass can be called only "collectible" as they are 20th-century commercial wares. In nearly every chapter, however, a wide range of objects made from the 18th century to the early 1900s is discussed. All of them are small in size. This does not make them necessarily any less valuable; portability and minimum space requirements for display in the home are important considerations for most collectors.

One long-range aim of the true collector is to gather as much information about the production of particular kinds of objects as possible. Reprints of manufacturers' catalogs may be helpful in this respect. Also useful are specialized volumes in which a scholar spreads out before the reader every detail of a form's historical development. In many respects, a museum exhibition may provide the same sort of perspective and basic information. Well-illustrated auction catalogs will sometimes give the collector further information on obscure kinds of pieces as well as a current feeling for the marketplace.

There is no substitute, however, for frequenting the real "schoolhouse" of antique collecting—the shop. There are thousands of such places in North America, and some communities are well-known for the wide variety of shops specializing in various antique objects. "Antiquing"—whether on the weekend or weekday—can be a very enjoyable and profitable exercise. Browsers are welcome almost everywhere and in the pleasant interchange of common interests one's store of useful knowledge can be greatly increased.

Many books on antiques include only examples from museum collections. The illustrations chosen for *The Woman's Day Book of Antique Collectibles* are drawn for the most part from shops or private collections. While some of the objects may in fact belong in a museum, they and the less exceptional pieces shown are representative of the sort to be found today in the marketplace. Few are one-of-a-kind. They are the type of simple decorative object, made to last, that were wrought for pleasure at a time when a work was judged as much by its aesthetic qualities as its commercial appeal.

Special thanks are owed to Val Tyler of the Frenchtown (New Jersey) House of Antiques for assisting with the photography for this book. Photographed in color at his shop, illustrated on the jacket and on p. 33, are the lusterware shown on p. 102, the Staffordshire blue and white china on p. 103, the lighting devices on p. 169, and the clocks illustrated on p. 207. Many of the objects shown in black and white are also from Mr. Tyler's collection.

Other color illustration credits are: Durand opaque art glass, p. 36, New Jersey State Museum, Joseph Crilley, photographer; china-head dolls, p. 101, Raggedy Ann Antique Doll and Toy Museum, Flemington, New Jersey; Wedgwood teapots, p. 104, Buten Museum of Wedgwood, Merion, Pennsylvania; calendar clock, p. 206, National Association of Watch and Clock Collectors Museum, Columbia, Pennsylvania. The remaining objects shown in color are from private collections.

Responsible for all black and white and color photography, unless otherwise noted above, is J. Michael Kanouff, staff photographer, The Main Street Press.

Sources for the black and white illustrations are, in addition to those previously listed for color: Nancy P. Olsson Antiques, Durham, Pennsylvania; The Tomato Factory, Hopewell, New Jersey; The Eagle's Nest, The Farmhouse, King's Row Antiques, and The Warehouse—all Mullica Hill, New Jersey; Virginia Kay's Antiques, Blawenburg, New Jersey; Auld Lang Syne Antiques, Moorestown, New Jersey; and *The Magazine Antiques*, for almost sixty years the serious collector's *vade mecum*.

1. China Figures and Groups

Just as children find a puddle an invitation to make mud pies, so potters seem never to have been able to resist turning out all kinds of figures. Almost every porcelain factory and innumerable potteries have displayed their skill at producing figures, figurines, and groups based on animals, birds, and people. Porcelain as well as pottery, chiefly various kinds of earthenwares and stonewares, contributed to the lavish output that made the eighteenth and nineteenth centuries so important in this field in both Europe and England. "Porcelain sculpture" was an eighteenth century term in Europe,

but was not accurate because a sculpture is carved and porcelain or pottery figures are molded or modeled, in several parts if the group is complicated.

Probably potters always had molded and shaped small animals and other figures from clay. The most spectacular advance was made after western potters discovered how to make porcelain. The porcelain brought in the 1600's from China to Europe was the first ever seen there and was admired greatly for its translucent beauty and clarity of color. It was not until about 1708 that Johann Friedrich Böttger in Dresden, Germany, succeeded in pro-

ducing a true hard-paste porcelain. Porcelain, whether hard paste or soft paste, is hard, white, vitreous, thin, lightweight and, when held up to the light, translucent. It is almost impossible offhand to tell a piece of hard-paste porcelain from a soft-paste one.

Not long after Johann Böttger had discovered how to make porcelain, Augustus the Strong, the ruler of Saxony, where Dresden and the Meissen pottery were located, purchased a palace, which he planned to convert into a showplace for porcelains. In charge of the work was Johann Joachim Kändler, who was appointed Modellmeister of the

Staffordshire bear in green, brown, and yellow glazes, 18th century.

Meissen factory in 1731. By 1732, Kändler had produced the notable "Goat and Suckling Kid," which is now in the Metropolitan Museum of Art in New York City. This porcelain "sculpture," 19⅜" high and 25½" long, is a masterful and exceptionally charming study of two marvelously realistic animals. But pieces as large as this were expensive and troublesome to make, so Kändler soon turned to smaller figures.

During his long and successful career, Kändler produced a versatile array of figures. For inspiration he drew not only on the court for figures of ladies in crinolines, of gallants and cavaliers in knee breeches and long coats, but also on everyday figures such as cobblers and carpenters, shepherds and huntsmen.

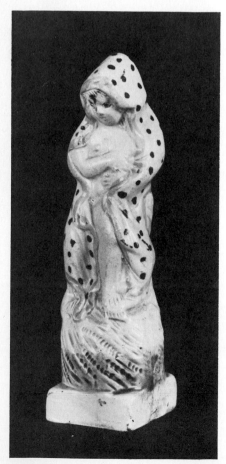

Pratt-type figure in green, yellow, and blue glazes, late 18th century, English.

Other ideas were based on the seasons and the months, mythological and allegorical characters. Although the Chinese influence in coloring and decoration was perhaps more pronounced in tableware, chinoiserie pieces were popular during the eighteenth century. Since chinoiserie is a European interpretation of Chinese style or decoration, many figures such as one group of people made at Höchst, Germany, is not quite Oriental-looking in spite of dress and architecture.

Elsewhere in Europe and England, potters followed the lead of Kändler, the great porcelain modeler. Germany and Austria became famous for hard-paste porcelain figures and groups, while notable soft-paste ones came from Chantilly and Sèvres in France; Chelsea, Plymouth, Bow and Derby in England. Porcelain figures and groups were skillfully glazed and colored.

A French innovation about 1769 were figures of biscuit, or bisque, a type of porcelain that was fired but unglazed and had been developed earlier in the century. Soon other countries were using biscuit for individual figures, such as a boy and a girl, each carrying a basket of leafy vegetables, and groups of two or more figures, such as a nurse with a baby in her arms and a youngster at her knees. Portrait busts of outstanding musicians and other personages were also made of biscuit. Biscuit can be either soft paste, which tends to have a creamy tone, or hard paste, which is likely to be whiter. During some periods biscuit figures were tinted appropriately with soft colors.

Pottery figures on the whole are less sophisticated than porcelain ones, but they are just as diverse and just as colorful. Because the various earthenware and stoneware figures produced in the Staffordshire District of England are so abundant as to be a story in themselves is no reason for not acknowledging the faience ones of France, delft of Holland and majolica of Italy. A zoo of smaller, more playful pottery animals would be more manageable than the magnificent porcelain ones. In the Staffordshire District horses and cows, dogs and sheep, bears and stags, lions and tigers, elephants and zebras and occasionally a camel were turned out by the thousands.

Cats, oddly enough, seem to have been made in lesser numbers than most other animals in Staffordshire, yet cats have been made in pottery typical of each country from ancient Persia to eighteenth-century France (one of the latter was white faience with green glass eyes). Although a variety of cats ranging from an old redware one covered with black glaze to a striped agateware one with a white face came from Staffordshire, they are hard to find now.

Most widely known of all Staffordshire animals are dogs and best loved are the pairs of dogs, made so that one faces right, the other left. Sometimes one of the pair is a female, who can be distinguished from her mate by the fact that she is slightly smaller in overall dimensions and has more details delineated on her face. Spaniels, poodles and, probably in the 1890's, pug dogs were molded realistically so that their fur ripples and their tails curl as they should and gold collars and chains can be seen. Some of these dogs hold baskets in their mouths. On spaniels the glaze

Bird whistle, Whieldon-type, green, tortoise, and yellow glazes, 18th century.

provides a cream or white body properly spotted with black, brown, russet or another tawny or red shade. For a time during the 1800's, spaniels had colored spots of gleaming luster. The finest of these pairs have glass eyes, glued in place, but by no means all of the spaniels do, particularly in the smaller sizes. The smallest spaniel I have seen is 3½" high; it is one of a miscellaneous group, each one different and ranging to 13" high, arranged along a friend's mantelpiece. The largest pair, 12½" and 13", stand on either side of the fireplace. Pairs of poodles sometimes were clipped, their upper halves covered with rough textured pottery granules described as coleslaw.

Staffordshire spaniels vary little in their expressions, whereas other breeds of dog, cats and other animals show more individuality in expression and pose. This is evident in smaller, single figures of such sporting and working dogs as whippets, greyhounds, setters, foxhounds, staghounds, springers, pointers and occasionally a Dalmatian standing, sitting or lying with crossed paws. A more active pose shows a whippet or greyhound carrying a dead hare.

Lions were another popular figure, some of them shown quite realistically, others being more stylized. They were also made in lesser quantity at potteries in Bennington, Vermont, starting about 1850. At first glance, a lion made in the United States and one made in England look much alike. Bennington lions usually were given a flint enamel glaze, which was brown with flecks and streaks of blue, green, yellow and orange. At Bennington, lions, poodles, and does and stags were made to face each other. Deer and poodles were either flint enamel or Rockingham, the mottled buff-and-brown glaze. Bennington poodles stood erect and usually held baskets in their mouths. Many of these standing poodles, an exclusive Bennington pose, have mustaches and topknots. Other Bennington animals including cows, sheep and horses in several poses, as well as birds, were made of Parian.

Parian is the nineteenth-century version of biscuit. This unglazed white porcelain was called Parian because it was considered to be as white as the marble quarried from the island of Paros and carved by Greek sculptors. Parian was developed and introduced by Copeland in England in 1846 and soon was being made throughout the Staffordshire District there and also in the United States. Parian statuettes and busts of children, young women with baskets of flowers, boys with baskets of eggs, and classical figures tend to be sentimental and rather undistinguished.

Other types of pottery figures from Staffordshire proved immensely popular at home and abroad. Many pottery figures, groups and pairs are charming or amusing, and some are rather gruesome. Probably the greatest years were from about 1750 to the early 1800's, when the Wood family were active in Burslem. From them and other potters poured figures and groups to please every taste. If little musicians, each about 6″ high and playing a different instrument, didn't appeal, there were sporting figures of boxing champions, cricket stars, or a couple preparing their cocks for fighting.

The potters capitalized on murders that aroused England, sometimes making two or three relevant pieces: the house where the murder occurred, the two or three people involved, and even the building where the murderer was hanged.

During the Victorian years, England's royal family was a never-ending source of figures. Queen Victoria and Prince Albert were shown in formal and informal poses, with and without one or more of their children at various ages. Small portrait figures in full color ranged from heroines such as Florence Nightingale and heroes such as Nelson and Garibaldi to actors and writers, from religious figures to rogues such as the highwayman

Staffordshire dog, 1860-90, one of a pair.

Dick Turpin shown leaning against his horse. Of course, there were anonymous soldiers resplendent in their uniforms, fortunetellers, figures representing the season—you name it, Staffordshire potters made it! Very different from this immensely popular earthenware but also coming from the Staffordshire District were the figures of animals and birds that Wedgwood made first from black basalt, later from jasperware that combined white and a pastel color.

Anything as popular as the pottery and porcelain figures of the eighteenth and nineteenth centuries was bound to be imitated. Best known of these imitations are the colored but unglazed plaster ornaments called chalkware, used chiefly as ornaments on the mantel. Chalkware figures were being peddled in cities in the early 1800's, but most of the ones found nowadays are believed to have been made between 1850 and 1890 either in this country or abroad. The Pennsylvania Dutch region has been a good hunting ground. Chalkware animals, birds, fruit, figures and occasionally a building were made of plaster shaped in molds.

The early ones were sized, and colored with oil paints; later ones were not sized and were colored with water paints. The colors, which probably were harsh when first applied, have faded through the years to soft, attractive tints. One fruit plaque, quite stylized, is now soft red, yellow, green and black. Since coloring was done by hand, the two pieces that made up a pair didn't always match exactly. Chalkware is porous, so it is a mistake to try to touch up faded colors because they cannot be matched and may run and bleed. Some of the chalkware animals

such as a perky spotted cat or a squirrel with a nut were almost life-size.

From the East Coast to the Pacific Ocean between the 1860's and about 1915, a home could hardly be considered complete unless it had a Rogers group, which was an American contribution to parlor ornament. John Rogers, who was born in Salem, Massachusetts, in 1829, studied sculpture in Europe but became discouraged and returned home. His first group, "The Checker Players," was produced in 1859 and was so well received that it started him on a new career. The originals of Rogers groups were not sold; the reproductions, produced in great quantity, were made of plaster of Paris and painted a sort of mud color. Between 1859 and 1893, Rogers created some eighty to a hundred different groups. One of the largest was "Council of War," which depicted President Lin-

coln, General Grant and Secretary of War Edwin M. Stanton. Many Rogers groups were based on legends or sentimental subjects: "John Alden and Priscilla," for example, and "First Love," which showed a boy and girl with arms entwined. Rogers groups are well modeled and tell a story in each piece, although they are more likely to be classed as folk art than as great sculpture in the future.

From Kändler's "Goat and Suckling Kid" to Staffordshire's "Red Barn" where murder occurred and Rogers' "The Country Post Office," figures and groups were made primarily for ornament and decoration. Relatively few served a purpose.

The bell woman, however, a rather primitive figure of salt-glazed stoneware made in Staffordshire in the mid-1700's, concealed a clapper under her flaring skirt. This was quite popular for a time. Throughout the eighteenth

Staffordshire greyhound or whippet, pen holder, c. 1850

"Huntsman," Staffordshire, c. 1855.

and nineteenth centuries, some china figures were made with slots so they could be used as banks; one really old one is an owl about 6″ high from the Whieldon pottery. Both Staffordshire and Bennington produced dogs sitting or reclining on cushions that could be used as paperweights. Another Bennington paperweight featured a lion, and an inkwell for two pots of ink was graced by a reclining dog. Candlesticks, usually quite old, were as simple as a pottery dog with a socket fixed to his back or elaborate porcelain figures so laden with flowers as to practically hide the sockets.

Potter's marks seem to be scarcer on figures than on tableware of comparable quality and age. I have owned and handled any number of Staffordshire dogs and have never found one with a potter's mark. Meissen products, on the other hand, always bear their crossed-swords mark. A number on the base is no aid to identification. Reproductions, unfortunately for the collector, exist in porcelain, earthenware and even chalkware. It often is claimed that reproductions are made from molds a century or more old, but this does not guarantee that the pottery or the coloring is the same as on the original. An expert in either porcelain or pottery is guided by coloring, glaze, character of the body, modeling, and decoration in order to judge source and age.

"Prince of Wales," Staffordshire, c. 1860.

2. Teapots

Even in these easygoing twentieth-century days when tea is so often prepared by pouring hot water over a tea bag, there are still people in the United States, and many more of them in England and parts of the British Commonwealth, who insist that tea can be brewed properly only in a teapot. The teapot used nowadays is essentially the same shape as the first ones brought from China in the 1600's. It is a vessel of some size, with a cover, a handle and a spout, in which tea is made and from which it is poured into cups.

The size and shape of teapots have varied during the two hundred and fifty and more years they have been manufactured in the western world, but here as in China the favorite material always has been porcelain or pottery. In the West, silver became second choice for families who could afford a teapot of this valuable metal. Pewter was used to some extent (until about 1850 in America), and copper and tin teapots were not unknown in some parts of the world. The occasional teapot of wood was an oddity and was probably displayed more than it was used. The general acceptance of tea and its increasing availability can be traced in the forms of silver teapots made from about 1700 to 1900, and the changing fashions of these two centuries can be seen in the more colorful pottery and porcelain teapots.

Staffordshire teapot, early 19th century.

The first shipment of tea leaves is said to have been unloaded at ports in Holland in 1610. By 1650, shipments were arriving quite regularly not only in Europe but also in England. The first tea merchants in London around 1660 stimulated interest by their advertising, which stressed tea's "scarcity and dearness" and mentioned presents "made thereof to princes and grandees." Since tea came from China, Englishmen as well as Europeans considered porcelain correct for preparing and serving the exotic beverage. Porcelain had been brought from China some time before tea and was the only kind known to Europeans during the seventeenth century. Silver became an acceptable supplement or substitute for porcelain in the West.

At first, all teapots were small because tea was scarce and expensive. The first silver teapots, made up to about 1710, were small and round; they usually had wooden handles and either straight or curving spouts. Another form of small silver teapot, which appeared by 1730, was pear-shaped. The bulbous lower section was encircled with a molded rib where it began to narrow. Pear-shaped pots had domed tops, curved handles and spouts. About 1750, teapots were being made in an inverted pear shape with the bulbous section toward the top; this form was usually footed and the rounded cover was not so high as on the pear-shaped pot. Straight-sided cylindrical pots, not much larger than pear-shaped ones, were new in the late 1700's. These were usually flat on the bottom and had a straight spout but a slightly curved handle. Similar but less austere were the gently curving lines of the boat-shaped teapot, which often was decorated with applied bands; it was introduced in the early 1800's. By 1830, teapots, even if silver, were being made in large sizes, and decoration such as gadrooning and fluting was becoming popular.

Attractive as metal teapots may have been, western potters turned out teapots in the earthenwares and stonewares of the time and redoubled their efforts to find out how to make porcelain. Success came first to Johann Friedrich Böttger in Germany. His first product was a refined red stoneware that was close-grained, hard, often eggshell-thin, and evenly colored. Small round teapots and handleless cups and saucers patterned after those imported from China were made from this red stoneware and often decorated with molded or applied ornament. By 1710, Böttger succeeded in producing porcelain of a quality comparable to that of Chinese porcelain; this achievement was the foundation of the Meissen pottery near Dresden, Germany, where many unusual and attractive teapots have been produced.

Porcelain tableware continued to be imported from China through the eighteenth and nineteenth centuries. When the Revolutionary War ended in 1781, the United States began to trade directly with China. To this country were brought the typically Chinese Canton, a porcelain with blue decoration, and Nanking, a somewhat finer porcelain more elaborately decorated and sometimes gilded. Then there was the Oriental, or Chinese-import, porcelain that was decorated in the western manner. Typical of the years after the Revolution was the straight-sided cylindrical teapot with, on one side, the monogram of the purchaser in a shield surmounted by a ship flying the American flag.

The eighteenth century began favorably for western potters

Castleford teapot, late 18th century.

with Böttger's discovery of porcelain. Before the century ended, other potters, especially English ones, had created many new and attractive kinds of earthenware and stoneware; a variety of teapots was produced in each one. In the first half of the eighteenth century, however, teapots in England were being made of delft, a tin-glazed earthenware, a lead-glazed earthenware called creamware, and salt-glazed stoneware.

Some of the most fascinating teapots were made of salt-glazed stoneware up to about 1760. This stoneware, originated in Germany, owes its distinctive glaze and color to the table salt that was thrown over it before the last firing (glaze in powder form was applied before the first firing). Because the salt vaporized, the surface of the finished pieces became pitted or bumpy. Around 1750, salt glaze of a rather gray-white tone was being molded to make teapots in such odd shapes as a house, a camel, a ram or a ship. The molded pattern, which often

was paneled, usually covered the article completely. A teapot molded in the form of a house shows windows, dormers and doors and has a chimney as the finial on the cover. With a spout curving out from one side and a handle attached to the other, it is a rather formidable utensil. Still another invention of this period was the double-walled teapot, also of salt-glazed stoneware, with the outer wall perforated in a design.

Some small teapots with floral decoration were made of English delft. Thomas Whieldon became noted for tortoiseshell creamware, an earthenware with a surface mottled and colored like its name. Tortoiseshell and marbled ware both had a rather brief popularity in the mid-eighteenth century; these two quite different kinds of pottery were made on a cream-colored base that was dusted over with various oxides that, in the firing, ran into the glaze to produce streaky and mottled surfaces. Agateware of the same period was made of different

Wedgwood black basalt teapot, c. 1780-1800.

clays kneaded or, as the potter said, "wedged" together so that the marbled effect goes right through the piece.

Probably the most inventive English potter of the eighteenth century was Josiah Wedgwood. His first achievement was a green glaze that proved indispensable in making the dishes shaped like fruits and vegetables that were so popular between 1760 and 1780. Green glaze, of course, was needed for the teapot shaped and colored exactly like a cauliflower; this was another variation of the small, round teapot. Another teapot of this period imitated a pineapple. By the early 1760's, Wedgwood introduced his perfected creamware, so attractive that it displaced previously popular earthenwares. Creamware was lightweight and lent itself to all kinds of decoration. The 1770's brought Wedgwood's two fine-grained, smooth stonewares, which he named black basalt and jasper. More teapots undoubtedly were made in the many patterns of creamware. However, a

black basalt teapot is stunning, whether its shape is traditional or the more unusual one of a helmet. Jasper ware is two-toned with white cameo decoration against a pastel background. Most familiar nowadays is jasper ware with classic figures against a

blue or green background, but in the late eighteenth and early nineteenth centuries teapots often had a mauve or lilac background. Round, cylindrical and helmet teapots were made for many years.

New techniques for decorating pottery also were introduced during the eighteenth century in England. Rockingham glaze, for example, appeared on pottery from Yorkshire about 1757. Pieces are recognized by the mottling in shades of brown and buff. Frankly, the glaze is more distinctive than the earthenware on which it was applied. A similar mottled glaze was used after 1849 in American potteries in Vermont, Maryland and along the Ohio River Valley. Of the many large teapots made here, perhaps the one most coveted by collectors is known as a "Rebecca-at-the-Well" teapot. Potteries in several states produced different versions: the scene on the side of the teapot, with the title underneath,

Pink luster Staffordshire teapot, mid-19th century.

shows up clearly against the dark glaze.

About 1775 the English perfected the technique of decorating pottery by means of transfer printing. This process, which involved little handwork, was used chiefly on earthenware. The number of teapots decorated with transfer printing that were exported to the United States between the 1780's and 1880's staggers the imagination. Shape, size and color changed from time to time. Con-

Blue and white Staffordshire teapot, mid-19th century.

sistently popular in America was the blue transfer printing, especially in flowing, or flowering, blue, where the deep, rich blue of the design has flowed into the background to tint it slightly, and in the commemorative ware. The latter is a general term for all the earthenware and stoneware transfer-printed with typically American scenes, events and designs; English potters made a definite search for such motifs as soon as the Revolutionary War was over. By 1830, teapots and

other ware from Staffordshire were being transfer-printed in light blue as well as deep blue, pink, carmine, lavender, green, sepia or brown, and black. Some teapots were decorated in two colors, chiefly green and rose or brown and rose. After 1830, too, these teapots were larger, one for family use often having a capacity of one and a half quarts. To hold this much tea, pots averaged seven inches high and were bulkier-looking than coffeepots. These large teapots were sometimes almost straight-sided, then again hexagonal or octagonal, or bulging and bulbous.

Also from the Staffordshire district came Gaudy Dutch and spatterware, made during the early 1800's chiefly for export to the United States. Both of these earthenwares were especially well liked by the Pennsylvania Germans, although spatterware was sold farther west. Gaudy Dutch is well named, for it was decorated with patterns based on butterflies, flowers, grapes and doves in red, blue and yellow. King's Rose, Cabbage Rose and Butterfly were three of the favorite Gaudy Dutch patterns. Spatterware, or sponge ware, is easy to recognize because the border was colored by daubing color on the white clay body with a sponge. A teapot usually was sponged or spattered all over with color, often blue, but somewhere it displayed a design against a white background. Popular motifs were roses, tulips or other flowers, eagles and peacocks.

Ironstone china was introduced by the Mason brothers in England in 1813. This was a type of stoneware that was glossy, hard, durable and, as produced by the Masons, handsomely dec-

orated with colored enamels and gilding. Less expensive ironstone was decorated by transfer printing, often with designs of flowers, birds and butterflies somewhat in the Chinese manner. Ironstone is the name given frequently to a type of china that should more correctly be called graniteware or white granite. This is opaque white, glossy and thicker than the original ironstone. Graniteware often is quite plain, but pieces may display a molded design of wheat, foliage or cornstalks. Teapots, seven inches to ten inches tall, were popular here in the mid-nineteenth century.

After 1850 so-called majolica teapots made in both England and the United States became popular. This majolica was a coarse earthenware with molded naturalistic designs set off with appropriate and often brightly colored lead glazes. One form was the cauliflower teapot that had been made in England a century earlier. Other popular designs were shell and seaweed and an open fan with bluebirds and flowers.

During the Victorian years, most families owned not only a good-sized teapot for everyday use but also a tea set. The simplest set consisted of a teapot, sugar bowl and creamer in any one of a dozen favorite patterns in some special pottery such as jasper ware or a porcelain such as unglazed white Parian. More complete sets for afternoon tea added a dozen cups and saucers and two serving plates. Then there were sets, probably used more often for Sunday night suppers, that had in addition plates about seven inches in diameter, saucedishes and a small bowl. Most popular were tea sets with luster decora-

"Garland" teapot, English, late 19th century.

tion, sprigs of dainty blossoms and leaves, and gold-banded white porcelain. The sprigged ware and the popular Blue Chelsea pattern, also called Chelsea Grape and Grandmother's Ware, with tiny clusters of blue or mulberry grapes, came mostly from England. White porcelain tea sets decorated with gold bands were both imported, some from Haviland in France, and made in the United States. Squat or round teapots are more typical of the Haviland tea sets, taller ones of the American gold-banded china.

Luster was a Victorian favorite, the tea sets called rose or pink luster being the most popular. A range of shades, most often pink or rose but sometimes orange or mulberry, was achieved by the application of a gold pigment. Gold luster designs were quite dainty, usually of flowers or fruit and foliage. Sometimes hand painting and gold pigment were combined, as for a strawberry luster tea set on which the berries are painted but the three-part leaves and border on each piece are a mulberry-colored luster. Teapots in these rose or pink luster sets were generally broad and rather squat. Silver luster, achieved by the application of a pigment derived from platinum, was made before gold lusterware

as a less costly imitation of real silver pieces. Small teapots, at first round or pear-shaped and later in fancier forms, were covered solidly with silver luster, which may be quite black now when they are found. Later a few copper luster teapots were made. These also were usually covered with the copper luster, perhaps broken with a flower motif or a transfer-printed border. Copper luster teapots were the larger sizes and shapes that came into general use by about 1850.

Luster and gold-banded tea sets are quite likely to have no potter's marks. Neither do a great many of the teapots that were used and loved even during the nineteenth century. Meissen in Germany and Wedgwood in England, founded in the eighteenth century, and Haviland, established in France about 1840, consistently placed their marks on the underside of each piece; by looking up the mark, you can find out the span of years during which the teapot or other piece was made. Considerable knowledge is required to interpret the clues that will help to identify and date approximately an unmarked teapot. These clues are shape, the kind of pottery or the type of porcelain and, if possible, the glaze, the style of decoration and how it was applied.

3. Pitchers and Tobies

Pitchers are one of the oldest utensils made and used by man. They are still as essential as they were when Rebekah carried her pitcher to the well to fill it with water, as related in Genesis. In the Mediterranean region, the seat of ancient civilizations, pitchers were being made of pottery, glass and probably metal even in Biblical days. And since that long-ago time, pitchers have been made of many materials, in several sizes and for various purposes.

A pitcher is a vessel which usually has a handle for holding or carrying it and a lip or spout for pouring out liquids. It does not have a cover as a general rule. A creamer is a small pitcher for holding cream. Still another variation is a ewer, which may be practical or decorative. The functional ewer is a large wide-mouthed pitcher that usually is kept in a deep matching bowl. The ewer and bowl combination used to stand in every bedroom to be used for personal ablutions. This sort of ewer, holding a gallon or more of water, was probably the largest pitcher made for household use and was heavy even when it contained no water. The word "ewer" also refers to a vaselike pitcher that usually has a long, narrow neck and a high, arched handle. The necks are too

Leather tavern Toby jug, probably 17th century, English.

narrow for these to be used for flowers, although they are ornamental enough to be vases. A jug is a swelling or cylindrical vessel with a small spout, a handle and a narrow mouth which is often stopped with a cork. It is made of pottery, metal or glass in various sizes.

With one exception jugs were likely to be plain and utilitarian. The exception is the character, or Toby, jug, first made in the 1760's in England. A Toby is a small pitcher, jug or mug shaped somewhat like a stout man who is seated and wears a cocked hat; one angle of the hat forms a spout for pouring. It was made originally of pottery covered with appropriate colored glazes. Toby jugs were gay pieces and probably were used more for ornament than for pouring. The Toby is entirely English in conception; the first ones are believed to have been derived from Toby Philpot, the subject of a song published in 1761. Soon, however, the character jug was taking other forms such as the Night Watchman who held a lantern; the Drunken Parson pouring liquor into a glass; or Lord Howe, made to commemorate his victory over the French in 1794. So it went throughout the nineteenth century, when Tobies made in the shape of Dickens' characters became popular. In recent years Tobies, in their inimitable style, have commemorated Winston Churchill, General Eisenhower and General MacArthur. A few female Tobies have been made, but these have been exceptions.

The first Toby jug, made in the 1760's, is believed to have been the work of Ralph Wood, who with his brother operated a pottery in Burslem, Staffordshire. Figures were a specialty of this

Whieldon-type Toby jug in brown, blue, and tan glazes, 18th century, English.

Toby jug, mid-19th century, English.

famous old pottery. Soon almost all potteries in the Staffordshire District were producing Tobies in various forms, and the appealing little jug also was copied by potteries in Europe, Japan and America.

Here in America Tobies seem to have been less colorful than those made in England. Most of the American-made Tobies were covered with the mottled buff and brown Rockingham glaze; few of them, however, displayed the slightly more colorful flint-enamel glaze which was brown brightened with flecks or streaks of blue, green, yellow and orange. Most American Tobies were nameless and even those that were called Benjamin Franklin or General John Stark bore little resemblance to the noted person. Tobies were being produced in the Bennington, Vermont, potteries in the late 1840's. However,

Staffordshire "Punch" Toby jug, early 19th century.

Rockingham or flint-enamel glazes are no guarantee that a Toby was made at Bennington, for potteries in other states, notably in the Ohio River valley, made similar jugs and used the same glazes.

Tobies made in larger sizes served other purposes. A Toby with a removable cocked hat in sizes from 3⅞″ to 5¼″ high was a snuff jar. A still larger Toby of painted metal with a removable but snugly fitting hat was a cracker jar.

Ordinary pitchers and creamers were made of porcelain and all kinds of pottery. Pitchers for water and milk were large enough, regardless of their shape, to hold at least one quart. Creamers were so small that they usually held only a cup or less. Sugar bowls and creamers were part of the tea sets and dinner sets that families acquired during the nineteenth century. In addition, both pitchers and creamers were made and sold individually. Still in use today in my house, for example, are an old Delft creamer, a larger but squat creamer (4″ at highest point) that was part of a luster tea set belonging to one grandmother, a slender milk pitcher (5¾″ tall) in another grandmother's gold-banded tea set, and a Royal Worcester porcelain creamer or jug decorated with field flowers which has bands and a handle covered in dull but rich-looking honey gold. A friend who lives nearby has the collection of copper-luster pitchers that she inherited lined up on her mantelpiece, and in her corner cupboard are an old creamware pitcher in pale blue with a

molded design, and a salt-glaze pitcher showing a calla lily and rope pattern.

Salt glaze is a type of stoneware that was glazed by throwing table salt into the kiln before the last firing. The salt vaporized and clung in drops, leaving the surface of the article pitted much like the skin of an orange. Salt-glaze pitchers were made in England and imported to America, particularly during the early 1800's. English salt glaze is typically gray-white, and pieces were made in molds in order to give them unusual shapes or relief decoration. Most talked about nowadays perhaps is the salt-glazed apostle pitcher; each of the arched panels around the sides frames one of the apostles. Other motifs that stood out in relief were calla lilies with flowers, buds, leaves and stems; other flowers and ferns; scrolls; rope, and basketweave. The gray-white pieces are found more commonly now than those that were touched with blue or were painted other colors.

Another very different sort of molded ware, made in the United States after 1850, was perhaps even more popular. This was an earthenware called majolica (it was not true *maiolica*). Highly colored glazes contributed to the naturalistic forms in which majolica pitchers were molded: a yellow and green ear of corn, brown basketweave with pink flowers and green leaves, an owl or a parrot.

Stoneware pitchers—not necessarily salt glaze with relief decoration but plainer ones ornamented with colored slip or painted—were preferred for keeping milk because stoneware is hard and nonporous. In this country, until the late 1800's, probably more pitchers for water

Staffordshire Toby jug with spatterware base, early 19th century.

and milk were imported than were made here, with England the most important source. Among those most popular during the 1800's and now prized by collectors are the transfer-printed ones, especially those decorated with American historical or patriotic scenes. In the Flowing Blue earthenware or stoneware that came from the Staffordshire District, the pitcher might show Lafayette at Franklin's or Washington's tomb. For the white or cream earthenware transfer-printed in black, for which Liverpool became famous, the favorite subject must have been George Washington. The English designers did know of other American heroes, for Stephen Decatur together with the frigate with which he won a naval victory during the War of 1812 was represented on pitchers. The American eagle was the chief decoration on many pitchers transfer-printed both in black and in Flowing Blue.

Another great favorite during Victorian days was lusterware, china decorated with metallic pigments. Luster tea sets including the creamer and covered sugar bowl were cherished, but luster also was used to decorate the odd but ever-useful creamer or pitcher. Real metals such as gold, platinum and copper were the source of the metallic pigments for decorating china, and the lusterware made in England

Rockingham-type pitcher, arm and hammer decoration, early to mid-19th century, American.

and imported to America during the nineteenth century falls into several color groups. Silver luster, which resulted from application of a pigment made from platinum, was produced as a less costly substitute for real silver pieces; this luster usually covered the entire creamer with no added decoration. A silver luster creamer found nowadays is likely to have darkened considerably. After 1820, copper luster became most common although gold or pink luster continued to be popular. Copper luster, derived from copper itself, also often covered the entire outer surface of a piece, but it was sometimes broken up by one or more bands of a transfer-printed or embossed design. Gold pigment produced several shades, most often pink or rose but also mulberry, purple and orange. Unlike copper and silver lusters, the gold or pink luster seldom covered the entire piece. Instead, the metallic pigment was applied to produce naturalistic floral or fruit patterns or perhaps a design of lines and scrolls on white china. Often green leaves were painted when the pink or rose-luster motif was a fruit such as strawberries.

Decorative ewers ranged from porcelain, with elaborate paintings of scenes or groups, to Parian ware with applied decoration. Ewers of Parian, the unglazed porcelain or bisque so popular during Victorian years, often displayed applied bunches of grapes. Decoration in relief distinguished ewers of basalt and jasperware in their typical colors. Ewers were chiefly an English and European product although some few were made in America.

Pitchers undoubtedly were among the earliest utensils made of glass. The first glassmakers in America produced pitchers that were either hand-blown or blown-molded; the latter technique consisted of blowing into a small mold, then removing the piece and expanding it to the desired size by blowing. The late eighteenth and early nineteenth centuries saw some handsome free-blown pitchers made here. They were likely to be broad at the base and ornamented with trails or threads of glass applied to form loops, waves, ribbons or perhaps a lily-pad design. Blown-molded pitchers of the nineteenth century are handsome, although they show only simple swirled, ribbed, paneled or quilted patterns; they are often brilliantly colored. After 1812 the blown-three-mold method became common here. For this, glass was blown into a full-size mold consisting of two, three or more parts hinged together. One way of detecting blown-three-mold pitchers is by the seam marks left where sections of the mold met. Blown-three-mold glass, offered as a less expensive substitute for cut glass, has an all-over pattern. The motifs were more limited than those that decorated cut glass, which were made by hand. Patterns on blown-three-mold pitchers were of three general types: swirls and scrolls known as baroque, combinations of geometric lines, and arches. Handles for both blown-molded and blown-three-mold pitchers were hand-blown and applied.

After the introduction of pressed glass in the 1820's, pitchers became plentiful in every household if only because this technique made them cheaper to buy. Creamers probably were more common than pitchers in the early lacy type of pressed glass, recognized by an allover stippled background that gives sparkle to the piece. When patterns became general, starting about 1850, most of them included both a creamer and a water pitcher. Water pitchers are large pieces to collect, but one couple of my acquaintance displays finds, totaling 482 at last count, on bookshelves lining the four walls of their living room. Most of their patterns are clear glass, although Emerald Green Herringbone blazes from one corner and there are a few water pitchers in custard, clam broth and various kinds of art glass.

Pressed-glass creamers vary in size and shape. For example, the creamer in Paneled English Hobnail with Prisms pattern is only 2″ high and 3″ wide and holds exactly one-third of a cup, while in the Cardinal pattern the footed creamer is approximately 5½″ high and holds a full cup of cream. Many patterns offered water pitchers in two sizes, quart and half-gallon; and at least one pattern, Diamond Point, had four sizes, ranging from a half-pint to three pints. In some patterns water sets could be purchased separately. For example, in Thousand Eye, Shell and Jewel, Daisy and Button, and Festoon, among other patterns, it was possible to obtain a large water pitcher, a matching glass tray, and water tumblers, lemonade tumblers or goblets, or perhaps all three kinds of glasses. If the pattern was made in colored as well as clear glass, pitchers and creamers were too.

Water pitchers and creamers were made in cut glass, especially during the Brilliant period (1876-1905) when this heavy and fancy glass became overwhelmingly popular. In fact, cut-glass patterns of that time included pitchers of both sizes. Wine or champagne pitchers also often were cut or etched, and these were much taller and slenderer than water pitchers. Lemonade pitchers were also tall and slim, but were more likely to be made in pressed or decorated glass, particularly a painted one, than in cut glass.

Creamers and sugar bowls, pitchers designed especially for water, milk, lemonade or syrup, and an occasional ewer were made in the many kinds of art glass so popular between 1880 and 1910. All of these different pitchers were common in the iridescent Carnival glass. Water pitchers, either globe-shaped or straight, were attractive in two-toned Amberina; Mary Gregory with its charmingly painted children; Pomona, noted for its delicate coloring and dainty floral decoration; and Crown Milano with its porcelainlike texture. Creamers, syrup pitchers and some water pitchers and ewers also were made of satin glass.

Syrup jugs or pitchers from 5″ to 8″ tall were quite different. For one thing, they had covers and often a matching plate. Syrup pitchers were made in pressed-glass patterns, cut glass and art glass. All glass ones had metal tops of pewter, tin or silver plate. The spout was incorporated into the metal top, which also often had a thumb-piece by which the cover could be raised. The handle, of course, was applied glass. Syrup jugs or pitchers also were made of china, silver and silver plate and perhaps pewter.

It has been recorded that by 1800 Paul Revere was turning out silver pitchers in three sizes. He is said to have modeled their form on that of the black-on-white transfer-printed earthenware pitchers made in Liverpool. Creamers or cream pots as they often were called, seem to have been more common than water pitchers during colonial days. Little silver jugs with covers and handles were known as hot-milk jugs. Some pitchers had been made of pewter, particularly during the first half of the nineteenth century, and the search to find an authentic antique pewter pitcher with attached cover is a worthwhile one. However, it wasn't until after 1850, when silver plate became accepted for flatware and hollow ware, that metal pitchers were as widely made and used as those in other materials.

4. Fanciful Dishes

In the eighteenth century Europeans were eager to own examples of the many new kinds of pottery being offered in England and Europe. If they could afford it, they bought porcelain that had just been brought from China and displayed it proudly in mahogany cases especially designed by Thomas Chippendale. The Chinese porcelain was profusely admired because it was so different from and so much more beautiful than any European pottery. Those who found the Chinese ware beyond their means settled for hard-paste porcelain made in Germany or the soft-paste pieces of France and England. Of the many new dishes being made of the various new kinds of pottery, none were more appealing than those molded and colored faithfully to represent vegetables, fruit, animals and birds. These began to appear in the 1740's and some, at least, were exported to America.

Some of these fanciful dishes, such as tureens shaped and colored exactly like an eggplant or a duck, came from China. Many other forms were made during the 1740's by the Meissen porcelain factory near Dresden, Germany, and copied in English potteries during the 1750's. At this time, the Meissen pottery was the natural pacesetter, for it had grown out of Johann Friedrich Böttger's discovery of how to make hard-paste porcelain as translucent, white and delicate in texture as that from China. Hard-paste porcelain from China had been brought to Europe before 1600, but it was not until about 1708 that Böttger achieved

"Cauliflower"-type, Whieldon or Wedgwood teapot in green and white glazes, 18th century.

the distinction of being the first westerner to produce real porcelain. China stone, the English equivalent of Chinese petuntse, and china clay, the kaolin of China, were needed to produce hard-paste porcelain. This was developed independently in England during the late 1760's and was being made at the Sèvres pottery in France by 1769. The English, however, went on to become famous for a different type of porcelain known as bone china, and hard-paste porcelain did not replace the soft paste, or *pâte tendre*, of the French until about 1800.

Meanwhile, soft-paste porcelain was creating excitement in France and England. (The terms "hard" and "soft" are related to the firing, "hard" referring to high temperature.) The desired qualities of translucency and whiteness were contributed by the addition of a glass substance before firing at a low temperature. Each piece then was decorated in colors, a lead glaze was applied and, finally, the piece was fired again

at still lower temperature. The firing on of the thick lead glaze apparently gave soft-paste porcelain its distinction by giving depth and richness to the decoration, which appeared to glow. Although soft-paste porcelain is creamy white and lacks the cold brilliance of hard paste, anyone but an expert usually finds it difficult to distinguish between the two types. Soft-paste porcelain is not nearly so resistant to liquids and stains as hard paste. Nor is soft-paste porcelain as hard, for its surface can be scratched easily with a knife. When this happens, the surface appears sugary, or granular.

Soft-paste porcelain was developed in France before 1700. Whatever the exact year, it was produced at many potteries by 1725. The first authenticated pieces of English soft-paste porcelain are believed to be the goat-and-bee jugs from the Chelsea pottery in London, perhaps as early as 1743. These jugs, in a sense, were the forerunners of the

naturalistic fruit and vegetable dishes that began to appear in quantity and variety in the 1750's. The soft-paste jug, taken from a silver one, was molded in relief. It consisted of two goats reclining head to tail and supporting an upper part decorated with flowers and a bee; the handle was shaped like a twig. Most of the goat-and-bee jugs were glazed with white and some had colored flowers.

The activity and experiments of potters led not only to porcelain but also to many improvements in long-familiar kinds of pottery. In France changes in decoration and firing of faience, the national tin-glazed earthenware, resulted in the finest of this ware being produced between 1709 and 1780. England was fortunate in having such an inventive potter as Josiah Wedgwood, who about 1759 created a lustrous and brilliant green glaze. He followed this in the early 1760's with an equally fine yellow glaze. He also perfected creamware, a lead-

Agate ware, Whieldon-type teapot, with shell on body, animal knop on lid, green-blue glazes, mid-18th century.

glazed earthenware so attractive that around 1765 Queen Charlotte gave him permission to name it queensware. Creamware was lighter in weight than any other kind of earthenware. The surface lent itself to painting and transfer printing, and the almost transparent glaze gave it a creamy color and texture. Other potteries in England and on the Continent were soon copying Wedgwood's creamware to such an extent that it displaced delft, the heretofore popular tin-glazed earthenware. Little more than a decade after fanciful dishes of soft-paste porcelain appeared in England, they were also being made in creamware.

Fanciful dishes were molded, yet owed much of their realism to color. Wedgwood's green glaze made it possible for him to introduce a distinctive group now often called cauliflower ware. By no means all pieces that fall into this category came from Wedgwood, for other potters in the Staffordshire district of England

Black basalt teapot, Wedgwood, bamboo design, c. 1779-80.

were prompt to follow his example. Cauliflower ware consists largely of teapots, hot-water jugs, creamers and other pieces chiefly for teatime use that were molded realistically with foliage in green and the rest of the body in a clear orange-yellow tint. The cauliflower was the favorite shape, especially for teapots. Pineapple and cabbage were other teapot shapes; a creamer consisted of cabbage leaves, even if it wasn't actually shaped like a cabbage; and the term applies to other pieces in the form of melons and maize, or corn.

In his cauliflower ware, which featured his green glaze, Wedgwood was merely producing in less expensive pottery, however excellent, the fanciful dishes that had been made first in hard-paste porcelain at Meissen in the 1740's and in soft-paste porcelain at the Chelsea, Bow and Worcester potteries, among others, in England in the 1750's. These porcelain dishes had more varied shapes and often more realistic coloring than pottery ones. Tureens, probably the most popular piece, had covers that were an integral part of the vegetable, fruit, animal or bird after which they were modeled. They also were made in several sizes. Some of the smaller melon-shaped ones were used for serving jam or preserves. Smallest of all probably were boxes in the size, shape and color of lemons.

Just as the cauliflower and pineapple were obvious favorites for teapots, so were the cauliflower, a bunch of asparagus and a melon for tureens. The cauliflower stood upright to form a teapot and on its side for a tureen. The Chelsea pottery was satisfied to have its cauliflower tureens of soft-paste porcelain in the shape and color-

Whieldon-type tea caddy, green, tortoise, and yellow glazes, 18th century.

ing of the vegetable. The Worcester pottery, also famous for soft-paste porcelain, embellished its cauliflower tureens with random moths and butterflies that were transfer-printed in black. Other vegetable forms were a head of cos, or romaine, lettuce lying lengthwise on a platter of overlapping green leaves, and squash and artichoke, usually life-size.

Melon tureens or dishes present many variations. English potters made them of soft-paste porcelain, creamware and salt-glaze stoneware. Decoration, coloring and arrangement of leaves and vine stem differed from pottery to pottery and add interest to the basic oval melon dish resting on a large underleaf or leaf platter. The broad end of the melon often was cupped with molded leaves. A creamware melon tureen from the Leeds pottery was likely not only to be colored realistically, but also to have the melon decorated with painted flower sprays. Wedgwood produced several variations; his creamware one might be utterly plain except for its tex-

ture and ribbing and have a simple oval knob on the upper section of the melon, which was the cover, or it might be a quite different melon appropriately tinted with green and yellow glazes. A salt-glaze stoneware melon dish is easier to identify than an earthenware one, for the surface is pitted or bumpy from the common table salt thrown over it before the last firing vaporized. Apples and clusters of grapes were other colorful fruit forms; the apples ranged in size from tureens to boxes.

Different indeed were some of the Chelsea tureens. One was a sunflower with the yellow petals edging the rim of the dish and the dark brown center of the flower forming the slightly rounded cover, to which a leaf handle was attached. Most charming of all, to my way of thinking, is the one in the form of a rabbit eating a cabbage leaf, now a museum piece. The white rabbit with colored spots on its body and color on its ears is not only eating a cabbage leaf but also appears to be

sitting on a cabbage, for leaves come up on either side of its crouched body. The Chelsea rabbit tureen may well have been copied from an earlier, similar Meissen one. Chelsea also made a long, slender tureen in the shape of a fish, probably carp or salmon.

Bird tureens, like those of vegetables and fruits, originated at Meissen in the 1740's and were made by several English potteries from the early 1750's to the late 1770's. These were shaped like sitting hens, cocks, ducks and drakes, swans, partridges and pigeons, but were not necessarily used to serve food linked to their form. Partridge tureens, which were the smallest, were used for sweetmeats. From China came duck tureens with markings and coloring meticulously accurate. Game or game-pie dishes in appropriate forms continued to be popular in England, although quality and modeling declined after 1770. Useful but certainly far less appealing was the covered game dish in the form of a trussed

Blown and molded, pressed, and brilliantly cut clear glass objects have been collected for many years. Enormous quantities of such American glass were produced in the 19th century, and much remains to be discovered. The useful forms—decanters, celery vases, salts, compotes, sugar bowls, goblets—and purely decorative objects, such as the eagle sculpture, are almost without count.

American colored glass of the 19th century—both blown and pressed—is widely sought today. The hues—canary, turquoise, cranberry, emerald green, cobalt blue, among others—possess a strength and clarity not available in modern glassware. Among the most prized pieces are those produced by the Boston and Sandwich Glass Co. (1825-1888) and various Ohio and western Pennsylvania factories. The canary sugar bowl and the vase, the turquoise-blue and milk-white lamp, and the cobalt-blue bowl in the "petal" pattern are probably Sandwich. The cobalt-blue candlestick is possibly an example of Pittsburgh glass.

Attractive appointments for salt were found at every well-laid 19th-century dinner table. Silver was the preferred material used in fine American households, but glass was also common. In the center is an American pressed clam-broth salt, and at far left and right are Stiegel-type cobalt-blue blown salts. The two footed silver pieces are English; the salt and pepper shakers are late 19th-century Gorham pieces. Since salt has a corrosive effect, silver containers were often provided with glass liners, most often blue in color. Resting behind the salts is a Staffordshire historical blue tray with an English view, another decorative item for the well-appointed dinner table.

Four opaque art glass vases from Victor Durand's Vineland Flint Glass Works
(1897-1931), Vineland, New Jersey. Made between 1924 and 1931, the
exceptional creations of the Durand "fancy shop" are among the last of the
great blown art glass pieces produced in North America. When the firm went
out of business in the Depression, similar objects could be purchased for $5
each; today, the price would have to be multiplied 50 or 100 times. This firm
also produced transparent art glass.

Queensware mold, Wedgwood, intaglio relief molding, c. 1770-1800.

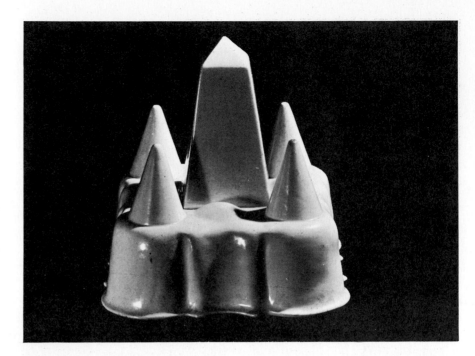

and brought to the table. There the mold itself, if not the dessert, was certain to cause comment, for the flower foliage or fruit sprays painted on all sides of the pyramid support could be seen and admired through the jelly. Eventually, a cone on a round base and a wedge on a rectangular base were added to the pyramid. This type of two-piece mold was made in some quantity for about fifty years, but is rarely seen now outside of museums.

The vogue for fanciful tureens and other dishes continued through the last fifty to sixty years of the eighteenth century, reaching its peak between 1750 and 1770. Whether they came from China or were produced in Germany or England, all the vegetable, fruit, animal and bird dishes are now cherished collector's items and often museum pieces. Meissen in Germany, Worcester and Wedgwood in England placed their potter's marks on practically all their wares. However, the many other potteries active along the same lines used either no marks at that time or else so small and obscure a mark that it is easily confused with a similar one of another pottery or difficult for anyone but an

Pearl ware jelly core mold and cover, Wedgwood, polychrome enamel decoration over the glaze, c. 1781-1800.

expert to identify. It also is quite easy to add an old mark or fake one on a piece of soft-paste porcelain.

Reproductions of some of these eighteenth-century dishes began to appear in the 1850's and were quite popular for a number of years. They were made by potteries in both England and America. Cauliflower teapots, dishes molded and colored like an ear of corn, and leaf plates and platters were especially common. However, these nineteenth-century vegetable and leaf dishes were made of majolica, a rather coarse earthenware with highly colored lead glazes. They are not to be compared in quality or decoration with those made in the eighteenth century of porcelain, earthenware and especially creamware, or fine stoneware.

5. Delftware

A small white china dish with blue decoration consisting of a windmill and fishing boats or flowers that look something like tulips brings a predictable reaction when shown to most people. Their eyes light up and they say quickly, "Delftware!" However, the chances are good that it is a piece of fairly modern delftware made in the Netherlands or some other country such as Germany or Czechoslovakia. Popular as this delftware is, it is quite different from the pottery that was being made in Holland by about 1525 and that either Dutch or Flemish potters introduced to England around 1550. Both Holland and England were producing it in quantity by the mid-seventeenth century. Potters in each country developed their own styles and decoration, although both were influenced greatly by the beautiful porcelain brought from China.

The delft made in Holland and England so long ago is tin-enameled earthenware. This seventeenth- and eighteenth-century earthenware was a soft type and was covered with a glaze of

Lambeth delft plate, mid-18th century.

39

lead that was made opaque by the addition of ashes or oxide of tin so that it resembled fine white enamel paint. On this white surface the artist or decorator painted his design or picture.

Neither the Flemish nor the Dutch invented tin-glazed earthenware. This kind of pottery originated in the Middle East and was brought to Spain by the Moors. Then, before 1500, it was taken to Italy from Spain by way of Majorca. Because the Italians thought this new and different pottery had been produced in Majorca, they called it maiolica. The town of Faenza became one of the centers where maiolica was made, so when this tin-glazed earthenware spread to France and Germany and was manufactured there it was called faience.

You may be thinking as you read this that the faience of northern Europe, the delft of Holland and England, and the maiolica of Moorish Spain and Renaissance Italy look nothing alike. It's true, they are different, but all are tin-glazed earthenware. They differ in appearance because each country developed its own typical style and colors for decoration. On the other hand, the majolica that was made in England and the United States during the nineteenth century and that is also sometimes called faience is not tin-glazed earthenware. Nineteenth-century majolica is a rather coarse earthenware characterized by molded naturalistic designs of flowers or birds set off with colored lead glazes.

Of the various kinds of tin-glazed earthenware, delft probably gained the greatest hold on people's affections both at home and abroad. Delft certainly became the national pottery of Holland, and English delft was not only popular in England but also was shipped in some quantity to other areas, notably America, until it was superseded by new and different earthenware in the late eighteenth century. The finest delftware was produced in both Holland and England from the early seventeenth century to about 1760.

Tin-glazed earthenware was made in Haarlem, Rotterdam, Amsterdam and Middleburg as well as in Delft. In fact, this earthenware had been made in northern Europe for almost a century before Delft came to the fore as a production center around 1650. Late as Delft was in entering the field, several factors led to its name's being perpetuated by the national pottery. Delft first was famous for its beer, which was so excellent that the two hundred breweries in the town sent their product throughout Europe. When their business decreased in the general upsurge of trade among all countries in the early seventeenth century, the potters took over the old brewery buildings. The flourishing industry they built up can be traced in large part to the guild of artists and other craftsmen, which was not only well organized with rules for apprentices and examinations but which also established a school of design. The skill of these Delft craftsmen in adapting the colors and designs of porcelain from China to their own earthenware was the foundation of Delft's success.

Potters in Delft were close enough to an international port to have access to the blue-and-white porcelain that the ships of the Dutch East India Company brought from China. This was extravagantly admired by both Europeans and the English, who had never seen porcelain before. The demand for Oriental china was so great that it could not be met. So the Dutch potters, and particularly those in Delft, made their tin-glazed earthenware as much like the porcelain from China as they could. As a result, delftware could be exported in quantity to be sold in other countries.

Because so much porcelain from China was decorated with blue, the Dutch made this the favorite color for decorating their earthenware. The second color used by the Dutch was purple. Later, probably early in the eighteenth century, polychrome porcelain from China and brilliant decorated ware from Japan offered quite different inspiration.

The Dutch often added a second glaze to obtain richness and depth. For both blue-and-white and polychrome, the colors were painted on the raw tin glaze and the whole was covered with a powdered lead glaze. Firing developed the glazes and the colors and produced a smooth and glassy finish. The new colors included yellow, green, brown and red, the last so little used in Europe at this time and so difficult that it was usually fired on separately. So proud did the Dutch become of their tin-enameled earthenware that they often referred to it as "porseleyn," and with its milky white surface and clearly delineated colors and designs, it bore well the comparison with true porcelain from China.

The early blue-and-white Chinese porcelain also inspired many of the designs with which the Dutch decorated their tin-glazed earthenware. Landscapes, plants and flowers, birds and figures were borrowed from the Chinese.

Sooner or later, some pieces of tin-glazed earthenware combined both Chinese and European motifs. During the eighteenth century the designs on delft became much more European, although decoration in blue only remained popular. Landscapes, scenes and figures reflected familiar sights and everyday living in the Lowlands. Large plates to hang on a wall, for example, displayed a road through a village leading to a windmill, and fishing vessels heading toward a wharf with civic buildings in the background. Portraits, biblical subjects and the seasons were other themes for large plates, platters and chargers, the last a large, flat and usually round dish. Pieces such as these may have been displayed on a dresser or against a plate rail more than they were used at mealtime. However, tableware ranged from mugs and other individual pieces to handsome tureens, trim butter bowls, creamers and caster sets. Spice boxes, tea caddies, bottles and

jars were as attractive as they were useful, and everyone seems to have enjoyed vases, slippers and shoes, and wall plaques with scrolled edges.

Probably more delftware was exported to America from England than from Holland since Bristol and Liverpool were not only important ports but also centers for tin-glazed earthenware. Other places where delft was made were Lambeth, Wincanton and Brislington. English potters also were influenced by porcelain from China and by the delft from Holland that imitated it. Although English delft inclined toward chinoiserie patterns, experts believe that on the whole the English did not copy Chinese designs and motifs quite so closely as did the Dutch. Floral patterns also were important. A good deal of English delft was decorated with blue or purple on white, but polychrome pieces probably were made in greater number than in Holland. Blues, light blue-green, greens, a red or

puce, leaf brown and yellow were the colors from which to choose for a polychrome piece.

Globular jugs are believed to be the oldest pieces of delft made in England; later, barrel-shaped jugs and mugs were decorated with birds and flowers in blue in the Chinese manner. English and Dutch potters made many of the same pieces, such as tableware and chargers. Blue-dash chargers are a famous English piece, distinguished by a border of broad dashes, usually blue, although the central design most often is polychrome. Subjects were as broad as those used in Holland for chargers: royal portraits, biblical scenes, floral and fruit decoration. English potters produced a considerable number of delft porringers, an article more commonly made of pewter or silver. Posset pots, used to prepare and serve a hot spiced and sweetened drink, and caudle cups for a sweetened or spiced concoction especially for invalids had two handles, a lid and a spout, and their decoration

English delft puzzle jug, mid-18th century.

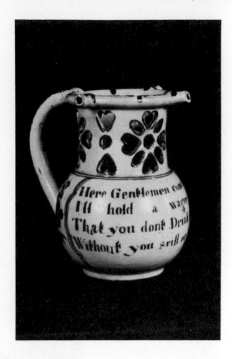

English delft puzzle jug, mid-18th century.

was sometimes simple, then again elaborate.

Both Bristol and Liverpool produced fine specimens of the indispensable eighteenth-century punch bowl. Liverpool in particular is noted for ship bowls—large deep punch bowls decorated with ships or naval equipment. Also typical of Liverpool is the wall pocket in the shape of a cornucopia. Wall pockets made in Lambeth were simpler in shape, more restrained in decoration. Candlesticks, which followed the forms of pewter and silver ones, were a specialty at Wincanton. Although details varied in each place, probably all English delft potteries produced "bricks," those rectangular boxes with perforated tops. They were used to hold flowers or an inkwell and quill pens.

English delft punch bowl, 18th century.

Tiles were an important output in both England and Holland. In fact, so popular were tiles in Holland that the making of them was almost a separate industry. Before the end of the seventeenth century Rotterdam, Haarlem, Amsterdam and Middleburg were noted for their tile production. In Dutch homes tiles were used on walls rather than on floors as in Spain and Italy. The entire wall in a kitchen or dairy might be covered with delft tiles, and in other rooms tiles usually faced the fireplace, overmantel or wainscoting. Single tiles, each with a complete motif, seem to have been almost as well liked as groups that were set to form a continuous pattern on the wall. The earliest motifs on delft tiles were fruits such as grapes and the Chinese pomegranate, tulips and other flowers, and animals such as the hare. Then came domestic motifs and scenes. In the late seventeenth century, tile decorators turned to ships, sea monsters and mythological figures as well as a large and varied roster of lifelike figures such as fishermen and farmers, peddlers and musicians, ladies and cavaliers and groups of children. The Chinese influence showed chiefly in the blue and purple monochrome tiles and in fretwork borders rather than in actual Chinese motifs and chinoiserie patterns adapted to tiles. But tiles were colorful, for potters turned to green, yellow and orange as well as blue.

So much did the Dutch like their tiles that entire pictures began to be made of them. Probably these had a special appeal to householders who could not afford oil paintings. Many were single tiles, considerably larger than those made for covering walls. There also were huge pictures made up of many tiles. For the latter, one of the favorite designs was a luxuriant bouquet arranged in a delft vase. Later, designs were adapted from engravings and paintings of Dutch interiors and landscapes.

Although not nearly so varied as the Dutch ones, English delft tiles interest collectors. Many English delft tiles were blue or purple monochromes displaying baskets of flowers in the Dutch manner, birds, figures or landscapes. Polychrome tiles often featured birds. Some transfer-printed delft tiles were made in Ireland, as well as in Liverpool, where this technique of decorating pottery was developed.

Dutch delft plate, early 20th century.

Obviously, except for transfer-printed ones, many English tiles could be mistaken for Dutch ones. And it may be difficult to decide whether many other pieces are English or Dutch delft. A Lambeth wall pocket, a Bristol brick or a Liverpool ship bowl is quite different from anything produced by Dutch potters, but a jug, a creamer, many plates and vases might all too easily be assigned to the wrong country. Potters' marks are one clue, although not necessarily a reliable one. It is helpful to know that English delftware was seldom marked, whereas Dutch potters placed their marks on the underside of a great deal of their delft. The style of decorating and the coloring can be safer guides for those who take the time to study and learn the characteristics of each country's tin-glazed earthenware. Remember that Dutch potters copied Chinese decoration quite accurately, whereas English potters tended toward chinoiserie patterns that were western interpretations of Chinese motifs.

Identification may be complicated by the fact that there have been imitations and reproductions, notably during the nineteenth century, and some of these can be mistaken easily for old delft. It can be immensely difficult to identify a good reproduction of antique delft unless the French or German potter added his own mark.

The introduction of creamware, or queensware, by Josiah Wedgwood in the 1760's soon made all kinds of tin-glazed earthenwares less important. English potters discontinued production of delft and turned to creamware or a reasonable facsimile of Wedgwood's fine product. Great quantities of creamware were exported, so production of tin-glazed earthenware in the Netherlands declined sharply. So-called delftware has continued to be made to some extent into the twentieth century in the Netherlands and a few other countries. The term is applied to china with an opaque white surface that is sometimes almost milky white, then again a hard shining white, and decorated with blue motifs that are considered typical of the Netherlands. The blue, incidentally, is often a poorer shade than that of antique delftware. Wherever it is made, modern delft bears little resemblance to the wares of the seventeenth and eighteenth centuries. In those years delftware was tin-enameled. Nowadays even in the Netherlands delftware is a hard-fired earthenware covered with a slip and painted under a lead glaze.

6. Lusterware

A pink luster tea set was one of the treasures brought out only for supper on Sunday or for guests on a weekday during the 1800's. Such tea sets were as popular in the United States as they were in England, where most of them were made. Any piece of pottery or porcelain that is covered or decorated with a thin film of metallic pigment is known as lusterware. Since lusterware was produced according to various formulas based on different metals, it offered a range of colors. A luster tea set that can still bring a nostalgic charm to a corner cupboard may be a shade of pink or rose, sometimes so faint as to be a delicate mulberry, again so brilliant as to be almost salmon or orange. And if these shades are not appealing, a variety of pieces can be found in brilliant copper or elegant silver luster.

When English potters began to produce lusterware around 1800, give or take a few years, they were developing a distinct type of their own. They were not, however, contributing anything brand-new to the decoration of ceramics. Credit for originating luster goes to the Near East, probably to the Persians, who were using luster, or glistening pigment made from metals, in the ninth century. Like the English so many centuries later, the Persians used copper and silver to produce handsome, colorful and iridescent lusterware. The luster techniques of the Near East were introduced by the Moors of Spain and from that country to Italy by 1500. Early luster of the Near East ranged from a dull yellow, golden brown and olive green to a metallic iridescence, while that of Spain and Italy displayed tones of ruby red, golden yellow and

Copper luster bowl, 19th century, English.

45

Copper luster goblet, 19th century, English.

rich blue, fading to an almost mother-of-pearl tint. Little of the everyday luster pottery of southern Europe has survived, but there are great plates, bowls and the like, displaying armorial bearings of Spanish and Italian families, in museums.

The nineteenth-century lusterware of England is as different as can be from the Hispano-Moresque pottery of the Renaissance. However, the luster pigments again were obtained from metals, and whether their finished appearance is an iridescent color or the color and sheen of a particular metal, it is easy to recognize. The actual color and appearance depend not only on the process but also on the skill with which the piece was fired. Luster should never be confused with gilding or silvering, very different ways of embellishing fine china. Nor should metallic luster decoration be confused with the pearly luster or iridescence typical of Irish Belleek and American Lenox porcelain; these nacreous wares reflect light, somewhat like mother-of-pearl.

The English applied luster to both pottery and porcelain. The finer kinds of earthenware, including the popular creamware, were widely used. Experts on luster state that soft-paste porcelain, pride of several English potteries during the eighteenth century, was not decorated with luster. However, bone china, which became the English equivalent of European hard-paste porcelain by 1800, often was given luster decoration. Many of the luster tea sets were bone china.

Silver luster was produced not

Silver luster sugar bowl, 19th century, English.

from silver but from platinum, for oxide of platinum produced a true silver color that did not tarnish. Nevertheless, when pieces entirely covered with silver luster are found nowadays, they are likely to look as though they need polishing. Gold luster, the source of several different colors, was made from gold oxide, and copper luster resulted from modification of the gold formula or from copper oxide. All three pigments were used in two different ways; they completely covered a piece of china, known as an allover, or they were used to decorate it in contrast to its white, cream or colored background.

Allover silver lusterware was one substitute for real silverware, particularly serving pieces, candlesticks and the like. One nickname, "poor man's silver," points up the fact that it was not only considerably less expensive than its silver counterparts but also less expensive than Sheffield plate, which consisted of silver fused over copper. Both Sheffield plate, which had been made since the 1740's, and allover silver luster, which began to be made in the early 1820's, declined when electroplated silver was introduced in the 1840's. Allover pieces of silver and gold luster represented considerable skill on the part of the potters, since they were decorated in the same manner as the real metal pieces. So exactly were the silver articles copied that the body of one silver luster creamer was molded to display the fluting that ornamented a real silver creamer of the period. For the most part, decoration consisted of the neoclassic motifs fashionable in the early 1800's. Fluting, beading and classical relief motifs, such as Wedgwood used on his jasper ware, were reproduced by the potters. Teapots as well as creamers and sugar bowls were made in the shapes and styles popular between 1800 and the 1840's; the first ones were small and classic in shape, but by the 1830's they were becoming larger and more rococo in outline. Silver luster candlesticks, jugs and other ornamental or useful pieces followed the style of real silver ones.

Oxide of gold made possible a variety of shades, chiefly pink or rose but sometimes orange or purple. The darker purple luster resulted from combining oxide of gold with oxide of tin. Another variation, basically pink, was the marbled, splashed, or mottled, luster that began to win followers around 1850.

Many of the pink or rose tea sets were gaily decorated with flowers and foliage, not necessarily too naturalistic and often combined with scrolls or a conventional motif rather like crosshatching or featherstitching. The luster pigment often was combined with enamel or paint. One colorful tea set has floral motifs of orange and rosy purple luster framed with luster lines and separated by large leaves painted

Copper luster pitcher, 19th century, English.

green and outlined with the luster. The strawberry pattern is one of the most coveted. Several potteries are known to have produced this. One of the most appealing I have seen has a wide conventional border of mulberry luster in which are embedded three-parted leaves of mulberry luster and berries painted red clasped in hulls painted green. Less sophisticated are the "cottage" tea sets, recognized by their design of a house, cottage or church. The building of pink luster has trees around it, a fence in front and a wide border.

Painting not only of tea sets but of other pieces was done with luster pigments against the ceramic body, on the lustered surface or in panels reserved for painting in enamel. Perhaps the most skillful painting was done by means of stencils, a technique worked out by Staffordshire potter John Davenport in 1806. Silhouette artists often were employed to cut out the paper patterns, which were pasted onto the glazed wares; the entire surface was then coated with wax. After the cutouts were removed, the design was exposed for painting with luster. When the luster had dried and the last bits of wax had been removed, the piece was given its final firing.

The reverse of stenciling is seen on resist lusterware, a decorating process developed by 1810. The white glaze or the ground color of the piece was used for the detailed pattern, which was set off by the metallic luster surrounding it. The design was painted over the glaze with a material that resisted the metallic oxide so that it did not adhere to the protected area. The resist later was washed away. This technique was used a great deal on silver luster pieces. Patterns were likely to be allover designs of fruit and vines, flowers combined with ivy and perhaps birds, sporting scenes and the like. One silver luster teapot in the helmet shape popular around 1800, for example, displays an intricate pattern of small fruits, vines, leaves and tendrils against its gleaming sides.

Transfer printing, the widely

Copper luster cup, 19th century, English.

used method of decorating table-wares in England, also was used on lusterware. Transfer printing involved far less handwork than any other type of decoration and was done in many colors. It was used on lusterware in at least three ways. Sometimes it was combined with resist decoration. Then again panels on the sides of a piece, such as a pitcher or a jug, were transfer-printed in black or another color and the remainder was decorated with pink luster or with bands of silver luster. A fair percentage of transfer-printed lusterware was made for sale in the United States, the transfer designs featuring an eagle with shield and stars, American patriots and statesmen, or scenes. Probably the most common examples of transfer-printed lusterware are the simple ones—that is, allover copper luster mugs, creamers and jugs decorated with bands of transfer printing in contrasting color. Often the bands were vivid blue; sometimes a wider band displayed a pattern of leaves or scrolls.

Pieces entirely covered with copper or gold luster are richest in color when the pigments were applied to a red-brown body that had been given a thin smear glaze. In the early years of the nineteenth century, copper luster ranging almost to bronze in tone was achieved by combining gold oxide with copper oxide and applying it to a dark body. Copper oxide alone was used starting in the 1820's, and the effect was neither as rich nor as fine. After 1840, copper luster was made in great quantity but poorer quality. The earthenware was heavy; the luster itself often is marred with specks or bubbles.

Silver, gold and copper luster-ware also was decorated with raised, molded or sprigged decoration. The effect was particularly good on allover pieces. Most of the earliest examples of raised or relief decoration against a luster background were done by hand, but later these were cast in molds. Two kinds of luster could be used on raised or sprigged ware, with the result that the ground tint usually was pink and the raised ornament a gold or bronze tone.

The greatest variety and quantity of luster probably were made for serving and drinking tea. A three-piece set consisting of tea-pot, sugar bowl and creamer was sometimes allover gold luster, more often allover silver or silver resist. Full tea sets were probably most common in bone china with pink or rose luster decoration.

Jugs and pitchers in various shapes and sizes were produced in all types of luster. There were even ewer-and-bowl sets for washstands and puzzle jugs. The pierced work, nozzles or piping concealed in a puzzle jug must be thoroughly understood before attempting to pour or drink from it successfully. Cow creamers were made in various poses, usually in marbled luster chiefly pink or glistening pinkish purple. Although less common than mugs, goblets and two-handled marriage or loving cups also were made and decorated with the various techniques common to luster; marriage cups seem to have been more popular in England than in America.

Appealing greatly to Victorians were luster plaques to hang on the wall. Each pottery plaque had a seascape or landscape painted on it or featured a text, axiom or moral admonition within a lustered frame. First choice for the frame seems to have been pink or marbled pink luster. Various lusters were used to make a variety of odd pieces. One of the oddest and most elaborate was the stand for displaying a watch, which took many fanciful forms. It wasn't enough, for example, to make a luster pottery tall-case clock with a hole where the watch could be hung in place of the dial; the clock had to be flanked with broken columns and figures where more luster could be applied. Other oddities were rolling pins for the kitchen, bulb pots, eggs to give on Easter and birthdays, knife rests, ink-wells, snuff boxes, tobacco jars, bell pulls, and furniture stops perhaps in the form of a lion's head and shoulders to prevent legs or casters from marking the rug.

The pairs of spaniels that became so popular in the nineteenth century—and are equally loved by twentieth-century collectors—often had luster markings ranging from a silvery mulberry to ruddy copper. Both busts and figures or statuary were modeled and covered with luster, chiefly for the English market, it seems. The busts usually were of a national hero such as Admiral Lord Nelson. Figures ranged from simple ones representing the seasons to an equestrian group representing Saint George and the Dragon or the Prussian Hussar.

Luster figures seldom are marked with the name of the sculptor or the pottery. In fact, potters seem to have been most reluctant to mark all kinds of lusterware, for most of it bears no clue to the maker. Some luster-ware made by such important potteries as Wedgwood, Leeds, Spode and Davenport did bear their marks. Yet the public demand for lusterware was met not primarily by a few of the important potteries but by many small and now forgotten ones. Some potteries produced a distinctive type of lusterware. Josiah Wedgwood II, son of the founder, sponsored before 1810 what the family pottery termed a moonlight luster; this was a pink splashed type, with orange-yellow speckling, that was usually applied to shell forms of vases, pastille burners and similar items. Knowledgeable collectors have learned to link other types of lusterware with the pottery that produced it. The Sunderland pottery in Durham, for example, became noted between 1807 and 1865 for the mottled, or splashed, pink luster and for certain designs. It takes time to learn about the types of ceramic body on which luster was applied, and the type of luster in which potteries specialized. Yet these are the facts that help to link a piece of luster to the pottery where it was made. To this day, a few English firms are said to use their own special formulas for the making of allover gold and silver lusterware.

7. Old Blue China

American housewives must have been overjoyed when gaily decorated sets of dishes began arriving in ports of the United States in the 1780's. Until then tables had been set with pewter and treen (woodenware) and only the most utilitarian articles were pottery. How much lovelier tables must have looked with the new sets of blue and white earthenware from England or blue and white porcelain from China! Wherever they came from, all kinds of dishes, as well as ornamental and useful objects such as vases, doorknobs and candlesticks, were soon being called china if they were made of baked clay, decorated with color and glazed.

The word china had been used first to distinguish the porcelain pieces that were brought from the country of that name to Europe and England in the late 1600's. The Chinese had been making beautiful porcelainware since the sixth century A.D., but Westerners had never seen it before. European and English potters who had been making only heavier and coarser kinds of pottery such as earthenware and stoneware were baffled by Chinese porcelain and it wasn't until 1709 that a German, Johann Friedrich Böttger, succeeded in producing

a hard-paste porcelain which was comparable in quality to the imported. His discovery was the cornerstone of the famous Meissen pottery works which was established near Dresden, Germany.

Potters in other countries experimented as much as the Germans did. As a result, many improvements were achieved in earthenwares and stonewares for dishes to be used on tables and eventually porcelain was being produced too. Because everything about Chinese porcelain was admired by European and

English potters, many of their dishes during the 1700's and early 1800's were decorated in blue with designs that imitated those on the Chinese ware. These are sometimes referred to as *chinoiserie*, a term applied to anything made in the Chinese style or with decoration that is inspired by Chinese motifs.

Blue and white china was easy to buy in eastern cities and towns of the United States; even in rural districts no house seems to have been so isolated but that a peddler could find it and sell at

Canton vegetable bowl, early 19th century.

51

Transfer-printed cup and saucer with silver luster, c. 1840, English.

least a tea set in one of the half-dozen styles or patterns that became so popular. Often the set was earthenware or stoneware and so was used as everyday china. Occasionally a person comes across an old blue teacup without a handle but with two saucers. However, cups seem to be the most breakable of all pieces and consequently plates, a platter or a large deep soup dish are more likely to have survived one hundred and fifty or more years of use. It is the old blue china made before 1890, and preferably in the early years of the nineteenth century, that collectors search for and that descendants who have inherited it cherish.

Old blue china doesn't have to be porcelain to be worth treasuring. Porcelain is white, hard, thin, lightweight and vitreous. Above all, it is translucent when a piece is held up to the light. Both earthenwares and stonewares are coarser and the finest quality of either is opaque in comparison to porcelain. Today's owner of the remnants of her great-grandmother's creamware

set might easily believe it to be porcelain, for creamware, which was also known as queen's ware and was developed by Josiah Wedgwood in the 1760's, was a vast improvement over earlier earthenwares. Still, even creamware is opaque, soft and porous. Stonewares are extremely hard and nonporous. Both porcelain and pottery for table use are decorated with a glaze poured molten over the clay body and baked at a high temperature to make the dish impervious to liquids.

The sets of blue and white dishes known as Cantonware were shipped from that port in China starting in the 1780's and a tremendous amount was carried in American clipper ships that crossed the oceans so speedily during the 1800's. It was not really expensive either in China or America and also was heavier looking than most porcelain, so most women used it for everyday kitchen china. Nowadays anyone fortunate enough to have inherited some Cantonware displays it in a corner cupboard and uses it on special occasions. Canton china was blue and white, although backgrounds inclined to a blue-gray and the shade of blue in the decoration varies considerably. Motifs are typically Chinese and any or all of the following are likely to appear on a single piece or to be repeated throughout a set: a tea house with pagoda roof, a bridge, willow trees, birds and landscape with hills or mountains. There is no one Canton pattern, and variations in its decoration are part of its enduring fascination.

Cantonware was made in very full sets for the table. These sets included covered serving dishes

and a covered butter dish, a tureen, plates and platters and open bowls in many sizes. A water bottle was not rare but sweetmeat dishes were. Any piece of Canton is cherished today, but experts claim that the finest quality is in really old pieces and collectors prefer those made before 1890 (since 1890 all tableware has had to be stamped with the country of origin in order to be imported into the United States).

By 1790 if a family could not wait for a shipment of dishes to arrive from Canton, they could purchase blue and white tableware from England. The popularity of Cantonware helped to establish the Willow pattern designed in England. Willow was made first of porcelain in Thomas Turner's Caughley pottery in 1780. It has been produced continuously ever since, chiefly in earthenware, by many other potters in England including the famous Josiah Wedgwood, and in the United States and lately in

"Madras", transfer-printed teapot, mid-19th century, English.

Japan. Strangely enough, whatever the quality of china and workmanship, the Willow pattern has remained basically the same. Placement of the several elements and decorative borders

Muffineer, or caster, c. 1825, English.

on rims varies, evidently according to the potter, and so do skillfulness of design and shades of blue.

The Willow pattern is true *chinoiserie* (the term is never applied to anything actually made in China). Needless to say, a legend has been spun to explain the Willow pattern. Traditional elements include a bridge, a river and islands, pagoda-like buildings, a boat, figures—usually two or three on the bridge—and two birds, sometimes called doves, overhead. The scene is framed with trees and shrubs that look exotic if not truly oriental. The figures represent a princess and the commoner whom she loves, usually shown on the bridge, followed by her father, a mandarin, and perhaps one or more of his associates. In fleeing from the irate father when the willow trees are in blossom, the lovers are drowned; the birds represent their souls.

Older than Willow is the blue and white porcelain pattern known as Meissen Onion, which was introduced by the Meissen factory in Germany before 1750. This also is classed as *chinoiserie* with a bit of humor. The Germans mistakenly identified the unfamiliar fruits, which they copied from the Chinese porcelain, as onions. They were really pomegranates. An immense quantity of Meissen Onion, actually a flower and fruit design, was imported into this country particularly in the late 1800's. Meissen Onion sets of tableware consisted of a varied and profuse number of pieces and the design ornamented an amazing assortment of household furnishings from bathtubs to candelabra and chandeliers. Since it was made for so long and so continuously, the pattern varies a little from time to time as does the shade of blue in which it was applied. About 1820, the soft blue of earlier years gave way to a bright, dark cobalt blue. The pattern was simplified around 1800 and even more so after 1900. On dishes made before 1800, onions in the border face the center, while after 1800 one onion faces in and the next one faces out. Some nineteenth-century pieces, including plates, had pierced or openwork borders.

Some English potters also made an onion pattern, but their sets are considered inferior in quality to the Meissen porcelain ones. All pieces made at the Meissen factory are stamped with its trade-mark which with the exception of the early years, always included crossed swords in some form. At the present time firms in England, Japan and the United States are making pottery sets with a pattern which recalls at first glance the traditional Meissen Onion pattern but which is hardly similar, let alone identical. The only genuine Meissen Onion was made in Germany and the earlier pieces are usually the most valuable.

By far the greatest amount of china came to this country from England, and much of it made

Adams sauceboat or creamer, rural motif, c. 1810-25, English.

Podmore, Walker cup and saucer, Washington vase pattern, 1849, English.

between about 1790 and the mid-1800's was intended especially to sell here. The Staffordshire District was the main source. Working in this county were the Clews brothers, the Mayer brothers, the Adams and the Ridgway families, Joseph Stubbs, Enoch Wood, J.&J. Jackson and many other potters whose names became familiar in American households because of their comparatively inexpensive yet attractive tea and dinner sets. Their work was often advertised in this country as "blue-printed," for the name Staffordshire became synonymous with transfer-printed decoration. Transfer printing by means of an engraved copper plate was originated in England about 1753 and the process made possible the mass production of a single design. Transfer printing was used chiefly on earthenware and to some extent after 1813 on ironstone, which was a type of glossy and durable stoneware whose white background had a blue tint.

Blue and red were the first colors used for transfer printing and

blue continued to be a favorite throughout the 1800's. The blue was deep, dark and strong from the late 1700's up to about 1850; thereafter the blues became lighter and sometimes looked almost faded. After 1830 other colors and sometimes a combination of colors were easy to buy.

Many people, and I am among them, consider old blue Staffordshire the most appealing of all the tea and dinner sets used long ago. Nothing else is quite like it. To bring to light a teapot of one-and-one-half-quart capacity, a couple of bone dishes or plates, a platter or a pitcher, guarantees endless enjoyment. A vast quantity of old blue Staffordshire made to sell in the United States was decorated with purely American historic or scenic views and was wreathed with flowers and foliage on the rims. Some of it was commemorative: the triumphal tour of Lafayette in 1824 was recorded on blue dishes from his landing at Castle Garden in New York City to his visits to Franklin's and Washington's tombs. The countless scenes chosen by potters

Blue and white spongeware pitcher, mid-19th century, English.

ranged from the inspirational to the sobering; in contrast to the Boston Athenaeum, the President's House in Washington and Harvard College, there was the Hartford Deaf and Dumb Asylum, Alms House in Boston and the Penitentiary in Allegheny near Pittsburgh. Potters went inland not only to Lake George and Niagara Falls but also to the Wyoming Valley, Pennsylvania, and the Shenandoah Valley in Virginia.

Some of the historic scenic dishes belong also to a group called Flowing Blue, Flowering Blue or Flow Blue, not just because they had borders of flowers and foliage but because the blue which was applied for decoration had a tendency to flow beyond the outlines of the design and tint the cream or white base. Yet the design stood out clearly without being blurred and the flow of the blue enriched the base color.

American views were only a small part of Flowing or Flowering Blue china. Flower and foliage patterns always were popular in this distinctive ware although the trend changed from time to time. Two large plates in my corner cupboard must have been made between 1810 and 1820 when shells were an important motif. In the center of each one, the largest of the shells is easily identified as a cowrie and is overhung with marine foliage. The decoration in deep rich blue is sharp and clear; Flowing Blue produced later in the nineteenth century often looks smudgy. Scenes and landscapes, often romanticized or perhaps oriental looking, also were common on Flowing Blue china.

Almost plain in comparison

Punch bowl, Wedgwood, late 19th century.

but well liked and widely used were the sets called "blue-edged" or "green-edged." They came from England too and were advertised in newspapers in this country as early as 1800. The only decoration was the narrow, feathery edging that looks as if it had been brushed or penciled on in blue or green; on some sets, there are simply narrow lines of blue or green. Undoubtedly these were kitchen dishes, but that is no reason to pass them by. Blue-edged dishes are as typical of their time as any of the old blue-printed ware.

The difficulty of telling whether

Blue and white spongeware bowl, 1880-1900, American.

a dish is ironstone or eartheware, creamware or porcelain is nothing compared to the difficulty of finding out where and when much of the old blue and white china was made. Cantonware, of course, is distinctive in background color and decorative motifs, and every piece of Meissen Onion ever made bears somewhere the crossed swords trademark of that pottery; other details of the mark changed slightly from time to time. But it wasn't until 1842 that the British Registry Office required that all pottery and porcelain be marked precisely and much that was produced before that year bears no mark, or only the pattern name or some small insignia on the underside. However, many collectors as well as experts can identify a piece of pottery almost at a glance, and perhaps after a little study can estimate approximately when it was made.

8.
American History on China

The Revolutionary War was hardly over before English potters began to export to the United States china decorated so that it would appeal to the Americans' pride in their new nation. Patriotic symbols and subjects, statesmen and heroes and, later, places and scenes in this country were colorfully transfer-printed on dishes to be used for tea and dinner. Shops in cities stocked this everyday earthenware, although it was neither the finest nor the most expensive china ever produced in England, and peddlers had no trouble selling it the length and breadth of the land. Most of it was manufactured in the Staffordshire district of England, a lesser amount in Liverpool, which was another pottery center. It is now referred to as Anglo-American ware and less formally as historical American china, commemorative ware or "old blue."

Whichever name you prefer for this distinctive china, it was decorated by transfer printing, a time-saving and inexpensive process that became synonymous with Staffordshire, although it was invented elsewhere in England. Transfer printing involved far less handwork than any other method of decorating china. Indeed, finishing usually involved no handwork at all because the design was engraved on a copper plate and thereafter could be reproduced over and over. Black was the first color used for transfer printing and remained a specialty with Liverpool potteries for many years. From about 1790 to 1830, Liverpool sent a flood of jugs and pitchers, bowls and plates with historical or patriotic American themes transfer-printed in black, perhaps with a luster border.

The Staffordshire potteries became known for blue or carmine-red transfer printing in the eighteenth and early nineteenth centuries. Blue of a rich, dark, brilliant tone quickly became the most popular color, at least with buyers in the United States. A

Staffordshire transfer-printed plate, "The Capitol," Washington, D.C.

dozen or more potters specialized in it. They were led by Enoch Wood & Sons, John and William Ridgway, J. & J. Jackson, Ralph Stevenson, James & Ralph Clews, Davenport & Co., the Mayer brothers, Joseph Stubbs, and the Adams family.

During the 1780's and 1790's it took more willpower than most Americans had to resist buying a beautiful deep-blue pitcher displaying an eagle with outspread wings and, in its beak, a long, fluttering scroll. (The eagle appeared on the Great Seal of the United States.) Other dishes and sets of the same period featured innumerable views of Mount Vernon, some of them including George Washington, and his horse; the Battle of Bunker Hill; and Franklin flying a kite.

The War of 1812 between Great Britain and the United States provided the English potters with new inspiration. It is amusing to note that they placed business above national pride, for they did not hesitate to make American victories the subjects of their transfer printing. Perhaps most often reproduced was Commodore Macdonough's victory on Lake Champlain, but not even the "Defense of Stonington, Conn. in 1814" was too minor to be overlooked. On the other

Staffordshire transfer-printed platter, "Lafayette at Washington's Tomb," Enoch Wood & Sons.

hand, a blue platter depicts the engagement between the U.S.F. *Chesapeake* and H.M.F. *Shannon*, which ended in an American defeat.

Lafayette's visit to the United States in 1824 was thoroughly covered in blue transfer-printed ware. It is a toss-up whether his "Arrival at Castle Garden" in New York or the "Landing of Lafayette" was produced in greater quantity. One or the other was turned out by every potter who was manufacturing dishes to sell in the United States. Lafayette's triumphal tour with its stops at scenes of the Revolution and at shrines erected to George Washington and its visits to the tomb of Washington and, according to the potters, the tomb of Benjamin Franklin was covered almost step by step and recorded on cups and saucers, tureens, creamers, plates and platters. Incidentally, tureens, sugar bowls and other pieces with either a cover or a tray usually showed two different scenes, not necessarily related: one on the tray or cover, the other on the container.

When patriotic subjects had been about exhausted, or perhaps only as good business practice, English potters fell back on engravings of American scenes that were starting to appear in books and periodicals in the 1820's. Then about 1830, transfer printing was being done in other colors, chiefly a lighter blue than the deep, rich blue used for so many years, pink, green, lavender, mulberry and sepia. In pink, for example, it was possible to purchase a plate showing "Schenectady on the Mohawk," "View near Conway, N.H.," or "Girard's Bank in Philadelphia." I am sure the color of one lavender plate was more pleasing than its scene, "Penitentiary in Allegheny near Pittsburgh." In sepia transfer printing, the choice was quite wide; for example, the "Headwaters of the Juniata," also available in blue or pink, and the "Water Works, Philadelphia." In green, a most attractive Staffordshire color, was "The President's House, Washington."

During the 1830's, James & Ralph Clews manufactured large

Staffordshire transfer-printed platter, "Esplanade, Castle Garden, New York."

*Staffordshire transfer-printed platter,
"New York from Brooklyn Heights."*

dinner services printed with American scenes in several colors. The Clews series was titled "Picturesque Views" and took most of its landscapes from William G. Wall's "Hudson River Portfolio." The idea did not originate with the Clewses. Another series of architecture views, named "Beauties of America," by John and William Ridgway, was produced in clear, dark blue during the 1820's. The tureen in this dinner service shows a strikingly sharp picture of the Boston Almshouse. The Medallion series by Ralph Stevenson is distinguished by four medallions on the rim showing portrait heads of men prominent in the 1820's. A Davenport series called "American Views" included scenes in Canada as well as the United States.

Although a scene, event or portrait dominated each piece of china, it was always surrounded by a handsome border. Some of these borders were quite elaborately designed and engraved and represent fine work. The com-

mon themes were flowers and foliage, oak leaves and acorns, and shells. Enoch Wood & Sons specialized in shell borders. In fact, two distinctly different designs of shell borders were used by this firm, who between 1819 and 1840 produced more historical china for America than any other potters in Staffordshire. However, just as Enoch Wood & Sons also used flower and foliage borders to some extent, so did other potters, such as Ralph Stevenson, occasionally use a shell border. The two shell borders used by the Woods are easy to learn to recognize; shell borders by other potters are quite different. Ralph Stevenson also did handsome oak-leaf and acorn borders.

All in all, more than eight hundred subjects were produced in transfer-printed earthenware for the American market between 1780 and about 1860. Not to be confused with this early historical china are the souvenir plates that first became popular around the turn of the century. It is still possible to buy cheaply at many resort and vacation spots a pictorial plate or perhaps a cup and saucer as a memento of the visit. The best ones are made in England and are modeled on the now antique American historical china. That is, decoration consists of a picture of the resort or landmark in the center and a border of flowers or foliage. On the whole, these souvenir dishes lack the unstudied charm of antique historical ware. The color is not as attractive and the transfer printing has a shiny look. The contemporary ones are sold individually, not in sets as the commemorative china was, and they always have a potter's mark.

Antique collectors disdain a

souvenir plate made in Staffordshire as recently as six months ago, even if it does have a view of New Hampshire's Old Man of the Mountains surrounded with a border of roses, thistles and shamrocks, both transfer-printed in blue. People have been collecting the late eighteenth- and early nineteenth-century historical earthenware for a good many years. It is still possible to buy examples, although prices are higher now than when collecting of it first began. Undoubtedly, too, there are still pieces to be found in out-of-the-way places.

A number of museums and restorations have fine collections. Old Sturbridge Village, the early nineteenth-century restoration in Sturbridge, Massachusetts, has a small but interesting collection of historical "old blue." Appropriately, two outstanding private collections were given to the Smithsonian Institution's Museum of History and Technology not so long ago. One gift comprised the nearly nine hundred pieces of Staffordshire earthenware, transfer-printed in various colors with American views, collected by Ellouise Baker Larsen and presented by her. The collection dates from the first half of the nineteenth century. The other, quite different, collection, gathered by Robert H. McCauley and dating from the late eighteenth and early nineteenth centuries, consists of over one hundred pieces of cream-colored English Liverpool-type earthenware decorated with transfer prints with American themes. Most of the pieces in the McCauley collection are pitchers (a specialty of the Liverpool potteries). The Larsen collection consists of tablewares of all sorts.

Staffordshire transfer-printed platter, "State House, Albany" and "Entrance of the Canal into the Hudson at Albany."

9. Picturesque Staffordshire Tableware

The Staffordshire district, a midland industrial county in England, has produced enough tableware since the seventeenth century to set the tables of the world. Staffordshire ware has been tremendously popular in the United States since the 1780's, when English potters started to decorate their wares to appeal especially to the ready market in this country. Mugs, jugs and sets of dishes came from such famous potters as Josiah Wedgwood, Josiah Spode, William Davenport, Enoch Wood, John Ridgway, the Mayer brothers and many others, all of whom worked within an area of approximately fifty square miles, only a small part of the county. In fact, by 1800 close to a hundred and fifty potteries were operating in the Staffordshire district. They produced earthenware, which is an opaque, porous pottery before it is glazed; hard and nonporous stoneware; and some porcelain, a thin, white, hard, lightweight, vitreous and translucent ware which originated in China and was not made by any Western country until 1708. Here, during

Queensware plate, Wedgwood, decorated over the glaze in purple enamel, c. 1769-77.

the eighteenth century, originated interesting new types of pottery such as basalt, jasper and Wedgwood's fine earthenware called creamware or queensware, along with a new porcelain that became known as bone china.

In spite of the variety of pottery and porcelain produced in the Staffordshire district, the name of this county has come to be synonymous, at least in this country, with the sort that was decorated by means of transfer printing. Before 1750 all pottery and porcelain had been decorated by hand, either with slip (a liquid potter's clay or paste); by painting or enameling; more rarely by molding, so that decoration was in relief; or by applying motifs. Then too, the glaze itself was a form of decoration. Glaze, used to coat a clay article, fuses with it at a high temperature to become glasslike and make the clay impervious to liquids. Colored glazes often were applied to earthenware. Overglaze decoration was not practical for everyday china, but underglaze decoration never wore off no matter how often a dish was used. Then in about 1750 transfer printing, the new and less expensive method of decoration, was developed. It involved far less handwork than any other kind of decoration, and furthermore, the design could be reproduced over and over. Developed in England, the process remained a peculiarly English type of decoration, although for a few years during the eighteenth century some of the continental European potteries also tried it.

Strangely enough, transfer printing was not invented in Staffordshire. Liverpool and London are the chief rivals for the discovery and development of this new process of decoration. Some experts insist flatly that the process was invented by an Irish engraver, John Brooks, and first used at the Battersea Enamelworks in London about 1753. On the other hand, John Sadler of Liverpool may have discovered transfer printing independently. In any case, when the company of Sadler and Green applied for a patent in 1756, they claimed to have been using transfer printing for several years. According to the story, which may be apocryphal, John Sadler, an engraver by trade, noticed a group of children who were playing with broken pieces of pottery. They were pasting still-wet impressions of discarded proofs from an engraving plate on the pieces; when they removed the paper, the ink impression remained on the pottery. Sadler immediately recognized the possibilities of what he saw for decorating china. For a few years after Sadler and Green were granted their patent, many Staffordshire potters, including Josiah Wedgwood, sent their wares to Liverpool to be decorated by the new process. Then, in 1763, Wedgwood applied for rights to do his own transfer printing and soon other potters, especially in Staffordshire, followed his lead.

Transfer printing was simple in both theory and practice. The desired design was engraved on a copper plate which was then inked with ceramic color, and a paper print was taken from it. While the ink on the paper or tissue was still wet, the design was

Queensware plates, Wedgwood, Queen's pattern, transfer-printed decoration in black, c. 1772-1800.

transferred onto the piece of pottery or porcelain. Next the piece was immersed in water to float off the paper, and finally it was fired to fix the color. Although in the early 1750's the famous porcelain factories of Bow and Chelsea in London did some decorating with transfer printing, in the 1760's the process was being used more and more on earthenware and stoneware to produce colorful, fully decorated and yet comparatively inexpensive tableware.

Black was the first color used for transfer printing. It remained a specialty of Liverpool potteries for many years. From 1790 through the first quarter of the nineteenth century, they sent innumerable jugs and pitchers, plates and bowls to the United States with historical and patriotic scenes transfer-printed in black. In the eighteenth century, Staffordshire potteries also produced black transfer-printed wares. The jugs from Staffordshire were lower and more globular, while those from Liverpool were barrel-shaped.

Carmine red and blue were two other colors chosen by Staffordshire potters during the late 1700's. Blue quickly became the most popular color, at least in America, and continued to be so through the 1800's. Well known is Flowing Blue earthenware and stoneware, which was made in many patterns, all of them having one thing in common: the patterns had run somewhat in the fire so that they gave the effect of being slightly blurred. The deep, strong blues that are so rich-looking were produced from the late 1700's up to about 1850; thereafter, the blue became lighter and sometimes almost faded.

By the early 1800's Staffordshire potters also used pink and rose, mulberry, lavender, green, and sepia or brown for an endless number of patterns. Two-color designs also had some vogue. Typical is one small green-and-pink plate in a corner cupboard in Connecticut, all that is left of a tea set made at Davenport potteries in Longport, Staffordshire, between 1805 and 1820. Pink-and-green transfer-printed designs have become one of the most popular color combinations hunted by present-day collectors of old Staffordshire ware. Among the monochrome pieces, a mulberry plate or platter in good con-

Tureen, Elijah Mayer and Son, early 19th century, English.

dition is probably rarest today, while lavender and green are less common than blue, brown, rose or red.

A good many of the patterns designed during the eighteenth century and in the early nineteenth century can be classed as chinoiserie. That is, they followed the style or imitated the exotic motifs of the greatly admired porcelain brought from China. The most famous chinoiserie pattern originating in England is Willow, introduced in 1780 by Thomas Turner of the Caughley porcelain factory in Shropshire. Willow always has been transfer-printed in blue, the color also inspired by the decoration on Chinese porcelain.

Other chinoiserie patterns sometimes were transfer-printed in colors other than blue. Mulberry, for example, was chosen by Podmore, Walker and Company in Tunstall, Staffordshire, for one of its chinoiserie patterns between 1834 and 1859. The pattern name, Corean, was incorporated in the potter's mark.

Pink, green, mulberry, blue, brown and black against a white background or a combination of colors were used for a group of patterns loosely based on European scenes. Castles, villas and

Sugar bowl, floral pattern, c. 1833-47, English.

vistas were not always typical of Italy, Spain or Switzerland despite pattern names which suggest definite locations in those countries. Pastoral scenes or a romanticized bit of landscape often were obviously English. Before 1842 it was not uncommon for the name of the pattern to be printed on the underside of each piece, often without a potter's mark.

An important segment of transfer-printed ware was designed to sell only in the United States. The American Revolution was hardly over before Staffordshire potters, including Josiah Wedgwood, began to decorate ornamental pieces and tableware with purely American motifs. Their selections were headed by the eagle and extended to

heroes and statesmen, historical and patriotic events and, by the early 1800's, to views of buildings, cities and countryside. Liverpool potteries sent over ware showing heroes such as George Washington and Stephen Decatur. Staffordshire potters also were inspired by the War of 1812, and by Lafayette's tour of the United States.

The most popular border for Staffordshire ware was floral. Sometimes the flowers can be recognized; oftentimes not. Foliage was important, entwined with flowers or alone. Shells were a popular motif for a few years in the early 1800's and Staffordshire potters like Enoch Wood and Sons sometimes used several kinds, especially to edge a marine design. At times during the nineteenth century, borders were based on geometric lines or calico motifs such as dots, diamonds and latticework.

A few firms such as Wedgwood have consistently marked every piece made at their potteries, using a succession of different marks for different wares and periods. Unfortunately, a great deal of the transfer-printed tableware made between the 1750's and early 1800's lacks an identifiable potter's mark. A mere small

Flow blue serving bowl, early 1800s, English.

crescent, a C or an X is a clue that is almost untraceable.

Less difficulty is encountered in dating and attributing a piece made in England after 1842. Starting that year, a system of marking was required by the British Patent Office. This Registry Mark not only indicates that the design was registered at the British Patent Office, but also makes it possible to find out what kind of ware it is, and the year, month and day on which the article was made. The Registry Mark is diamond-shaped with circles or curved lines at the corners to set off the key letters and numerals. One group of symbols was used for the years 1842 to 1867, another for 1868 to 1883. These keys can be found in many books on pottery and porcelain. In addition, many potters continued to print their own trademark. Any piece of transfer-printed ware that bears the words "Made in England" under the potter's mark was imported after 1891, when a law passed by Congress made it essential to state the country of origin.

10. Souvenir Spoons

Shopping for gifts to take home to family and friends was hardly burdensome for the traveler during the 1890's. The solution was simply to buy souvenir spoons of the place a person had visited. It was as easy to buy a sterling silver teaspoon of unique design in Ouray, Colorado, or Miles City, Montana, as it was in New York and Boston, although the choice of appropriate designs was much wider in the large eastern and midwestern cities. Travelers to these cities also often had a choice of teaspoon, coffee (demitasse) spoon or orange spoon. An engaged daughter might be collecting coffee spoons; and no two would be alike in the dozen they were aiming to acquire. These cherished spoons of the 1890's are collected almost as avidly today as they were then.

The first Americans to become acquainted with souvenir spoons were the ones who took the Grand Tour of the Continent in the last quarter of the nineteenth century. They learned it was a simple matter in Nuremberg, Germany, a cathedral town visited by every traveler, to purchase an apostle spoon, so-called because its handle was topped with a miniature figure of one of the saints. In Wittenberg, a spoon depicting Martin Luther could be bought. By the time the traveler reached Italy and Rome, he might select a spoon with a turned-over handle ending in the neck and head of a goose. Happily, tourists also discovered that a silver spoon was easy to pack, that a half dozen required little more space than just one, and that all of them arrived home in perfect condition.

The plunge into making souvenir spoons in this country was taken in the late 1880's by M. W. Galt Bro. & Co., jewelers in Washington, D.C. This firm copyrighted designs for two spoons: the handle of one ornamented with a bust of Martha Washington; the handle of the other, with George Washington. It was Daniel Low, jeweler and silversmith in Salem, Massachusetts, who really sensed the latent market here. After a trip to Europe during which he, like other tourists, bought souvenir spoons, it occurred to him that a spoon decorated with a witch and her devices would be a most appropriate souvenir of Salem, where witchcraft trials were held in the early 1690's. The resulting teaspoon sold for $2; the coffee spoon, for $1.25; and an orange spoon with its deep, narrow, irregularly shaped and pointed bowl, for $2.25. The same spoons

Souvenir spoon, sterling silver, "New Jersey."

Souvenir spoon, sterling silver, "Niagara Falls."

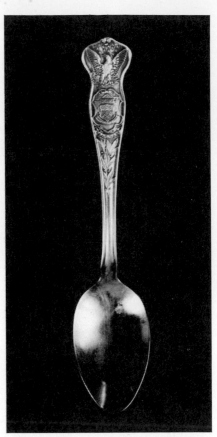

Souvenir spoon, sterling silver, "Colorado."

with gold bowls sold for 25 to 50 cents more. Nowadays one of them sells for $60-$70. The design on the handle was simple but effective—at the top, above the word Salem, a furious-looking witch wearing a pointed hat and carrying a broom; below, three crossed witch pins (straight pins witches used to prick their victims). The spoon sold so fast that soon the design was being made in fifteen other pieces, including forks, knives and other kinds of spoons.

So popular was the first witch spoon that a second one was designed, again for Daniel Low. A more elaborate handle displays all the symbols of the witchcraft delusion of Salem residents. At the base a cat stands with its back arched; a rope twining around the handle encloses "Salem, 1692"

and three witch pins; and topping all this are a new crescent moon and the witch with her broom. The same motifs are seen on the underside of the handle. This second witch design was made not only in the usual three spoons but also in bonbon and sugar spoons, a sardine fork and a paper knife. Both these witch spoons were of heavy sterling silver and display fine workmanship.

Inspired by Salem, silversmiths in Boston, Lynn, New Bedford and other nearby cities started producing appropriate souvenir spoons. Springfield, Pittsfield and Hartford were among the western New England cities that eventually had their own souvenir spoons. From New England, the fad spread to New York City, and from that point, south and west to the far corners of this country. Thousands of different designs were turned out; some places had only one, but large cities, such as Buffalo and Chicago, had a half dozen or more.

The majority of the souvenir spoons made during the 1890's were of sterling silver. Although plated silver had become acceptable for flatware and hollow ware, few of the souvenir spoons were made of it. This may have been because so many of the souvenir spoons were designed and made by the Gorham Company, which had been producing silverware in Providence, Rhode Island, since 1831. It was probably natural that their first souvenir spoons were based on landmarks of New York City, since they had a retail store there. The first one had a handle tipped with a miniature replica of the Statue of Liberty. Several versions of this spoon differed chiefly in the bowl. Some

had actual coins, such as a dime; a quarter or a half-dollar, inserted in the center. The bowl of another early Gorham New York souvenir spoon consisted of a silver dollar hollowed or curved slightly to a semisphere; the handle was tipped with the coat of arms of New York State. Gorham also produced souvenir spoons to be sold in other cities, such as Baltimore and Detroit, and for special events. However, local silversmiths became active in behalf not only of their own city or town but also of neighboring ones.

Less is known, even by collectors, of the souvenir spoons made by the equally famous Tiffany & Company, jewelers and silversmiths who had their fine store in New York and their workshops in New Jersey. Tiffany & Company produced a considerable number of souvenir spoons between 1891 and 1920. Their series blanketed New York City and environs with such designs as Brooklyn Bridge, the Metropolitan Museum of Art, several churches, more bridges, and other spots beloved of tourists.

Designs for all souvenir spoons were original and often unusual. It is amazing, too, how many different designs based on the same motifs could be worked out. Sometimes they were restricted to the handle; sometimes both handle and bowl were used. A coffee-spoon souvenir of Boston is covered with eight motifs. The bowl depicts the Old State House. On the flared end of the handle is the State House and under it, successively, are Paul Revere on his horse, a pot of beans with that word on it, and Boston spelled out vertically. On the reverse of the handle are Faneuil Hall, Old South Church and Bunker Hill Monument.

Many souvenir spoons had fancy gilt handles or gilt or gold-washed bowls. Some had enamel decoration. One of the handsomest is a sterling silver teaspoon from Toronto, Canada. The tip of the handle is covered with white enamel, background for a maple leaf in autumn colors and a

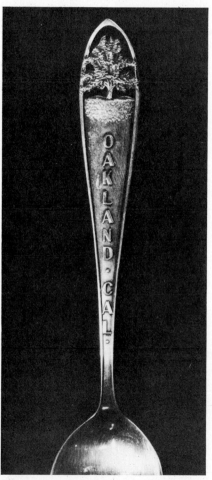

Souvenir spoon, sterling silver, "Oakland, California."

green banner with Canada in gold letters. On the gilt bowl Toronto is above the coat of arms of Canada, both in relief.

Presidents and poets, explorers and soldiers, and celebrities in general were well represented. H.G. Hudson in Amesbury, Massachusetts, brought out four different spoons honoring John Greenleaf Whittier. One had Whittier's head in relief terminating the handle; another showed his birthplace; the third, his home in Amesbury; and the fourth showed "The Captain's Well" of the poem of that name. All four spoons displayed a facsimile of his autograph. Harriet Beecher Stowe was depicted on an *Uncle Tom's Cabin* spoon, and Susan B. Anthony and Moll Pitcher of Lynn (not to be confused with Molly Pitcher of Revolutionary War fame) had spoons of their own.

Famous persons, cities and resorts, and historical and current events, such as the Columbian Exposition in Chicago in 1893, offered plenty of opportunity for creative decoration. When inspiration flagged, designers turned to fraternal organizations, holidays, games and sports, Indians, animals and other wildlife. There were whist and euchre

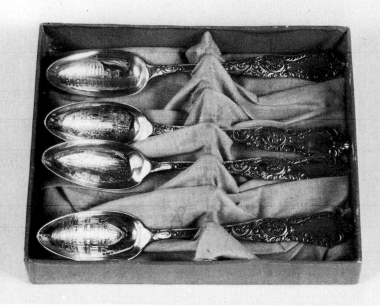

Set of four demitasse sterling silver souvenir spoons, "Columbian Exposition,"
1893.

spoons, a seaside souvenir spoon and good-luck spoons. Special spoons were designed to be given as a token of love, a reminder of friendship, and for engagement, wedding and silver-anniversary presents.

The original price of souvenir spoons seems a mere pittance by present-day standards. Collectors still find them reasonable, for the majority sell for $15 to $25. Souvenir spoons can still be purchased in Europe and new ones are still brought out occasionally in this country. Alas! The current ones made in the United States are likely to be plated silver, not sterling, and the workmanship in execution of the design is seldom as fine as that on souvenir spoons made here during the 1890's.

11. Silver Spoons

Silver spoon by John Edwards, Boston, 1700-1725.

Silver spoons have been made for centuries in many countries. Golden ones are mentioned in the Bible. Bronze, brass, pewter, tin and iron ones have been common and such unusual materials as ivory, horn, flint and slate have been used at various times and places. Many a household still has at least one wooden spoon among its kitchen equipment, but it is the silver spoons that always have been treasured, counted and handed on from one generation to the next.

In America, spoons have been made to some extent of horn but chiefly of wood and several metals. The silversmiths who were kept busy during colonial days melting down Spanish dollars and other silver coins turned out tankards, beakers, mugs, candlesticks and many other handsome and useful household articles, but rarely silver spoons. Yet some silver spoons were made in the late 1600's. Proof of this is the collection of silver funeral spoons at the Museum of the City of New York. They had been made for a bereaved family to present to mourning friends

who came to the funeral. These 300 year old spoons had large bowls and rather straight handles with notched or trifid (three-pointed) tips; on the handle in script was recorded the date and reason for the gift.

Spoons made during colonial days had large bowls so wide that they were almost round; handles were straight, short and almost stocky. The first great change in spoons was brought about by the vogue for drinking tea, a beverage that had been introduced into Holland in the early 1600's, into England by 1650 and soon after was brought to America. Tea drinking required smaller spoons than any previously made. Teaspoons also were lighter, easier to balance and to manage with teacup and saucer. The so-called five o'clock teaspoons, which were smaller than current teaspoons, were made through the Victorian era but not longer.

Other kinds of spoons also were originated to facilitate the making and enjoyment of tea. First of these, after the teaspoon itself, was the tea-caddy ladle; then about 1780 came the caddy spoon which resembled a short-handled scoop. These were used to dip the tea leaves out of the canisters in which they were stored. An occasional one had a small hook on the underside so it could be hung in the tea chest. The earliest caddy ladles were in the form of scallop shells and sometimes the flutes of the shells were embossed, perhaps with a floral design. Many caddy spoons had smooth bowls which might be decorated, and during the 1800's some were made in odd shapes such as a jockey cap, a bird or a fish. Typically, caddy spoons had short wide handles which might be decorated on one or both sides.

Sugar spoons are more common today than sugar tongs, which were made first in the 1690's. Sugar spoons always have had a rather wide, flaring and shallow bowl. A fluted scallop-shell form used to be common for sugar spoons, which were kept in bowls of sugar.

A distinctly odd looking piece of silver that became essential to the tea paraphernalia during the 1700's was the mote-skimmer or strainer teaspoon. This slender spoon became common in England and undoubtedly was demanded by American women whose husbands could afford to import them. The mote-skimmer had a long, narrow, tapering handle that was barbed or pointed at the end and a fairly narrow and long bowl that was pierced ornamentally. The pointed handle was used for clearing tea leaves from the spout of the teapot and the perforated bowl for skimming leaves from the tea after it had been poured.

Quite different and appearing much later were tea-ball spoons with the bowl covered and pierced; tea leaves could be placed therein for making a cup of tea. A tea-ball spoon was included in a set of the sterling silver pattern Strasbourg, introduced in 1897. This pattern is still made but the teaball spoon is not. And long before tea-ball spoons appeared, many changes had taken place in other spoons.

It was about 1700 when individual spoons were added to equipment for the dining table. By the early 1800's in England and America, tables were being set with a soupspoon, a dessert spoon and a teaspoon for each person. Considering that a spoon has only two parts, it is amazing that so many changes appeared during the 1700's and 1800's. They occurred in the size and shape of the bowl, the length and shape of the handle, the shape and curve of the handle's tip, the ornamental engraving or lack of it and the placement of initials or monograms. These characteristics often indicate the decade or the span of years when a silver spoon was made; they can be as important as the marks of the silversmiths on the underside and are far easier to trace.

In the early 1700's, bowls were still large but oval rather than round, and the comparatively thin handles usually had a notched or trifid tip. This was the period of the rattail spoon which had a tongue or reinforcement of silver fastened down the back of the spoon to the bowl. The smaller teaspoons were becoming better known too. After 1750, for some reason or other, tips turned down. Bowls became narrower and slightly pointed, handles wider with more shaping. The 1790's brought quantity production of teaspoons and other individual spoons. Although made of silver, they were so thin and lightweight that many found nowadays show teethmarks or are bent. Between 1790 and 1830 handles became wider and tips were rounded, tapered or squared off to form the clipped coffin tip.

By the 1830's when pieces were stamped Coin or Dollar, C or D, to certify their silver content, spoons still had narrow pointed bowls but the handles were likely to be fiddle-shaped; the tips turned up again, for good. Many fiddle-shaped spoons had decorations on the tips of the handles, usually a shell, a sheaf of wheat or a basket of flowers. Or the fiddle outline was emphasized with a slight ridge, called a thread, just a fraction of an inch from the edges. At this time, tipped spoons appeared with no decoration other than a simple indentation at the tip of the handle. Tipped handles, threading, and shell shapes continued to be popular throughout the nineteenth century and into the present one, in spite of the many fancier patterns in which both sterling silver and plated silver were made after 1860.

Owners' initials or family crest were placed on colonial silver as a means of identification. Around 1700, initials or monograms were placed on the back of the handle. But by the 1790's, they began to appear on the front. In the 1830's,

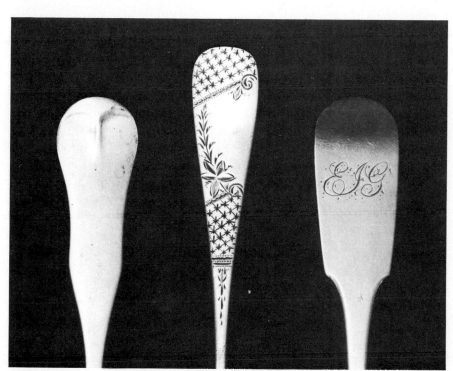

Sterling silver spoons, mid- and late-19th century, American.

it was not uncommon for a bride's monogram to be placed on the front of the handle and her married surname on the underside, both written in script.

Not subject to these changes was the marrow spoon which was used much more in England than in America. Its purpose was to extract marrow, considered a great delicacy, from bone cavities.

Marrow spoons were made from the late 1600's to the early 1900's, and during the 1800's came to be known as marrow scoops. Each one had two bowls or scoops, one at either end, and because they were different sizes they could be used for small or large bones. Incidentally, a cheese scoop, which was a serving piece and much larger than a marrow scoop, was part of many silver patterns made in America after the 1870's.

Some of the colonists brought apostle spoons to America. So far as I know, they never were made in this country. The handle terminated in the figure of one of the apostles and a full set consisted of a dozen spoons, each one ornamented with a different apostle. These spoons were christening gifts during the fifteenth and sixteenth centuries. Starting in the 1600's, many figure-top spoons were made in Holland and Germany. The terminal figures on the handle represented Biblical personages such as the Virgin and Child, or mythological characters such as St. George and the Dragon. Figure-top spoons gradually lost any religious significance and became less elaborate. Among heavy Dutch silver spoons of the nineteenth century, one was topped with a windmill having vanes that turned, and another had a bird atop a handle modeled to resemble tree bark.

Many of the souvenir spoons that became so popular in the United States in the late 1800's recall the earlier and larger figure-top spoons. For example, a teaspoon that was a souvenir of Watkins Glen, New York, was topped

with the cutout figures of an Indian and his dog; another one from Buffalo, New York, terminated in a cutout buffalo and showed Niagara Falls on the bowl. By no means all of the souvenir spoons made between 1880 and 1910 had cutout figures. More of them probably displayed appropriate motifs in low relief on the bowl and on one or both sides of the handle. Thus a demitasse spoon, souvenir of Mount Vernon, shows a bust of George Washington on the tip, Washington spelled out vertically along the handle and a view of his home, Mount Vernon, on the bowl. Thousands of souvenir spoons were made in sterling silver or plated silver, honoring cities, towns and resorts in the east, midwest and far west.

The early 1700's had brought small personal spoons to the fore, but for centuries before that large spoons had been important for cooking and serving. The 1700's also brought changes and additions to this group, notably in serving spoons in various sizes and shapes, and ladles for several purposes. Early in the century, silver basting spoons with handles up to eighteen inches long were plain and simple yet handsome. Gravy spoons had

shorter handles and smaller bowls, of course, and some had perforated bowls to strain pieces of onion and other solid ingredients from the liquid gravy. Special large spoons began to be made for removing stuffing from the meat to a plate, and for serving various foods. By the early 1800's, American families were offered a wide choice of silver spoons from little ones three and one-half inches long for salt dishes to soup ladles twelve inches or more long.

Ladles were perhaps the most enduring of the eighteenth-century innovations. Although sauceboats with spouts for pouring had been used for a long time, it wasn't until the 1700's that ladles were considered necessary accessories. A ladle is recognized by its cuplike bowl and handle bent to fit the curve of the spout against which it is to rest. Like spoons, many of the earliest ladles had scallop-shell bowls, and as the fiddle, thread, shell and other ways of decorating were developed for other spoons, they were copied in ladle designs. By the late nineteenth century, the gravy spoon had been superseded by a gravy ladle. At least six different sizes of silver ladles were being made in the United States during Victorian years. The largest was for serving soup, the smallest for relishes or mustard. In between were special ones for oysters, gravy, cream and punch.

The Victorian years brought more kinds of serving spoons as well as more rococo styles and patterns. Tablespoons, averaging eight and one-half inches long, were not new. Their bowls, handles and tips had changed as had those on individual spoons. Around 1800, tablespoons had narrow pointed bowls and the tips of their handles turned down but, by the middle of the century, bowls were oval and tips turned up. Similar, except for its perforated bowl, was a pierced serving spoon for moist vegetables. A berry spoon, deeper and rounder than a tablespoon, was desirable for serving a fruit dessert and the indispensable pudding spoon had a scoop, often fluted, rather than a bowl. A slender spoon resembling a teaspoon, except that its handle was longer and narrower and its bowl was pierced decoratively, was a relish spoon. Still another small spoon was for jelly. The exceedingly decorative nut or bonbon spoons, with shallow pierced bowls and handles to make them about five inches in over-all length, came to stay, but the special spoons for macaroni or ice are no longer made.

All kinds of silver spoons were produced in this country, and in ever-increasing quantity after 1790. Whether they were thin lightweight teaspoons with turned-down tips, utterly simple tablespoons with pointed bowls, marrow spoons or macaroni spoons, pudding spoons or ladles, an identification mark was put on the underside. Many books about old silver contain pages of

Sterling silver spoons, late 19th and early 20th centuries, American.

silversmiths' marks. In England, craftsmen's guild rules had required silversmiths to stamp their wares with hallmarks that indicated the maker, his town, the year, the reigning monarch and the sterling quality of the metal. In early America the only mark was customarily that of the maker, either his initials or his last name. Between 1830 and 1860, silverware was stamped Coin, Dollar, Pure Coin, or with the letter C or D to guarantee that it was of the quality of silver coins from the United States Mint (nine hundred parts of pure silver out of one thousand parts). Since 1860 the word "sterling" has verified that a piece consists of ninety-two and five-tenths per cent pure silver. Plated silver, introduced in the 1840's, was so stamped and often stated the grade such as Triple Plate or Quadruple Plate in addition to the maker's name.

12. Household and Personal Silver

Porringers, candlesticks, teapots and other gleaming articles of real silver were one sign of a family's wealth during Colonial days. They were fashioned by the silversmiths working in America from the silver coins a family managed to amass. These pieces were identified by the owner's monogram or crest and stamped underneath with the silversmith's mark, which was his guarantee of the value. It was not until mid-nineteenth century that the majority of families in this country were prosperous enough to afford silverware. By that time, they could choose between sterling silver and less expensive silver plate, introduced here in 1846.

The word "sterling," which came into use after 1860, stamped on a piece of silver is a guarantee that it is .925 fine, or consists of 925 parts of pure silver out of 1,000 parts. Between 1830 and 1860 silverware had often been marked with "C," "D," "coin," "dollar" or "pure coin" to indicate that it was the same quality as the silver coins from the United States Mint; that is, .900 fine, or 900 parts of pure silver out of 1,000 parts. Silver-plated ware, of which several grades were made, often stated the quality, such a "triple plate" or "quadruple plate," near the maker's mark on the underside. Still another mark stands for the kind of base metal that was coated with pure silver by electroplating. Britannia, a type of pewter, often was used in the early days of electroplating here; later, a white base metal was preferred. Silver plating had been invented in England and was introduced here by the Rogers brothers, Connecticut silversmiths.

Some of the articles that had commonly been made of silver during the eighteenth century in America had gone out of fashion by the time the technique of silver plating was introduced here.

Silver-plated coffee urn, 19th century, English.

Tankards, beakers, caudle cups and various other kinds of cups, and even porringers were no longer in demand by the 1850's. On the other hand, baskets and plates for cake, punch bowls, pitchers for various purposes, as well as innumerable serving dishes and ornamental pieces, were made in greater quantity between 1850 and 1900 than ever before. Many of them were available in either sterling silver or silver plate, thus offering a price range to fit family resources. Some Victorian silverware may be puzzling, but the pieces are worth polishing and, if they can't be put to good use, are impressive to display.

There is, for example, the "large coffeepot" friends purchased at an auction a couple of years ago. It is silver plate, which has polished up beautifully, and about the shape and height of a silver coffeepot with a hinged lid and a handle. It also has a porcelain lining, whose purpose, according to my friends' reasoning, was to keep the coffee hot. It took a while to convince them that their piece is an ice pitcher. Innumerable ones were manufactured between the 1850's and 1900, when the demand petered out.

A number of patents for a double-wall pitcher in which ice

74

could be placed to keep water cool had been granted in the early 1850's. The first ones were made of britannia metal with a space between the inner and outer walls. Later, ice pitchers were made of silver plate and improved with an inner lining of porcelain. Some ice pitchers were made on a stand so they could be tilted; others could be bought with matching goblets.

Serving liquids and foods in insulated silver containers was not a new idea with Victorians, although they undoubtedly had many more pieces of this sort than were available a century earlier. The predecessor probably was the argyle, first made in the eighteenth century. Because John, fourth Duke of Argyll, disliked the congealing gravy that was passed in open sauce boats after the meat had been carved and served, he designed gravy containers that were heated internally. Silversmiths in England began making them in the 1760's and sold them as argyles, misspelling the inventor's name. This dish resembled a small teapot with a long, narrow, curving spout. It was heated by one of four methods: a hot-water jacket, a central box-iron, a central hot-water chamber, or a lower hot-water compartment. Argyles changed somewhat in shape periodically, as did teapots and coffeepots, but were made of both silver and silver plate and were popular for about a century.

The origin of chafing dishes can be traced back even farther, for they were in use in England during the reign of Queen Elizabeth I. Apothecaries at that time recommended to their wealthy patients that they drink from silver cups and cook in silver skillets

Brittania teapot, 19th century, English.

and saucepans because of the danger of food poisoning from copper and brass utensils improperly used and cared for. The cooked food still in the covered pan was carried into the dining room on a burning charcoal brazier. These skillets were also known as chafers and with their charcoal braziers were called chafing dishes. By the end of the seventeenth century a spirit lamp was substituted for the charcoal brazier. These silver saucepans or skillets were small, often no more than four inches in diameter and

less than that in height. Chafing dishes such as these were made in Boston, New York and Philadelphia during the eighteenth century. They are smaller and daintier than the modern chafing dish, usually pierced decoratively and have wooden balls under the feet to prevent the table from being marred.

A highly acceptable gift in this country during late Victorian years was a silver-plated serving dish with an inset of glass or porcelain that was heat-proof. This baking dish was slipped into the silver-plated container with its cover before it was brought to the table. Round and oval dishes of this sort, family size, were popular here. Earlier, probably, were large dishes for bringing various kinds of meat to the table. They had a hot-water compartment in the base and sometimes a cover or hinged lid too. Victorians also liked their round or oval vegetable dishes to have a hot-water compartment in the base. In fact, Victorians carried their preference for warm food to such a point that silver toast racks were made with a hot-water chamber in the base. By 1800 an urn of a size and shape for tea or coffee and with a spigot was being made to fit over a spirit lamp. A variation was the coffee biggin, which worked on the principle of the drip pot, over a spirit burner.

The practicality of the Victorians may have been exceeded by their love of ornaments, which led them to display and cherish large pieces for dinner tables and sideboards. Some of these, such as epergnes and punch bowls, were traditional, but their availability by the late nineteenth century in sterling silver or silver plate made it possible for more

Silver-plated gallery tray, 19th century, English.

families to own them. The epergne, which had been known for almost three hundred years, reached its peak of popularity here during the Victorian years. The term refers to an ornamental piece that was usually tall (some were three feet high) and consisted of a large center basket, perhaps with a canopy, with decorative arms or brackets from which were suspended small baskets or dishes. The latter, which were filled with flowers, fruits, nuts or bonbons, were usually detachable. Epergnes as a rule were made of silver, although the little baskets sometimes were lined with glass. Openwork was characteristic. Before American silversmiths started to make epergnes in the nineteenth century, owners in this country had imported them from England or France. One of the new forms that appeared during the 1800's consisted of a bowl into which a series of slender vases to hold flowers could be fitted. Another had a central wirework or pierced basket on a high stem of foliage or a figure. Others stood on a mirror plateau or silver plinth on which were placed side baskets or classical figures.

The sideboard in American dining rooms wasn't complete without a fruit bowl on a silver-plated stand. By the 1880's, an art glass was often used for the bowl. Rococo as it is, I prize one that was a gift to a great-grandaunt, for her name is engraved across the top of the gleaming silver-plated base. On the stand, stamped, "quadruple plate" on the underside, are two cupids holding a silver-plated saucer into which fits a satin-glass bowl. The irregularly shaped bowl with its crimped edge shades from rose to pink inside and is white on the exterior, which is encircled with a branch of brambles. Enameled red raspberries and blue-black blackberries hang from gold stems with gold leaves.

Punch bowls, made since Colonial days, also became fancier during the Victorian years. Early punch bowls were made with two handles. These large deep bowls with or without a cover and often with a foot were likely to be decorated with chasing, engraving and embossing. Designs ranged from simple panels of embossed flowers to allover scenic designs that became general in late Victorian years. A variation of the punch bowl, also made from Colonial through Victorian times, was known as a monteith. A monteith differs from a punch bowl in having a notched or scalloped edge from which footed glasses could be suspended in order to chill them. Some monteiths were enhanced with a crown or removable rim from which glasses could be hung. This type of bowl is said to have been named for a Scotsman who wore a cloak with a scalloped edge.

Silver cake baskets and dishes were handsome and so were silver-plated ones, although some of the latter were elaborately deco-

Sheffield cake basket, early 19th century, English.

rated. A cake basket, whether of old silver, sterling silver or silver plate, had a fancy but serviceable handle and stood on four small feet, a footed pedestal or a shallow base. Pierced baskets, especially those made in the eighteenth century, are as charming as they are rare. Both baskets and broad, shallow dishes for serving cake became immensely popular during the nineteenth century. Two or more decorative techniques, such as fluting, gadrooning, chasing and beading, often were combined to decorate

these round or oval pieces.

The Victorian penchant for silver extended to personal accessories after 1870, when it became commonplace for men and women to own silver-backed and silver-handled brushes and other small articles of sterling silver or silver plate for their chiffoniers, dressing tables and bureaus. Each piece usually bore the monogram of the owner in script letters. The silver was decorated with scrolls, ribbons, ferns or foliage, often combined with roses, water lilies or other flowers. Straight handles were common on mirrors, but occasionally one is found with a loop handle.

Although they were not required to do so, American silversmiths during Colonial days customarily marked their wares with either their initials or their last name in a depressed oval, shield or other geometric form. Coin silver also usually had a maker's mark as well and, of course, sterling silver is stamped with that word and the silversmith's mark. Silver plate bears the manufacturer's name or symbol; often the grade of the plate is stamped nearby and there may be a design or manufacturer's number. A great many marks can be identified in one of several books.

13. The Luster of Pewter

Pewter is one of those things about which most people feel strongly; they either like it a great deal or won't have any in the house. For more than two decades, whenever an auctioneer has announced a piece for sale, a ripple has gone through the audience and bidding has been spirited. The enthusiasm of collectors approaches that of American housewives from colonial days to about 1850, for during those years pewter was perhaps more popular in America than anywhere else in the world. Certainly it was in general use longer here.

Pewter, unlike silver, is not a precious metal. It is an alloy of which the chief constituent is tin; the other ingredients may be copper, bismuth, antimony and lead in varying proportions. Tin deposits in Asia made it possible for the Chinese to produce beautiful articles of pewter more than two thousand years ago, and those in Cornwall, England, supplied the Romans with the main ingredient for pewter plates and dishes before the birth of Christ. By the thirteenth century, it was indispensable in houses and churches in England and, within another hundred years, was almost as common in Europe. Pewterers began to emigrate to the colonies

in America before 1700. The first ones came to Virginia, but others soon were established in every important city. New settlements and rural areas were served by peddlers who included pewter and tinware in their varied stock. So great was the demand for pewter that fully as much probably was imported from England and Europe as was made here.

It was not easy for a pewterer to follow his craft in colonial days, for at that time tin, the chief element, was mined in England and

Wales and was exported only under a heavy tariff. To help out the pewterers, customers often traded in scarred and dented pieces for shining new ones. These badly worn pieces were melted down by the craftsmen and used to make new ones, and it has been said that even peddlers carried melting pots and spoon molds the better to serve their customers. As a result, very few of the pieces used during the 1700's in America are to be found, even in museums. Collec-

Pewter charger, Edward Danforth, Middletown, Ct., 18th century.

Pewter basin, English, 19th century.

tors consider themselves lucky to come across pewter made between 1810 and 1860.

Because pewter is so much softer than silver and brass, it can be dented, bent and scratched easily. Pewter also corrodes and develops tiny pockmarks. Consequently pewter, unlike silver, cannot acquire patina with age and handling. The surface is one of the best ways to decide whether a piece of pewter is an authentic antique. Although the surface will look smooth, it will feel rough to the touch since old pewter is bound to have at least minute scratches from the use it has had. Again, because of the softness, the piece is likely to be somewhat uneven.

A plate, platter, mug or beaker of pewter was far less expensive than the same article made from silver, and pewter candlesticks, inkwells and buttons were less costly than those of brass. This accounts for the great diversity of things made from pewter. Table and household articles of pewter were a natural preference over treen (wooden) ware, which was what most people had to use to set tables and serve food until well along in the 1600's. It wasn't until ten years or so after the Revolution that earthenware dishes became quite readily available and began slowly to replace pewter on tables. At that, pewter still remained popular for other household utensils and accessories and for personal adornment.

Spoons, plates, platters and chargers, which were large, flat, round dishes for carrying meat, and other tableware were made in one piece. Anyone who has visited a restoration where old-time crafts are practiced can recall how fascinating it was to watch the pewterers pour molten metal into a mold to form a teaspoon. (Incidentally, never place any piece of pewter over direct heat, for it will melt). Teaspoons, however, were only one of a dozen or more different kinds that were common; there also were large cooking and basting spoons, ladles of various sizes, tablespoons and serving spoons, tiny salt spoons and sugar spoons. Teapots, tankards, porringers and other items that had to be cast in two or more pieces and soldered together became known as hollow ware, a term also applied to silverware.

For centuries, pewter was fashioned by casting and turning. The hot, molten metal was poured into a mold to shape it and then was turned on a lathe to smooth the surface. Many pieces also were hammered to give them strength and perhaps to achieve some simple form of decoration. The hammer marks on old pewter, however, can hardly be detected in contrast to the fairly large ones clearly visible as a sort of allover decoration on some modern pewter. Finally, workmen must have cleaned or polished their pieces to an irresistible luster.

Two changes that occurred shortly after 1800 made pewter more popular than ever in this country. An alloy, appropriately called britannia since it had been originated in England, was introduced here and by the 1820's it had replaced, for the most part, the old type of pewter. Britannia resembles pewter so closely that it is impossible to tell one from the other unless pieces are so marked on the underside. Britannia also

Modern copy of Revere-type pitcher of late 18th century.

is an alloy, chiefly tin with some antimony and copper. It was considered an improvement over the old pewter formula, not only because the finished metal was brighter but also because it was more durable and did not bend so easily. By 1825, pewter and britannia were being made by a different process known as spinning. This technique eliminated casting and hammering, and made possible a greater variety of shapes and pieces.

On the whole, American pewter was far simpler than that made in other countries. With this soft metal, such decorative techniques as chasing and *repoussé* or embossing, which were common on silver, could not be used. However, English pieces of pewter often were engraved and many European ones were cast in relief, while in the Orient inlay of other metals and semiprecious stones was not uncommon. In comparison with European and Oriental pewter, that of England and America was plain.

One popular piece, the porringer, had one or two fancy handles. These handles were pierced in an openwork, rather geometric pattern or had elaborately scrolled designs, or they might take the shape of a simple tab or ear. A fairly deep dish, the porringer had a nearly flat bottom, upright sides and occasionally a cover, and was originally used for individual servings of porridge.

Some pewterers became noted for one or two pieces and confined their output largely to them. All pewterers in New York City were noted for the tankards, which varied in the design of the cover, handle, terminal of the handle and the thumbpiece by which the lid was raised. Many had dolphin terminals on the handles. One of the New York pewterers, Frederick Bassett, produced the largest tankards, holding three and one-half pints, ever made in this country before the Revolution.

Teapots, coffee pots, pitchers, sugar bowls and other hollow ware followed the shape, size and general style of comparable pieces of silver. However, styles and shapes were simplified and slower to change in America than in England. Small pear-shaped teapots, for example, are a Queen Anne style that appeared in American silverware from about 1725-1750. But pear-shaped pewter teapots were still being made by the Boardman brothers in Hartford, Connecticut, in the early 1800's. The spinning pro-

Pewter lighthouse coffeepot, signed "Calder," early 19th century, American.

cess not only made teapots and especially water pitchers more plentiful in britannia than they had been earlier, but also introduced larger teapots. By the 1820's, cylindrical teapots, often with straight spouts, became fashionable. Then during the early Victorian years, they became even larger and more rococo in shape, and had curving spouts and handles. Tea services consisting of a teapot and matching or similar creamer, sugar bowl and tray also were made to some extent during the early Victorian years. Utilitarian, although usually plain pieces of good workmanship and with good lines, were tea caddies. At a country auction last fall, competitive bidding quickly pushed up the price of a pewter tea caddy, which was about 8" high with a cover plus an inner lid that fit snugly into the mouth. It probably was close to one hundred and fifty years old.

All kinds of drinking vessels were made of pewter. Flagons for wine, tall with a handle, spout and sometimes a lid, and steins, beer mugs that usually held a pint, were more common in Europe than America. Here tankards were much more common in pewter than in silver. The pewter ones varied in size and capacity. Some of the earliest ones were pear-shaped, also called tulip-shaped, but most American tankards were inclined to have straight sides and domed tops. Mugs, which are much smaller drinking cups with a handle, were usually cylindrical. Beakers were perhaps more common in pewter than any other material; these are large, wide-mouthed drinking cups sometimes footed or on a standard.

Pewter measures were an everyday necessity in kitchens, dairies and barns as well as taverns. A pewter collector in Florida who has specialized in measures has gathered examples typical of various regions of France, England and Scotland as well as of the Channel Islands, Ireland and America. A set consists of seven measures in graduated sizes from one-half gill to a gallon, but it would be unusual to obtain a complete matched set. A one-quarter gill size is rare. Measures made in this country were not likely to have lids as did the English baluster-shaped ones. Other popular shapes were pear, pot-bellied, cylindrical or straight-sided.

Pewter mug, early to mid-19th century, American.

In addition to plates, platters and chargers, bowls or basins ranging from 4" to 14" in diameter were common. Most of them were quite plain and perhaps had a molded rim. Salvers on a low foot were another coveted piece. Salt dishes took the form of large, open trenchers in the eighteenth century, but by the time britannia was general in the nineteenth century they often were low footed dishes, pierced to show a colored glass liner.

Candlesticks and chambersticks with their simple turnings often were as handsome as those of silver. Wall sconces to hold one or more candles, and chandeliers with several candles were valued

Pewter inkwell and pen holder, early 19th century, American.

highly. Probably the first type of pewter lamp was the little peg lamp, which had a projecting end so that it could be placed in a candlestick, or a hook to fasten it in wood. In the early 1800's pewter lamps to burn whale oil were small and quite simple, but by 1830 larger and more ornamental ones of britannia appeared. Some miniature night lamps were made too. Pewter also was considered decorative enough for inkwells and inkstands, picture frames, door latches, buttons and snuff-boxes.

Pewterers in this country were not required to mark their wares as were these craftsmen in England. However, marks were quite general here and identify the pewterer and often the place where he worked. Books on pewter usually reproduce a sampling of these makers' marks or touches. Instead of identification, some pieces have a quality mark that indicates the grade of alloy. Britannia eventually became a base for silver plate; its use for this purpose can be determined from the silversmith's mark. Silver plate suited people's purses and fancy, and as a result the 1850's saw pewter and britannia disappearing into cupboards.

With time and neglect, pewter and britannia darken and may develop black spots. They can be cleaned, but cannot be polished until smooth. If special pewter polish is not available, it is safe to use a good silver polish. Avoid a gritty polish or a liquid one with an abrasive action. Water will dull and spot the finish, but if pewter is dried carefully after cleaning and washing it should retain its own inimitable luster for many months.

Pewter basin, American, late 18th century.

14. Versatile Porringers

A porringer is a small dish, deeper than a saucer or saucedish, with one or two handles, like tabs, attached at the rim. Some of the oldest porringers have straight sides, usually with a rolled edge. Much more common, particularly in pewter, were curving sides, contracted at top and bottom. The bottom had a domed center, rising slightly from a circular gutter. This is sometimes called a porringer basin. Of the many porringers produced in America by silversmiths and pewterers, few had covers.

The words *porringer* and *porridge* are closely connected, and the porringer was used originally for eating porridge and cereal. It was ideal for serving any liquid or semiliquid food, from broth to stew. The American colonists are said to have used their porringers for eating berries and milk too. Porringers were equally handy in the sickroom, although any patient who saw a porringer being used while the doctor was bleeding him, according to the practice of the times, could not have been entirely happy about eating broth or custard later on, even from another porringer. In any event, porringers remained popular in America at least seventy-

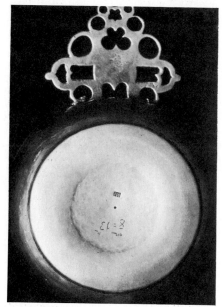

Silver porringer, John De Nys, Philadelphia, early 18th century.

five years longer than in any other country, but dropped out of use about 1850, when a variety of china dishes took their place. They came back into fashion about twenty-five years ago as gifts for newborn babies.

Porringers were made of both silver and pewter. Pewter ones were not only less expensive but also softer and less durable than those of silver. As with other pieces of pewter, porringers were melted down when they became badly dented and marked, and the metal was fashioned into a

new piece needed by the household. Pewter had pretty well replaced treen (woodenware) for table use in average homes in England by the early 1600's, when the first colonies were being settled in America. Eventually it became more popular in America than in any other country, and pewter pieces of all kinds, including porringers, were used here longer than anywhere else.

Silver porringers were made in America during the seventeenth century, but pewter ones were produced in greatest quantity between about 1750 and 1850. Before that, probably more pewter porringers were imported to the Colonies than made here. There were good reasons for this. In the first place, the Worshipful Company of Pewterers in London discouraged emigration, if only because they wanted to conduct trade with the Colonies. In that they were successful, for as late as the mid-eighteenth century the value of pewter ware shipped to America compared more than favorably with that of other important commodities. In the second place, England, in the interest of her trade in finished products, was reluctant to sell tin, one of the chief ingredients of pewter, to the Colonies. Of course, pew-

Pewter porringer basin, late 18th century, American.

terers did come to America from countries in Europe and eventually from England. Added to these were the young men who served their apprenticeship in America, some of them probably during the seventeenth century. By 1788, there were enough members in the New York Pewterers' Society to make a notable impression when they marched in the parade in New York City celebrating the ratification of the Constitution.

Both silver and pewter porringers were made in several sizes. Diameters ranged from 2½″ to 6″. The most practical sizes were from 4″ to 6″ in diameter. The smaller porringers from 2½″ to 3½″ in diameter were common in European countries with extensive vineyards, where they were used as wine tasters. Some diminutive porringers were made and signed by pewterers working in America, but they are believed to have been used as measures or toys. Certainly one less than 3″ in diameter was neither large enough nor stable enough with its handle to hold food. A contemporary reproduction in sterling silver of a porringer made by Paul Revere probably represents an adult's porringer. This one has straight sides, 1¾″ high including

the rolled edge, and is 4¾″ in diameter. Its pierced handle is 2¼″ long and 2″ at the widest point.

Porringers and spoons were two of the commonest articles in Colonial silver, according to the experts. Arthur and Joanna Mason of Boston must have been delighted to receive a silver porringer as a wedding gift in 1655—flattered and appreciative too, for it must have taken a considerable number of silver coins to make the porringer after they were melted down, and to pay the silversmith. Their gift bears the marks of John Hull and his partner, Robert Sanderson. Robert Sanderson had immigrated to Massachusetts in 1638 after he had served a nine years' apprenticeship at his trade in London. John Hull, who had come to Massachusetts with his family when he was ten years old, learned the trade of goldsmithing, as it was generally called, from his half-brother in Boston.

The porringer for the Masons was simple but handsome, a large round one with a handle pierced in a keyhole design. The porringer is now in the Museum of Fine Arts in Boston.

From France and Holland also came craftsmen who became famous in the Colonies. A silver porringer by Appollos De Rivoire, whose work is overshadowed by that of his son, Paul Revere, is in the Metropolitan Museum of Art in New York City. This family were Hugeunots who fled from France to the island of Guernsey before coming to America. Another silver porringer in the Metropolitan Museum's collection represents a different heritage. This is a superb one with two elegantly pierced handles and cover, made by Jan van Nieuwkirke, who worked in New York from 1708 to 1716.

Both silver and pewter porringers were cast in two parts, the bowl and the handle. Although pewter porringers cost far less than silver ones, the brass molds in which the molten metal was cast were expensive. The prized brass molds were commonly handed on from one generation to the next, and it was customary for a pewterer who had completed his apprenticeship to go into business with a set of used molds that had been inherited or purchased. Secondhand molds

Sterling silver porringer, Gorham, 20th century.

often were advertised for sale in newspapers.

If it had not been for the high cost of the molds, the independence of craftsmen in America might have spurred every pewterer to have his own special design for the handle. As it was, more than twenty different handles were made in this country. This is far more than were produced in other countries, and many of the American ones were quite different from those common in England and Europe. The pierced handle was typical of England,

while the solid tab became traditional in Europe. Both types of handle were made in America, but the pierced, or perforated, one became the favorite. The shape and design of the handle make it reasonably easy to decide whether a porringer was made in this country or was imported, as uncounted numbers, particularly of pewter, were.

The shape and design of the handle also are a clue to the region of America where the craftsman worked. The silver porringer made in Boston in 1655 by John Hull and Robert Sanderson had a pierced handle. Some variation of the pierced handle became common throughout New England and in the southern colonies, all of which had been settled primarily by families from some part of England. In areas where settlers came from one of the European countries, craftsmen made solid handles in one form or another. It is interesting that the design of a handle on a silver porringer was likely to be adapted as much as fifty years later to a pewter porringer.

The solid handle in its simplest and plainest form was general in southeastern Pennsylvania, where Germans settled. It relied on its shape for interest; otherwise, there was only a small hole so that it could be hung in a cupboard or on the wall. Solid handles were usually oval, sometimes rather long, sometimes more of a square with rounded corners. In Newport, Rhode Island, a distinctly pear-shaped handle appeared about 1770. Newport, however, was sufficiently cosmopolitan that the solid handle was made in competition with the pierced handle.

The decorative piercing was

done after the handle had been cast but before it was applied to the bowl. The earliest handles on both silver and pewter porringers are said to have been pierced with geometrical designs, such as a square, diamond, triangle, circle and crescent. Two or perhaps three of these shapes were combined in one handle. After 1725 handles were pierced in various scroll patterns. One of the oldest and most familiar of these is the fairly simple keyhole design, recognizable by the roundness of its piercing. Handsomest of all is the flowered handle, which was pierced with elaborate scrollwork and sometimes attenuated almost to a point. The flowered handle flourished in New York, the Connecticut River Valley and Rhode Island. There were many variations of scrolled piercing that fall between the simplicity of the keyhole handle and the intricacy of the flowerered one.

Unusual in this country were handles in the form of a crown or dolphin. The crown handle, pierced to emphasize its shape, was popular in England, much less so in America. Any American porringers with crown handles are almost certain to have been made before the Revolutionary War. A cherished porringer with a dolphin handle, now in a private collection, was made by pewterer John Danforth of Norwich, Connecticut (1741-1799). The handle consists of two dolphins flanking a shield, with geometric piercing between and above them. One handle was enough, evidently, for most silversmiths and pewterers in America. Porringers with two handles were far from unknown, but four handles were unusual, contrary to English and Euro-

Silver porringer, René Grignon, c. 1692, New England.

pean custom. Richard Lee, pewterer working in Springfield, Vermont, between 1802 and 1823, did produce a 4"-wide porringer with four handles that are extremely decorative but look disproportionate.

Handles frequently displayed on their upper side the initials of the person for whom the porringer had been made. The style of the initialing isn't always a clue to the age of the porringer, for this personal touch sometimes was added years after it had been made. The craftsman's, or maker's, mark was sometimes on the underside of the handle, sometimes on the bottom of the porringer. Many, but not all, pewterers marked their wares. Silversmiths, as a rule, marked their work with their names or initials plus their mark in relief against a depressed oval, shield, rectangle or other shape.

I suspect that most of the antique silver porringers made in America are already in museums or private collections. The number of enthusiastic pewter collectors in the last decade may have unearthed many of the pewter porringers too. Pewter, even brand-new, was never as lustrous and bright as silver. Any pewter porringers found now are likely to be not only dented and perhaps corroded or pitted but also quite black. Nothing can or should be done about surface damage, but there is no reason for not making the pewter lustrous again with a special pewter polish. The age and region of a pewter porringer can be determined by the maker's mark or, if there is none, then less definitely by the shape and decoration of the handle.

15. Brass
All Through the House

Brass ware adds a cheerful glow to any room, although articles made of this metal are no longer so essential to the smooth running of a house as they were two hundred and even one hundred years ago. In the days when America was being settled and a young nation was being founded, the brazier was more important to a town than a silversmith. This was because the brazier produced so many practical articles that were needed throughout the house to make daily living more comfortable. His handcrafted articles almost without exception served a useful purpose, but however utilitarian, they added a gleam of beauty. Although so many different things were made of brass, there is no superabundance of really old pieces around nowadays. Many of the articles that it was nice to own in brass could also be made of other materials. Measures were quite as likely to be of copper or pewter as of brass, door knockers of iron were common before brass ones became popular, many more candle boxes were wood than brass, and candlesticks or candle holders could be purchased in any of a half-dozen materials, depending on the buyer's purse.

Articles of brass were less expensive than those of silver and more durable than those of pewter, which is much softer. Brass is an alloy consisting chiefly of copper and zinc in variable proportions. The resulting metal is ductile and malleable, hard and durable, easily joined, and takes a high polish. As a result, articles of brass have not deteriorated as have those made fully as long ago of some of the other metals. Some silversmiths and many coppersmiths worked with brass as well as their chosen metal. Paul Revere, who won lasting fame as a skilled silversmith, is known to have worked with both brass and copper. Less well known is William Heyser of Chambersburg, Pennsylvania, who left a copper teakettle, signed with his name and dated 1825, as well as a large hammered brass kettle. Maker's names and marks were the exception rather than the rule on brass. Unlike silversmiths and most pewterers, who marked their products, braziers seldom identified their work and almost no records of their names exist. The demand for brass must have been great, for although braziers established themselves in all the colonies, a considerable amount of brass ware was imported from Europe. A brass milk can might

Brass tobacco jar, late 18th century, English.

Brass incense burner, 19th century, Middle Eastern.

have come from Holland, brass candlesticks from England, yet they would look very much like the same pieces made in America. Braziers came to America from England, Holland and France and worked here in the styles they had learned in their native land. Although braziers are known to have worked in America since the 1660's, most of the brass that people find nowadays was made and used during the nineteenth rather than the eighteenth century.

It was in the eighteenth century that well-kept houses, particularly in a Colonial city such as Philadelphia, Pennsylvania, or Newport, Rhode Island, began to be furnished with many brass accessories. The first example of the brazier's skill often was the gleaming door knocker or rapper. Brass ones of good size began to replace simpler ones of wrought iron by the early 1700's. Frequent polishing revealed the beauty of these early brass knockers. An elongated S, which became a classic design of the eighteenth century, was really a rapper. The piece in the form of an S was hinged to one of two brass disks on the door so it could be pulled forward and rapped on the second disk. Two other popular designs of this cen-

tury were the shell and the vase; these forms were fastened to a door and had attached brass loops that could be clanged against them. By 1790 the eagle was as popular a motif for knockers as it was for furniture decoration. Eagle knockers with attached loops were made in several poses, some worked into more elaborate designs than others. The urn and the lyre were other popular designs for knockers during the neoclassic years of the early 1800's. Cast-iron door knockers in more fanciful shapes became common after about 1850 but never completely displaced the rich-looking brass ones. Incidentally, door knockers were fastened only to the outside door, never to the doors of rooms inside the house.

Fully as decorative and much more varied were candlesticks. These ranged from the chamber stick on an attached saucer with a ring handle for carrying it around the house and from short brass ones four inches or so high to heavy sticks seven to nine inches or more tall. Except for chamber sticks, candlesticks were usually made and bought in pairs. Brass ones followed the changing styles and forms of silver ones. An early and now rare form had a domed base. Tall candlesticks with baluster stems and round or square bases were popular in America during the eighteenth century, particularly during the Queen Anne period (1725-1750). From about 1800 to 1840 neoclassic designs favoring slender, tapering stems were preferred. Until the late 1600's brass candlesticks, wherever they were made, were cast in a solid piece. But from about 1680 to 1790 they were cast in two pieces and the hollowed halves were soldered or brazed together; the seams on this type of candlestick are a clue to its age. After 1790 candlesticks were again cast in one piece.

To increase the illumination of a room after dark, a pair of brass sconces was often attached to a wall, or a candelabrum holding two or more candles was kept on a side table. Brass sconces undoubtedly were more common than candelabra. For a household that burned candles every evening, an extinguisher or snuffers was essential and usually was of the same metal as the candlesticks. An extinguisher is simply a cone to be held or dropped over the candle to put out its light; it was often attached by a chain to the rim of a brass or silver candlestick. A snuffers was a scissorslike tool with an open box attached to one pointed blade and the fourth side of the box terminating the other blade. A snuffers extinguished the flame and, more importantly, clipped off burned portions of the wick so the candle would burn more evenly and brightly. The clippings were caught in the box so they would not fall and mar wood or cloth. Snuffers were often purchased with either a small tray or an upright stand on which they were kept.

Near the fireplace or under the mantelpiece might hang a cylindrical brass box to hold candles. If this box was embossed decoratively, it probably had been imported from Holland. From the mantelpiece might hang a small portable lamp with one wick to burn whale oil, its back turned over to form a hook so it was easy not only to hang but also to carry. Brass seems to have been used far less than other materials for lamps. The two most popular styles appeared after kerosene had been generally accepted as the best fuel. These were the student lamp, introduced about 1875, and the Rayo, with a round font on a footed base and a dome shade of glass, which became popular in the 1880's. Many Rayo lamps were nickel-plated over brass.

A much older and simpler type of lamp, called a *lucerna*, is a curiosity worth looking for in brass. The *lucerna* was displaced in America in the early 1800's, but it was used in Spain as late as the 1870's (*lucerna* is the Spanish word for lamp). The *lucerna* has a tall standard over which its several parts can be slipped. Lowest is the arm that permits the height of the light to be adjusted. Above the arm is a small drip pan on which rests the two-part oil font, around the lower part of which are four equidistant spouts for wicks. Tiny conical brass extinguishers and sometimes a clipper for the wicks were attached by chains to the arm. *Lucernas* must have given not only little light but also poor light. Animal fats or vegetable oils in small in-

Brass candle snuffer and tray, 18th century, English.

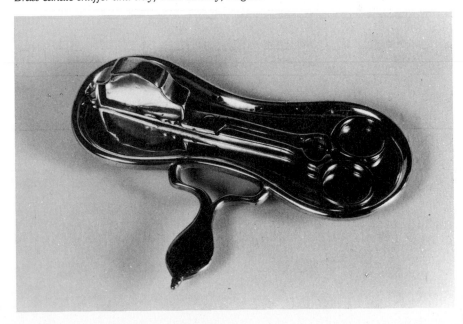

land communities and fish oil along the coast might be all that was available to burn, and all these smoked and smelled.

The fireplace was a focal point for brass, and the most important fireplace in the house had a full complement. For some of the fireplaces the andirons consisted simply of a horizontal bar and shaft of iron with the shaft tipped with a knob or finial of brass. The most prized andirons were those with brass shafts and legs. Extra-fine andirons also had a lower brass shaft about three inches behind the tall shaft, and the iron between the two was overlaid with brass. During the eighteenth century brass shafts or uprights were usually baluster-shaped and tipped with an oval or pointed finial. By 1800 tapering and square-sided shafts terminated in classic urn finials. After 1815 the American Empire period brought rounded shafts topped with good-size round balls. The tongs, poker and small shovel that made up a set of fire-tending tools usually were of iron. However, good sets had brass handles. Other bits of gleaming brass were jamb hooks to hold the tools These all-brass hooks had two holes in their back plates for screws to fasten them in the frame on either side of the fireplace.

Brass fenders probably never were as common in America as they were in England and Europe and, in any case, were not used in this country before the late 1700's. Then they were placed chiefly in front of fireplaces of well-to-do urban families. A fender presumably prevented sparks or embers from flying out into the room, but because they were only six to eight inches high they were more decorative than they were a

safeguard. A fender is rigid and either curved at the ends or serpentine along its length. Fenders usually were pierced decoratively and often had a pierced or open scalloped rim across the top.

After about 1850, when coal and then gas began to be used for fireplace heat, andirons were replaced by grates. These grates, or fire baskets, of iron sometimes were decorated with brass finials and facings. Coal scuttles and coal boxes were made of brass to stand beside the fireplace. The

coal scuttle, or hod, often was hammered to form a surface pattern and the lid of the coal box usually was embossed decoratively.

The main fireplace of the house provided both heat and a center for cooking. Here were hung and used all manner of cooking utensils, from pots and kettles to skillets and teakettles. Here also were kept tools for stirring and testing, such as a long-handled fork, ladles, perhaps a pancake turner or a dipper; handles were

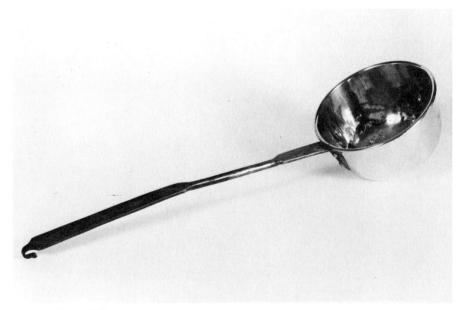

Brass and iron ladle, early 19th century, English or American.

often iron. Standing or hanging against a wall near the fireplace was likely to be a warming pan, or bed warmer. This flat pan with a cover had a long handle, usually of wood, so that it could be pushed quickly between the sheets to take the chill off a cold bed. The flat cover often was engraved with flowers, birds or geometric designs. Bed warmers often had pans made of copper instead of brass. Smaller boxlike foot warmers, or foot stoves, with a carrying handle weren't always made of brass, but they also were kept near the hearth.

A brass mortar and pestle was as common in kitchens as in apothecary shops until late in the nineteenth century. At home, the mortar and pestle was used to grind herbs and spices. Coffeepots and chocolate pots, pitchers, measures, skimmers and scoops were also traditionally made of brass. Although people cooked with brass, they did not eat from it, and so brass, unlike pewter, was not used to make tableware. On the other hand, during the 1800's it seems to have been largely a matter of personal preference whether a housewife bought utensils such as dippers, pitchers, mugs and measures of copper or brass.

Ranking high on the list of products from the brazier was furniture hardware, particularly drawer pulls. Both drawer pulls and keyhole escutcheons were customarily made of brass from the late 1600's to about 1840. During this hundred-fifty-year span, shapes of drawer pulls changed whenever furniture styles did. In the early 1800's additional metal decoration on furniture might have included brass paw mounts tipping the legs of

Large brass gilt curtain tiebacks, late 19th century, American.

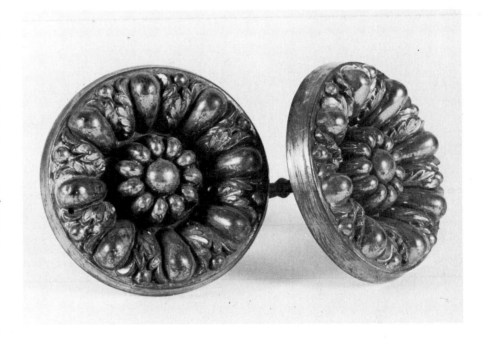

chairs and brass stars around a table. Clock dials, those handsome ones on tall case clocks, were made of brass up to about 1770; the numerals and perhaps part of the dial itself often were engraved.

Curtain tiebacks, which became so popular during Victorian years, sometimes were made of brass. They were bought in pairs, and each one consisted of a disk about three inches in diameter of ornamented brass that screwed or slipped onto a spike that was inserted in the window frame. Easier to recognize is the

tall umbrella stand that stood in the hall and often was brass. Also popular in late Victorian years were jardinieres to hold potted palms or Boston ferns. They often had a hammered surface or a pair of handles in the form of a lion's or stag's head. Fern dishes to be used on the dining-room table were lower and smaller, sometimes footed, and perhaps pierced or hammered. Brass trays also became quite common during Victorian years but these are likely to have been made in other countries and imported.

During the nineteenth century

likely to be brass.

It is usually impossible to tell not only by whom and when an article of brass was made but also whether it was made in this country or abroad. One of the exceptions is the spun-brass kettle, which was manufactured in Connecticut starting in 1851 and sold by peddlers. Concentric circles are typical of a spun-brass piece and there usually is an identifying stamp on the bottom. It also is extremely difficult to tell a reproduction from an antique, particularly a piece of cast brass.

An old piece of brass that looks dingy can be polished with little effort to its original sheen and luster. Old brass never seems to become red when it tarnishes, as do later pieces. After polishing, old brass is a rich shade of softly gleaming golden yellow. Color is probably the best indication of antique brass ware, but it must be seen and fixed firmly in mind before it can be recognized.

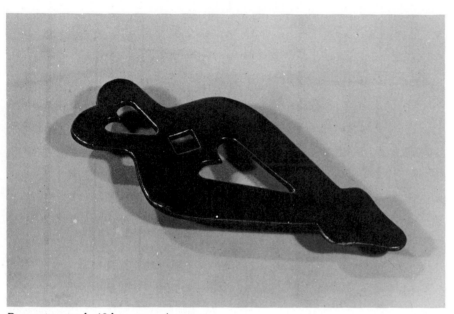

Brass trivet, early 19th century, American.

and early years of the twentieth century, horse and pony brasses were turned out in more patterns than ever before in their long history. From about 1850 onward horses often wore as many as twenty decorative brass amulets. Eighteenth- and early nineteenth-century brasses were shaped by hand and flattened with hammers and on genuine antique brasses of this era the marks of the hammer used to flatten the disks could be seen on both sides. The introduction of casting about the middle of the nineteenth century led to the

production of more and different designs. People eagerly bought the new designs carried by peddlers. Collectors should beware of reproductions.

Braziers kept busy turning out all manner of useful articles. For the men, they made bullet molds, powder horns, spurs, stirrups and bootjacks. For the women there were sewing birds and thimbles. Then there were buttons and buckles, inkwells and inkstands, and some trivets. The ship's bell, school bell and dinner bell, with wooden handles, and some of the bells worn by horses also were

Brass watering can, 20th century, American or English.

16. Bells of Joy

Of all the outward symbols of Christmas, the most joyous is the ringing of bells. The mellow sweet-toned ones in church steeples and belfries all over the world have heralded the tidings of Christmas since Medieval times. The real bells of Christmas are those in churches and cathedrals although there are many smaller secular bells that add "to the tintinnabulation that so musically swells" in a glorious crescendo at midnight on Christmas Eve.

Bells had been made and used for various purposes long before the birth of Christ. Bronze ones have been unearthed in Assyrian tombs and bells of both bronze and pure copper have been found among the remains of the Inca civilization. In China, two thousand years before Christ, large and small bells were used in religious ceremonies. All over the world in every country, bells evidently have been made ever since man discovered that one of the qualities of metal is resonance.

Christmas had become quite well established before bells became an important part of the celebration. The first large bell for a Christian church is believed to have been originated by a bishop in Campania, Italy, in the fifth century A.D. Throughout the Middle Ages and for centuries afterward, people regarded their church bells as almost living things. Before being hoisted into the belfry, bells were solemnly named and dedicated. Church bells have not only called people to worship, but also they told the

Brass cowbell, 19th century, American.

time of day; they pealed for marriages and tolled for deaths; they were rung to warn of disasters and to celebrate victories, homecomings and peace.

But the high point of every year was the ringing of church bells during the Christmas season. This became well established in England, if not elsewhere, during the Middle Ages. The joyful clamor of bells started at vespers on the first Sunday in Advent and the tidings were repeated on the following Advent Sundays. On the three mornings before Christmas Day, happy peals were rung as a reminder to everyone within hearing. At sunset on December twenty-fourth and every hour thereafter until sunset on December twenty-fifth, bells rang out their message. A few merry peals might be heard any time on Christmas Day for no particular reason.

Most important of all was the hour that the bells tolled before midnight on Christmas Eve, tolling as they might on any day or night when someone was dying. This hour of tolling was known in England as "The Old Lad's Passing Bell," the Old Lad being a nickname for the devil. At midnight the tolling changed to great joyous peals announcing the death of Satan and the birth of the Christ Child. In the melodious tones of their church bells, people believed they heard the "songs of the angels" on that night so long ago.

Casting of the largest and finest church bells was begun during the fifteenth century. Probably these bells had an unusual sweet

95

tonal quality, for it was during the sixteenth century that England became known as "the ringing isle." It has been said that bells are as much the national music of England as bagpipes are of Scotland and the guitar of Spain. The ringing of bells was a familiar, everyday sound in America too, at least until the present century.

At Christmas time, however, it is often possible to hear some of the most famous bells in this and other countries over radio and television. Never to be forgotten by the millions who have heard them are the tones of Big Ben, the thirteen and one-half ton bell in the Parliament clock tower in London. Other English bells almost as cherished are Great Paul, sixteen and three-quarters tons, in St. Paul's Cathedral, the eleven ton Great Peter in York Minster and the seven and one-half ton Great Tom in Oxford. Special Christmas messages come from the bells of Notre Dame in Paris and the Church of the Nativity in Bethlehem. Here in this country, the bells of St. Thomas Church and the carillon of Riverside Church, both in New York City, are perhaps the most famous. Certainly it would be interesting to hear one of the bells cast by Paul Revere and his sons between 1792 and 1818. Thirty-seven churches in Massachusetts, Rhode Island, New Hampshire, Vermont and Maine have Revere bells. The one that hangs in King's Chapel, Boston, is, according to its inscription, "The sweetest bell we ever made, Paul Revere & Son. 1817."

The largest bell in the world, known as the Great Bell, the Tsar Kolokol or Big John of Moscow, was cast in the 1730's but has never been heard. Soon after it was hoisted to a frame at one end of the Kremlin, fire destroyed the timbers and a piece came out of the bell itself, which fell thirty feet into the ground. More than a hundred years later, the bell was lifted and made into a chapel. Big John might not have had as sweet a tone as many of its contemporaries, because so many people contributed gold and silver to the melting pot. These two precious metals dull the resonance of a large bell.

The famous bell of St. Patrick, now in the National Museum of Ireland, probably wasn't musical either. It was a little quadrangular bell of iron fastened together with iron rivets and bronzed. Since it was only 6″ high, 4¾″ across at the shoulder and 5″ across at the base, it was meant to be rung by hand. This is much the same shape as the cattle bells that later became common, especially in Switzerland.

Christmas carols are often played on carillons. A carillon is a set of bells, each one tuned to the intervals of the chromatic scale. They are played either by hand or by mechanisms attached to a clock. Carillons as we know them are only about five hundred years old. They hang in church belfries, clock towers and bell towers, and are as typical of the Low Countries as bells are of England. It was the Dutch, Flemish and Belgians who brought carillons to their high musical status. Dunkerque had a carillon by 1437 and by 1540 a huge carillon of sixty bells hung in the cathedral at Antwerp. Among modern carillons, the one in Riverside Church in New York City consists of seventy-four bells and its twenty ton bourdon (deepest-toned bell) is the largest tuned bell in the world.

Quite different from the bells in most American belfries are those in the steeple of St. Michael's Episcopal Church in Charleston, South Carolina. They are a "change-ringing peal," a set of bells tuned to the tones of the major scale and rung in continually varying order. The St. Michael's peal is the oldest in the United States. A ring or peal of bells is less musical than a carillon yet has a sonorous richness of its own; change ringing is based on a mathematical pattern and is, regrettably, becoming a lost skill in this country. When at rest, a ring of bells stands upside down and each bell must be tipped individually to make a sound; in other words, a ring of bells at rest hangs just opposite to the way most church bells do.

Most church bells are the classic shape; that is, a hollow vessel shaped like an inverted cup with a flaring mouth. The majority have a clapper or tongue to make them vibrate. Most people agree that the finest ones were made of either bronze or bell metal, an alloy that is a variety of bronze. However, some people insist that smaller bells of almost pure silver tinkle more melodi-

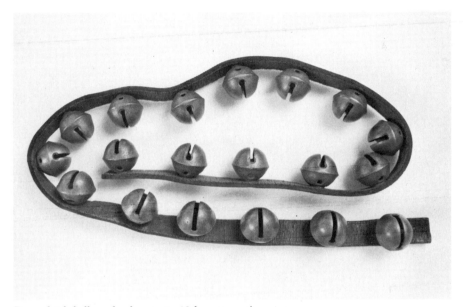

Brass sleigh bells on leather strap, 19th century, American.

ously than any other kind. Bell-making, even back in the Bronze Age, always has been an art. A bell founder, as a man who casts bells is known, tried to shape bells in a set so that each one had a different note yet all would be in tune. Tuning was sometimes desirable, although alteration of the bell, by hammer and chisel in the old days, was apt to damage the quality of its tone.

Bells were made of other metals, chiefly iron, copper, brass and silver and, later on, of china and glass. Many bells of the Bronze Age were quadrangular as was St. Patrick's bell. Most an-

cient of all shapes is the crotal, which is the little round bell with small holes in its sides and a tiny ball within. Some very old crotals were pear-shaped. The balls inside once were stones, later metal. The golden bells for adornment mentioned in the Bible were crotals, but the ones most familiar to Americans are sleigh bells.

Not only sleigh bells but also all kinds of bells worn by animals are interesting to collect. And if only because a horse, an ox, a mule and a goat were in the stable at Bethlehem with the Christ Child, these bells deserve to be brought out at Christmas time.

Brass schoolhouse bell, wood handle, 19th century, American.

These four are not the only animals that have worn bells. It seems as though all the familiar ones from elephants to camels have worn their own special style of bell in one century or another and at one time or another.

Always associated with Christmas in America is the merry tinkle from strings of bells attached to harnesses of horses that drew cutters over snow-packed roads. Dozens of little bells on strips of leather overlay all parts of the harness. Some strings have as many as forty bells. Most valued by collectors are strings of bells graduated in size. The best quality are attached to the leather with shanks and cotter pins and some very fine ones have engraved decoration. Some are brass, others iron or silver-colored metal. Many sleigh bells are crotals, but some are flaring bells no more than 1½" long.

Horses have worn some bells during all seasons and in all countries since ancient times. There have been hame bells, larger bells that could be attached to the collar, and also frames of bells that were mounted on the collar in an upright position. Special arrangements of brass bells on wrought-iron frames were attached to the collars of horses and oxen that drew the Conestoga wagons across the plains. These frames were made in sets of six: the two for the lead horses had five bells, those for the next pair had four bells and the last two had three bells. In most countries, oxen wore bells only when driven to market. Mule and pony bells usually were crotals but might be of silver, bronze or brass depending on the country. Donkeys often wore the same kind of bell camels did; instead of having a clapper, it consisted of a smaller bell inserted inside a larger one.

Bells varied in size, shape and tone for cows, goats and sheep. Cowbells have disappeared gradually, at least in America. They weren't always as melodious as the bells horses wore, but they had their distinctive notes. Cowbells usually were quadrangular and of quite good size although made of a single sheet of metal. Some from Switzerland and other countries are decorated with ornaments in relief. Bells for goats and sheep were smaller. Goat bells, small and shrill in tone, were made in pairs. The smaller bell was for the nanny goat, the larger and deeper bell for the billy. Only one sheep, the leader of the flock, wore a bell.

Tradition has it that St. Nicholas carried a hand bell on his annual visits to children. Hand bells with wooden or metal handles are almost as ancient as crotals and were made in many sizes. Most familiar in this country is probably the bell of brass with a polished wood handle. Town criers carried a large hand bell as they made their rounds. Street venders often were recognized by the tones of the hand bells they carried. Small but beautifully made hand bells were rung for funerals and in other religious ceremonies. Among the many services of plain but nonetheless pleasant-toned hand bells was summoning children to school and farm hands to dinner.

Tune-ringing with hand bells is a specialty, and a performance by a skilled group of bell ringers can be thrilling to hear. One person may perform with a set of twelve to twenty bells. Better known are groups that play in one of two ways: ringers may hold two to four bells in their hands (two bells in each hand), or may be responsible for a certain number of bells set before the group on a table, picking up each bell at the point its note is called for in the music.

Table bells of china or glass as well as silver and other metals are still being made to some extent, although not now in the quantity and diversity they had been for centuries. These are small bells, 3″ to 5″ high, that were used primarily to summon servants. One invariably stood at the mistress' place at the dining table and there might have been others in strategic places throughout the house. As is true of hand bells, the handle of a table bell usually equaled about half of its height. Little china bells with dainty decoration, and glass bells, either cut

Crystal table bell, 19th century, American.

or colored, are much more recent than metal ones. Reputedly, the finest table bells were made of silver which rang sweetly and with an unmistakable tone.

During the Renaissance in Italy, silversmiths turned out magnificently decorated table bells of gold as well as silver. In England, silver table bells have been made continuously since the days of Elizabeth I. On the earliest ones, handles were silver and baluster-shaped, but by the late seven-

teenth century they took the form of a figure such as a rampant lion, a crest or a classical half-figure. This development led to the figure bell and handle, for which the most natural design was the one cast and chased in the form of a serving woman wearing a wide skirt and apron with her hands clasped in front of her. This figure has been made over and over again since about 1700 in England and elsewhere. It is sometimes called a crinoline bell. Another natural form was the flower, the flaring bell having its outside rim scalloped and marked somewhat like petals. During some periods, ebony or ivory handles replaced silver ones. Styles of decoration followed those on other and more important pieces of silver so that, during the nineteenth century, silver bells usually were decorated with allover designs of flowers or grapes and foliage and the more elaborate motifs that became popular during Victorian days.

Not necessarily table bells but some kind of call bells were those made in the shape of figures and people. Like table bells and hand bells, these "people" bells seem to have been made in many countries and hence reflect not only history but also different customs

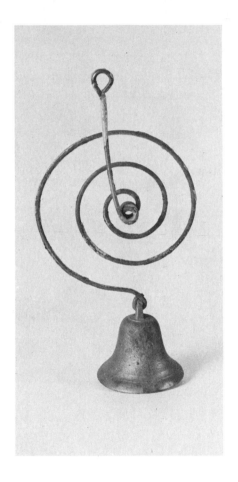

Brass doorbell, 19th century, American.

and beliefs. Bells portraying in miniature Queen Anne and James I were made in England, an Indian maid beating a drum came from France, while the famous Hemony family of bell founders in Holland produced a handsome bell that is undeniably a queen. A bell cast in the form of a Madonna or a St. Christopher carrying Christ is representative of the many that are religious in appearance.

Front doors of houses now have electrical bells or chimes instead of the bell that pealed all through the house when its handle was turned or pulled. And few stores now have bells that tinkle when the door is pushed open. Yet not so long ago their pleasant tones blended into all the jingling and the tinkling, the tolling and the pealing in "the joyous welcome of the Christmas bells."

Nineteenth-century dolls with china heads are highly valued by serious collectors. Considered exceptional are those from Germany illustrated here. The seated girl and the blonde boy date from c. 1860. In the center is a doll with a rare painted brown-eyed china head said to have been made from 1840 to 1850. The remaining doll is the "Dolly Madison" model, perhaps made as early as 1800; a similar head was produced in 1880.

Lustre ware was produced in great quantity during the first half of the 19th century in England, much of the production being shipped to North America. Illustrated are three of the most common metallic finishes—copper, silver, and pink. Also produced were gold, lilac, canary yellow, and bronze. Some of the silver and gold wares were made in obvious imitation of the precious metals; silver lustre (as seen in the teapot, sugar, and creamer) was often manufactured in the same molds as solid silver.

Belleek figures from Ireland have an unglazed porcelain body similar to Parian ware made in England and the United States. The two bird figures have a soft marble-like appearance; the one at left is marked "Just Hatched." At the far right is a small Staffordshire bird figure.

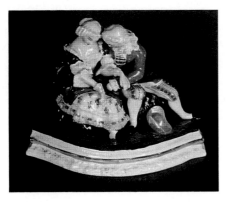

China figures and groups are among the most charming of the 18th and 19th century antique collectibles. The earthenware figures made in the Staffordshire district of England are deservedly popular. The beautifully modeled and decorated "Lovers" is one familiar Staffordshire motif.

China novelty items for the parlor whatnot or fireplace mantel delighted the Victorians and attract the interest of many modern collectors. The variety of objects made is without count. At left is a Staffordshire bird whistle, and next to it is another English object, a flower bedecked box. The two miniature vases at right are probably of American manufacture.

Old blue china made in the Staffordshire district of England during the 19th century was shipped to North America in great quantity. Some carried Chinese motifs; the Willow pattern, among the most popular, appears on the tureen seen here. Blue and white wares were transfer-printed with scenes of English, American, or Oriental views or with highly ornamental floral patterns. Darker shades of blue predominated until the mid-1800s, and thereafter the color gradually faded.

The domestic wares made by the Wedgwood firm during the late 18th and early 19th centuries are justly famous on both sides of the Atlantic. Josiah Wedgwood was the most gifted of the Staffordshire potters who contributed to the development of modern decorative and utilitarian objects for the home. Teapots are among the most practical, but this quality does not make them any less decorative in the hands of a true artist. Illustrated, from left to right, are an 18th-century blue and white Jasper teapot with bas-relief decoration; a caneware teapot with molded relief decoration from the early 19th century; and an 18th-century encaustic-painted black basalt teapot.

17. All Kinds of Candleholders

Candles, like lamps, have been known since earliest times. Candles haven't been essential for illumination after dark since kerosene proved to be such an excellent fuel for lamps about 1860, but people have been loath to part with candlesticks or candelabra, particularly antique ones. If any excuse is needed for keeping them fitted with candles, someone usually half-heartedly mentions that after all, a person never knows when a thunderstorm or an ice storm or other blackout of electric power will make everyone in the house thankful to have candles handy. Nowadays most people agree that candlelight is romantic, at least for a dinner table, but during the 1700's and a great part of the 1800's candles were more fashionable than lamps for nighttime lighting. Anyway, families who could afford candles much preferred them to the guttering, ill-smelling lamps.

The forerunner of the candle was the rushlight, which was made simply by dipping the cylindrical stem of a rush into household grease. Rushlights were not uncommon in colonial America, where they usually were clamped to a wrought-iron holder. The candle actually is a rod of fatty or waxy material with a fibrous wick through the center (the improved plaited or braided wick came into use around 1820). Tallow-dip was another name for a candle that was made by dipping a wick into talow; candles of beeswax, long ago prescribed for church use, were poured and then rolled. Then in the late 1700's spermaceti candles became available. These finest-burning ones of all were made of the white crystalline wax

Iron candlestick with brass candle push-up, late 17th century, English.

"Barn" candlestick with hanging hook, iron and wood, 18th century, English.

tipped with a pricket, or spike, on which the candle was secured, and had a saucer or bowl underneath to catch the drippings of wax or tallow. By 1700 the pricket candlestick had given way to the one with a socket. As a result, a small, round glass disk, or *bobèche*, which was removable, rested on the socket to catch any blobs. Many an early candlestick had a slot just below the socket from which a knob protruded. By pushing this up, the stub of the candle could be dislodged easily. If there was no knob, something with a sharp point could be poked in the slot to remove the stub.

The average candlestick was 4" to 8" tall with an occasional metal one 12" or a little higher and an adjustable wooden one from 30" to 5' or so. Only wealthy families could afford silver candlesticks during colonial days. Silver candlesticks were made in America, but by far the majority of silver and Sheffield-plate ones were imported from England. They followed changing styles of other pieces of silver. For example, candlesticks made in the early 1700's usually had baluster shafts, while neoclassic columns became fashionable in the late 1700's and early 1800's. Pewter candlesticks, which were less expensive, were somewhat simpler than silver ones although they followed the same general forms.

A good many brass candlesticks were imported from Holland as well as England. Undoubtedly many more pewter and brass candlesticks than silver ones were made in America, and the pewterers and the braziers here followed the styles they had been making in their native countries. Silver candlesticks

made in America before 1800 are either in museums or restorations, or else are cherished by the families who have inherited them. However, excellent reproductions are being made of silver, pewter and brass candlesticks that were widely used during the eighteenth and early nineteenth centuries. Antique silver and pewter ones can be distinguished from their reproductions by the makers marks, antique brass ones

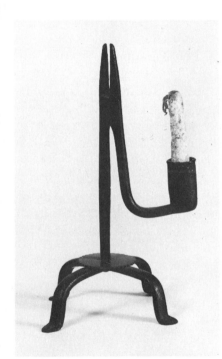

Iron candle and rushlight holder, 18th century, English.

obtained from the head cavity of the sperm or right whale. After 1785, when American whalers were sailing the seven seas, spermaceti candles became more and more plentiful in this country. Candlesticks and other means of illumination with candles were made in greater quantity and in greater variety than ever before until about 1860.

A candlestick, whatever its material or style, consisted of a base, a shaft and a socket or cup for the candle. An older style was

Brass chamberstick with candle push-up, early 19th century, English.

by the color. Old brass when polished is a rich golden shade very different from the harsher tone of present-day brass. An antique candlestick of any metal also is bound to show small dents and other signs of constant service.

People with little money to spare also needed sticks for candles, and so many were made of tin, wrought iron or wood. There are many interesting ones to be seen in restorations, and antique ones can be purchased occasionally. One simple wrought-iron candlestick didn't have to stand on a flat surface: this one looked like a long spike with a point at one end, a loop handle at the other and a socket midway; it could be stuck in a crevice between beams or in any convenient place. Equally clever was the wooden candlestick which had a shield-shaped front concealing the socket and which was fastened at a right angle to a thin board that could be slid under a beam. More conventional wood candlesticks, 4" or so tall, were often beautifully turned.

Tall candlesticks to stand on floor or table were made of wood or wrought iron, occasionally of tin. The wrought-iron ones were likely to be quite gracefully designed; some of them were trimmed with brass, and many could be carried by means of a loop handle. Although many tall wooden candlesticks or, more correctly, candlestands, were rather crude-looking, they had the built-in advantage of permitting the height of the light to be adjusted (this was possible with many wrought-iron ones, too). Their maximum height was about 5', and they had a tripod, crosspiece or solid base which supported a turned shaft on

which the crossbar with sockets could be screwed up or down. Most wooden ones held two candles, but wooden or metal ones could have sockets for one to four candles.

Hog-scraper candlestick with brass rings and push-up, 19th century, American.

Candlesticks of pottery and porcelain appeared in some quantity during the 1700's and 1800's. These ranged from blue and white Holland Delft to Meissen porcelain ornamented with tiny applied flowers; from English creamware, often in flower or figure forms, to unglazed Parian. Pressed-glass candlesticks became immensely popular in the United States starting in the 1820's. Most famous of all of these is the one with a dolphin as its shaft. This was made from about 1830 to 1910 in clear, colored, milk-white and opalescent pressed glass as well as combinations of any two kinds. Other details differed with the manufacturer, particularly the base, which could be a square, hexagon or the high round shape called a petticoat. One of the first firms to make dolphin candlesticks was the Boston and Sandwich Glass Company, which was also a leader in making candlesticks of colored glass and with lacy glass sockets. Later, candlesticks were made in such early patterns of pressed glass as Excelsior, Sawtooth, Flute, and Diamond Point. Cut-glass candlesticks always were prized because their cuttings reflected and thus enhanced the candlelight, and they

Silver chambersticks with extinguisher, thumb handles, late 18th century, English.

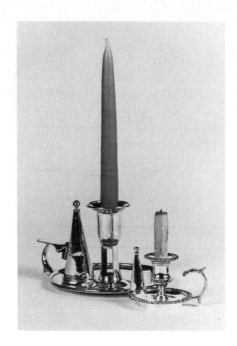

came into quite general ownership before the nineteenth century ended.

All of the familiar materials from silver to tin and pottery eventually were used for the chamber candlestick or chamberstick that was introduced during

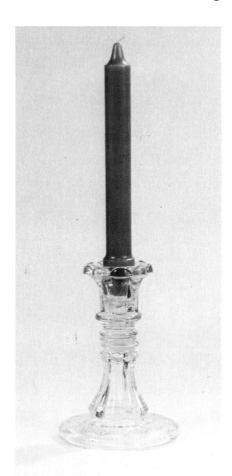

Clear Sandwich glass candlestick, 1860s.

the 1700's. This short candlestick had a socket above a saucerlike base to which a scroll or ring handle was attached; it was meant to be carried from room to room, to light the way upstairs and to provide some illumination in a bedroom. Before the eighteenth century ended, housewives prided themselves on the small table in the downstairs hall on which chambersticks stood so each person could take one to his room. For convenience a master candlestick or taperstick was kept burning on the table, and the candlebox nearby held wax candles, if the family could afford them, because they did not sputter and drip like those of tallow.

Much older than the chamberstick was the taperstick, a sort of miniature candlestick about 4″ high with a deep, narrow socket. This was made chiefly of silver, brass or glass. The slender wax tapers made to burn in them gave too little light for general illumination but served many other purposes. Tapersticks were common on tea tables and, because men used them to light the tobacco in their pipes, they often were called tobacco candlesticks. The smokeless tapers also were used to melt sealing wax for letters. Spermaceti tapers were preferred not

only because they were nonodorous but also because they seldom required snuffing and so could be left unattended without fear of their guttering.

The finest and largest of candles provided only weak illumination. One of several methods devised to increase the amount of light was sconces. These brackets or fixtures that became so popular during the 1700's were attached to the walls, often in pairs. Probably the majority of sconces held only one candle, but a good many had sockets for two and an occasional plain tin or wood sconce was shaped so that it held three candles. Backplates were 6½″ to 12″ high. Brass sconces often had a projecting arm that was scrolled. Pewter and tin sconces were either of two general shapes: a narrow backplate arched at the top, or a round backplate which was plain and saucer-shaped or which perhaps had a crimped edge. On the whole, sconces used in this country were fairly simple, yet they were as decorative as they were practical. None illustrates this better than the sconce with a backplate covered with small pieces of looking glass, each one reflecting the pinpoint of candlelight. To increase the illusion of light, metal sconces often had reflectors. Thin pieces of pewter or a small plaque of bright tin were added, if appropriate, or a shining medallion polished on a silver or brass backplate.

An obvious way to obtain more light was fixtures such as candelabra and chandeliers that held a group of candles. A candelabrum is a footed, branched candlestick with sockets for two or more candles. A chandelier is a branched candlestick or cluster of candles that is suspended from the ceiling by means of a chain or other device. Candelabra were made of glass, silver, Sheffield plate, brass or other materials popular for candlesticks. Chandeliers of glass, or glass and a metal, graced many houses with their light and sparkle, while less expensive ones of tin, wood or pewter with arms for four to six candles did very well for families that did not entertain a great deal.

Chandeliers, particularly those of glass or silver, glittered when all of their candles were lighted. Their brilliance seemed even greater if glass pendants known as crystal drops or prisms hung from each socket and perhaps from other places on the chandelier. Prisms also were used lavishly on candlesticks and candelabra where they hung with tiny hooks from the socket or *bobèches*. Because they were made of glass cut in various shapes and faceted, prisms also increased the illusion if not the actual amount of light. Around 1800, prisms were fairly

Three-branch brass sconce, early 19th century, American.

short and round, or oval. After 1820 long rectangular prisms became fashionable. At other times they were cut and faceted, and were pear-shaped, spear-pointed or in other forms calculated to scintillate.

Much simpler ceiling fixtures were large, decorative lanterns fitted for one or more candles. These were by no means uncommon here before 1800. One style consisted of a hanging glass bowl with a socket for a candle in the base, suspended from the ceiling with chains and having a circular glass disk called a smoke bell inserted in the chains below the ceiling to prevent the latter from being stained. True lanterns, often 20″ long, had four- or six-sided frames of brass or painted tin enclosing panes of glass, and usually a decorative top consisting of metal arms or some other pleasing arrangement which terminated in the ceiling chain. Some few lanterns had carefully-cut wooden frames.

More numerous, perhaps, were the smaller lanterns for carrying a

lighted candle outdoors. In order to shield the flame of the candle and also to permit the light to shine out, many lanterns for outdoor use were pierced tin. Best known of all now is the cylindrical tin lantern with a pointed top and pierced design which is often mistakenly called a Paul Revere lantern. Actually, this style wasn't made before the 1820's. On that famous night in 1775, Paul Revere probably carried a tall rectangular lantern with a metal frame, four panes of glass, and a round, pierced cap on top. Other outdoor lanterns were hexagonal or octagonal, and some had horn instead of glass panes.

Candlelight at its best couldn't be enjoyed without some equipment in addition to various kinds of holders. Shades, for example, were made first for candles. Oldest of all are the large, slightly shaped cylinders, open at both ends, known as hurricane shades or wind glasses. These were 14″ to 18″ tall so that they could be slipped over a candlestick with its candle to protect it from drafts and, of course, to make its illumination safer. The first ones were plain glass, but in the early 1800's some had delicately cut or engraved designs. By 1800 a shorter but graceful lily-shaped shade of clear glass often was fitted into the specially designed socket of a candlestick or sconce. The idea of placing a large circular metal shade over a candelabrum was borrowed from the French in the early 1800's. Here the shade was likely to be of painted tin, but similar ones were made of brass, copper or silver and decorated lavishly. The height of this shade could be adjusted with a key. This distinct style of shaded candelabrum was called a *bouillotte* since it was ideal to place on the table where a popular card game of that named was played.

There had to be some convenient way to light candles. One of the oldest was a small, round tin box with a handle on one side, which held tinder, steel and flint for lighting the candle fitted into the socket on its cover. This was practical, but not at all attractive. Many gadgets were developed in various parts of the country. However, almost every household kept on hand a supply of spills, slender rolls of paper or slips of wood to be lighted in the fireplace and used, in turn, to light the candles. After 1820 they usually were kept in footed spillholders of pressed glass.

Fully as important was a neat, safe way to extinguish the flame of a candle. Both extinguishers and snuffers were indispensable, the extinguisher often being hooked onto the candlestick. An extinguisher is small cone of metal which was dropped over a candle to put out its flame. Later,

Tin lantern, 1860s, American.

Tin and iron tinderbox and candlestick, c. 1810, probably American.

when shades came into general use, a handle long enough to reach down inside was added. Snuffers were more likely to be kept on their own trays or upright stands of matching metal. Snuffers of brass or silver look like scissors, approximately 5½″ long, with a three-sided box on the longer, pointed blade; the fourth side of the box terminates the shorter blade. Most snuffers had three small mounts, about ⅜″ high, on the handles and long blade. Snuffers extinguished the flame, but the real job was trimming the burnt wick that the candle would burn evenly and brightly. The ends of the wick were caught in the box.

18. Trivets

The trivets that housewives bought for two hundred and seventy-five years were only one small demand that kept blacksmith shops and later, iron foundries in business. These three-legged stands of iron were invaluable in the days when cooking was done at a fireplace, as it was for so many years. A trivet standing over the coals was just right to hold a pot or kettle and keep the food in it hot. Since a trivet was equally good on a table to prevent the surface from being marred or stained, smaller and lower ones were made for this purpose. As the years passed and

women kept finding more and more uses for this simple convenient tool, trivets were made in all sizes, shapes and heights as safe resting places for anything hot. Not least important was the distinctly shaped stand which was designed especially to hold the hot flatiron used to press clothing.

As stoves replaced fireplaces and electric irons the heavy hand ones that had to be heated over a fire, trivets disappeared from kitchens. Unless they were contributed to scrap metal drives during war times, the once indispensable trivets settled into dim,

Wrought-iron trivet with wood handle, 18th century, American.

Cast-iron trivet, early 20th century, American.

dark corners of cellars, dusty drawers and closets or wherever unwanted items accumulated in a home. When an old trivet comes to light, it may be bent and certainly will be as rusty as the one a boy who had been digging around an old foundation brought home one day. After identifying it for him, his mother suggested that he smooth away the rust with a wire brush and steel wool to bring out the design. Soon they could see clearly a spread eagle framed in a classic laurel wreath, a pattern first made over a hundred years ago.

A couple of coats of black paint dressed up this old trivet so that it could be hung on the front door as a knocker. By the way, experts on old metals frown on painting trivets and suggest that a more appropriate finish is obtained by covering them with old-fashioned black stove polish or with coachman's black thinned with turpentine. When dry, either one can be buffed to a dull luster. Old trivets were used so constantly that they seldom were gleaming bright. Battered and rusty as old ironware may be when a piece is found in some unlikely place nowadays, it is easy to see that the blacksmith took time to fashion a cooking pot in a pleasing shape

and to make the trivet ornamental.

The designs of hand-wrought trivets were copied when cast iron ones began to be made in foundries in the 1830's. After 1850, cast iron trivets appeared in countless patterns that reflected the events, personalities and pursuits of the time. Not even small trivets, roughly triangular in shape, that were made to hold smoothing, pressing and pleating irons and cast flatirons were plain. Their designs were likely to be simpler than those of trivets meant to support all kinds of pots and dishes over fireplaces or stoves and elsewhere through the house, but it seems as though everyone who worked with iron couldn't help but make it into something decorative. Most of the flatiron stands or trivets were produced by foundries.

Three feet, an almost literal translation from the old French word *tripied*, are what most of them have. However, the New England blacksmiths who were hammering out articles in the mid-1600's from local deposits of iron were true craftsmen who seldom made any two trivets exactly alike. So it isn't strange that some of the oldest of these stands had four feet or legs. These are correctly known as quads. Quads and trivets served the same purpose and the only difference is the number of feet.

Quads made during the 1700's and first years of the 1800's often consisted of two pieces of iron that crisscrossed in the center and had the ends bent into scrolls that were turned down to form the legs. The comparatively few quads of cast iron after 1850 displayed patterns similar to three-legged ones. One cast iron quad made in some quantity consisted of a circle enclosing a spray of leaves, another was a rectangle in a most Victorian pattern of bunches of grapes and leaves. This last one had a handle.

More quads probably were made from wrought iron than were cast in the late 1800's. Trivets were wrought iron until the 1830's when some began to be made from cast iron and by the 1850's practically all trivets were cast iron. A couple of trivet collectors have told me that it is possible to tell the difference between the two forms of iron. They insist that really old wrought iron trivets made during the early 1800's are much rougher to the touch than the later cast iron ones.

More trivets than quads seem

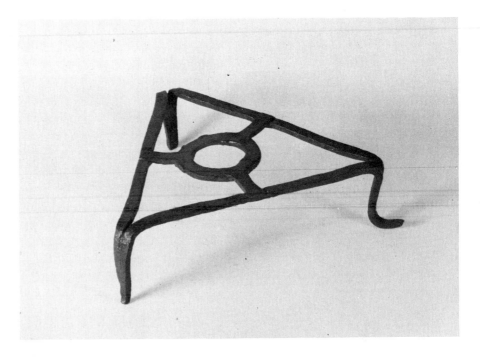

to have handles. Some of the old wrought iron trivets have long handles, probably so that a person would be less likely to burn her arm or hand in lifting the trivet or pot on it off the embers in the fireplace. The handle also was convenient for hanging the trivet against the fireplace or wall when it was not in use. As designs for trivets became more diversified handles became more decorative, usually with some motif in the pattern adapted to this small portion. The short handles of trivets made after 1850 are in good scale. On a trivet between 5″

Cast-iron trivet, 18th century, American.

and 6" long or about 5" in diameter, the handle averages 2½" to 3" in length.

Legs or feet differed in height too. The variation is greater among the old wrought iron ones made to be used over fireplace coals. Some of these have legs that place trivets 3" or higher over the embers. After trivets were made of cast iron and were less likely to be used at the fireplace, legs conformed to a more or less standard height. They were ½" to ⅝" high on large trivets, about ⅜" on small ones.

Feet were essential and handles were common whether the trivet was round, rectangular or triangular. Blacksmiths' designs for trivets of the 1700's were uncomplicated and based on such forms as a scroll or two, a cross within a circle, a heart or a triangle with rounded corners. The horseshoe, a symbol of good luck, also was adapted by blacksmiths to trivets. These same forms were the basis of many more elaborate patterns that prove the appropriateness of iron lace as a synonym for trivets and other articles made of cast iron. The horseshoe outlining a cast iron trivet enclosed openwork of ovals, lattice, loops or stars or perhaps a rose. Involved scrollwork formed other patterns, circles were entwined, swirls arranged to form a peacock's tail.

The heart was used alone or with other motifs for many patterns. A border of open hearts circled a star on a round cast iron trivet. The large heart centered in a triangular trivet was pierced by two arrows and another triangular style consisted of two hearts laced together at their tips. Hearts, like circles, were entwined and also combined with

tulips and other popular motifs.

A trivet displaying hearts and tulips might well have been made in the Pennsylvania German section of southeastern Pennsylvania. The hearts, flowers, birds, angels and peacocks which these people painted on their furniture and worked into the hex signs on their barns also were adapted to trivets. Flowers and fruits were worked into patterns for trivets that foundries made to sell in all parts of the country. Most popular were roses and grapes that had been carved on early Victorian furniture. Foliage, a fern leaf, grain and agricultural motifs also were the basis for any number of patterns. A distinctive rectangular design, for example, consists of a bold stalk of grain down the center flanked by scrolls; the pattern is known as Tassel and Grain.

Natural motifs for trivets were an eagle, a lyre and stars which had been widely used to decorate various pieces of furniture made during the early 1800's. Some openwork trivets are lyre-shaped and any number of patterns included a small lyre. Patriotic motifs in addition to the eagle and stars were a profile of George Washington, symbols and references to other early Presidents and patriots. At the time of the Civil War, cannon, swords and a shield with stars and stripes dominated some patterns. During the 1850's when popular concert singer Jenny Lind was touring this country her likeness appeared on more than one style and shape of trivet. Then there are the various patterns inspired by the insignia of several fraternal organizations.

Although the trivets that were flatiron stands were always tri-

Cast-iron trivet, late 19th century, American.

angular, the shape did not limit patterns. Nor did their size, from 5″ to 6″ long and 4″ to 4½″ at the wide end. Many of these trivets have a rim known as an iron-guard around their upper surface. If the iron-guard was plain the design might be no more than groups of small circles pierced through the flat surface. A scalloped or decorative iron-guard framed a more involved pattern. I distinctly remember one of my grandmother's heavy flatiron trivets whose flat top was more open than closed with its three rows of circles graduated in size around a lyre cutout. Finishing it and guaranteeing that the iron wouldn't slide off was a neat little scalloped rim. Triangular ones in lacy patterns without iron-guards are sometimes referred to as Cathedral trivets, probably because of a slight resemblance to an arched Gothic window.

It was not unusual for both plain and fancy flatiron trivets to carry lettering indicating that they were given away as premiums or for advertising. A late 19th century one with an openwork center combined with a small lyre and a pineapple has the lettering "Mrs Potts Crown" along one side and "Iron Phila Pa" on the other side. From a short distance the lettering looks ornamental. On many the manufacturer's identification was the only attempt at decoration. In the late 1800's more and more large trivets began to carry advertising lettering. For example when stoves were fast replacing fireplaces, many manufacturers made cast iron trivets with advertising which were given to customers who bought their stoves or which were sold at modest prices.

Quite different from flatiron stands, although some were the same shape, are miniature trivets. Small sizes in various shapes were a natural development, particularly to use almost anywhere except in the fireplace or on the stove, since large trivets standing over a fire became too hot to carry to the table. Miniatures were made in all of the accepted shapes and many of the familiar patterns. The eagle with laurel wreath, for instance, formed a trivet 5½″ in diameter with a handle 3″ long and a miniature one 3″ in diameter with a 2″ handle. At least one miniature was uncommon in being oblong. Fitting the shape was the design of two hearts back to back tapering to simple scrolls at the pointed ends. Some triangular trivets were only 4″ long with 1½″ handles. Trivets smaller than this usually were toy ones. Toy trivets, irons and stoves with which little girls could work along with their mothers were made from the early 1800's and in considerable quantity during the 1880's and 1890's.

There is no end to the trivets that may be found with a little searching. Old ones turn up in the most unlikely places. One old one cleaned up and on display inevitably leads to others and often influences relatives and acquain-

Cast-iron "heart" trivet, 19th century, American.

tances to turn over their finds. The house with the trivet door knocker now has a half dozen hanging on the wall over the kitchen stove (electric). One is the miniature of the large eagle with laurel wreath on the front door. Another in this wall group is a flatiron stand with advertising and one of the large ones is known as the President Adams pattern. Most if not all of the trivets in this house were made before 1900.

The condition of an old trivet will depend on where it has been hidden for so many years. Perhaps it won't be thick with rust but it certainly won't be the smooth allover black of the many good reproductions now being made. Old trivets of either wrought or cast iron are heavier than the contemporary iron ones even though the patterns are exactly alike. A better test is to turn a trivet over, for an old one usually is rough and worn on the underside and the feet scratched.

Approximate age and the place and maker of an iron trivet is almost impossible to determine. Trivets like other utensils made of iron were seldom marked by the maker. A wrought iron trivet in a simple design probably was made before 1800 and the more elabo-rate the pattern of a cast iron trivet, the more certain that it was made after 1850. Flatiron stands continued to be made in quantity during the early 1900's. Advertising on trivets may be a clue if it includes the city or town as well as the manufacturer's name. But a search through old city directories to learn when this firm was actively in business requires many hours spent in a library and a great deal of time and patience.

19. Victorian Jewelry

The woman who doesn't enjoy owning and wearing jewelry is rare. Many women, in fact, do not discard the simple pieces given them during childhood that have been outgrown, and the more valuable ones received later on Christmas and other special occasions are cherished and handed on after considerable thought to children and grandchildren. Men are far more modest about wearing jewelry nowadays than they were two and three centuries ago or even during the Victorian era. Jewelry of one kind or another came into such general ownership during the long, prosperous Victorian years (1837-1901) in both America and England that almost every family now has a few pieces: a couple of stickpins or other decorative pins, a pair of cuff links or a long gold watch chain with jeweled slide. Such odds and ends are not likely to be worth a fortune today, but they often are attractive enough to wear occasionally or to be converted to present-day use.

A great deal of the Victorian jewelry may seem unimportant at first glance. However, the gold used for settings was a rich, soft, deep golden yellow that is most attractive. Two of the most popular stones were coral and turquoise, now fashionable again. Semiprecious garnets, moonstones, amethysts and topazes were used lavishly, but these and gems such as diamonds, sapphires, emeralds and opals often were quite small.

Much of the jewelry that women wore a hundred years ago was made from beautiful deep gold decorated with enamel. Cobalt-blue or black and white enamels in carefully executed designs were striking against the gold. Women of all ages proudly wore handsome enameled bracelets, pins and earrings, or earbobs, as the little pendants that dangled from pierced ears usually were called. The last time I visited my eighty-eight-year-old aunt, the collar of her dress was fastened with a round gold pin on which most of the original black and white enamel could still be seen. This round gold brooch, 1¼" in diameter, has a garland of tiny berries and leaves etched and highlighted with black enamel in the center and a fancy scalloped edging accented with white

Carved cameo and gold-filled chain, late 19th century, American.

enamel. In addition to a simple pin on the underside, this brooch has a small ring so it can be worn on a chain around the neck. Many Victorian brooches had not only the pin clasp and the ring but also a hook from which a watch could be suspended.

Victorians seem to have owned pins appropriate to wear on any occasion. One kind features naturalistic flowers. Examples range from etched gold pins with a flower and leaves to enameled pins with blossoms, a bird or a butterfly decorated with tiny flashing gems. Another charming sort of Victorian floral jewelry is made up of mosaic pins and ear-bobs.

Victorians loved sunburst and star pins set with either semiprecious or precious gems. For evening, everyone who could possibly afford it wore a sunburst, star, crescent or bowknot of diamonds or diamonds and pearls. The pearls might be natural ocean or fresh-water pearls, or paste.

Rings were worn generally by both men and women during the Victorian era. Many men wore signet rings with an intaglio design, or gold rings with their monogram. However many rings a woman wore customarily, her most important one was her wedding ring. Styles of wedding rings have changed periodically, even during the last one hundred and fifty years, from bands close to a half-inch wide to those so narrow they can hardly be measured accurately. Sometimes the familiar gold band was decoratively chased, engraved or carved or set with one or more stones. All Victorian wedding rings were simple compared to those used during earlier centuries.

Older than the custom of be-

trothal rings is the art of carving cameos, which the Victorian esteemed highly for jewelry. All cameos are carved in relief. The more valuable ones are those that have been carved on a hard stone having two or three layers differing in color such as onyx, agate or sardonyx. By far the greatest number of cameos have been carved on shells. Preferred for the purpose were shells that could be carved to show red on a sardonyx tint or a white layer that could be cut down against a background of claret, orange, pink or other color. Some stones but many more shells were the base of the cameos used for necklaces, large pendants and brooches, earrings and bracelets worn by many Victorians. Classic profiles and mythological figures, alone or in groups, were the two major designs. Less common was a scene. Early in the nineteenth century the gold settings were quite plain, but during the Victorian years many were wreathed with fine gold rope or dainty filigree. Small pearls or perhaps garnets or diamonds were sometimes worked

Hand-painted brooch, late 19th century, American.

into the gold settings. Collectors of cameos cherish unmounted specimens.

Many women owned a set of cameo jewelry that included brooch, necklace, earrings and two bracelets, but probably few called this a parure. The parure, an eighteenth-century innovation, consisted of earrings, a brooch, necklace, ring and sometimes shoulder brooches or clasps.

A set of jewelry was the prized possession of most Victorian women. Young ladies loved their matching necklace, earbobs and bracelets of cameos, garnets or carved coral roses mounted in gold leaves. Bridal sets of jewelry were vastly important. One Virginia family cherishes an exquisite set of seed pearls on mother-of-pearl that has been worn by each generation of brides since the late 1700's. It consists of a shimmering necklace, earrings, two bracelets and a brooch. By the 1860's brides often were given garnets; the minimum was a brooch and earbobs, but usually there were two matching bracelets. The garnet brooch, averaging 1¾" in diameter, was either round or star-shaped.

Victorians wore jewelry not only when they were married but also during periods of mourning. Since mourning jewelry had to be black, jet or onyx was preferred. Bracelets, pins, earrings and other personal adornments woven from human hair were worn as memorial pieces or mementos of a loved one. Memorial rings, which may have originated earlier, were not unusual during the seventeenth century. These often had elaborate designs around the hoop and always included the name and date of death enameled in black and white.

Everyday jewelry also was made of glass and pottery. Not long after Josiah Wedgwood introduced his popular two-color jasperware in 1774, small pieces were produced for ornaments. The white decoration in relief, usually against a Wedgwood-blue background, was reminiscent of a cameo. These jasperware pieces were mounted, the earliest ones in cut steel, to be worn as lockets, rings and bracelets. Parian ware, the unglazed porcelain so white and so similar in texture to rough marble that it was named for the Parian variety, lent itself to trinkets that Victorians, young and old, enjoyed wearing. In the potteries in Bennington, Vermont, during the 1850's, the white Parian base was decorated with tiny applied blossoms. Crosses, pins in various shapes, stickpins, pendants, earrings, and pieces that could be strung on ribbon and worn as a bracelet were popular. Millefiori, literally glass of a thousand flowers, was a process that had been perfected for paperweights. The colorful millefiori bits also were arranged effectively under clear glass for brooches, earbobs and other small pieces of jewelry.

Amethyst glass bead necklace, early 20th century, American.

A string of gold beads meant as much to women of the nineteenth century as a string of pearls does to their twentieth-century descendants. These beads are likely to be twenty-four-karat gold. Chokers usually were strung with gold beads of the same size, but slightly longer strands often consisted of beads graduated in size. By the 1880's, ladies were wearing gold watches about 1⅜" in diameter. These watches had closed cases with a monogram on one side and sometimes a jeweled decoration on the other. They were either pinned to the shirtwaist with a bowknot or other simple pin designed for the purpose or worn on long gold chains and tucked into the belt. The long gold chains, single or double, had a slide that might be plain gold with beaded edge and initial or monogram, or jeweled with opals and pearls, garnets and moonstones. Lockets on gold chains almost as long as those for watches were widely popular. The locket usually was a sizable gold heart, unadorned except for the monogram, enameled in color, or decorated perhaps with small entwined hearts outlined in turquoises and pearls.

Early nineteenth-century bracelets and gold chains sometimes fastened with golden clasped hands, ornamented by a garnet or turquoise on the ring finger. Clasped hands remained a favorite motif throughout the

Polished-steel belt buckle, late 19th century, American.

Victorian years. The heart was used for pendants, lockets, and earrings and as the main motif for bracelets and necklaces. A plain gold heart, no more than ¼″ long, even dangled from an oval chased-gold pin. Victorian serpent bracelets and necklaces can still be found—some with flashing eyes of tiny emeralds or rubies.

Gold chains have returned to fashion again and Victorian ones with their slides may still be strong enough to wear. Some owners have had the long gold watch chains converted into bracelets with the jeweled slides as ornaments. Stickpins are likely to be appropriated now by women who have five to seven grouped together and made into an important pin. Among the simple pins were gold bowknots, a single pearl or a small pear-shaped amethyst. Then there were gold stickpins studded with garnets, moonstones, topazes, opals or any of the stones favored for women's jewelry. Gentlemen's cuff links almost as varied as their stickpins, usually can be converted to clip or screw-back earrings. The handsome gold fob and the seals which every solid Victorian gentleman wore on his watch chain now often turn up on charm bracelets. However small or odd the piece of Victorian jewelry, its rich gold and excellent workmanship make it worthy of consideration for use today.

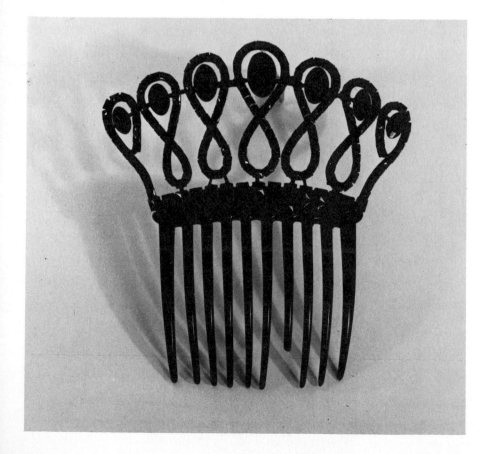

Jeweled tortoiseshell comb, early 20th century, American.

20. Weather Vanes

In the days before weather forecasts were published in daily newspapers and announced over radio and television, it was important to many people to observe which way the wind was blowing. Such knowledge helped the farmer regulate his sowing, harvesting and dozens of other chores. The farmer's house had to be located so that the prevailing winds would carry away from it odors from barns and other buildings. A knowledge of winds was equally important to fishermen and mariners. In fact, men and women in both seacoast cities and inland settlements were helped in planning their work if they could look at a weather vane and note the direction of the wind and conclude its possible effect on the weather.

Present-day weather vanes, though small in number and primarily decorative, continue a great American tradition. For somewhat more than two hundred and fifty years, weather vanes were produced here, first by amateur woodworkers and then by skilled craftsmen in wood and metals. Antique weather vanes now are classified as folk art of the finest sort, for both their construction and the originality of their designs. No country has ever been brightened by a more diversified lot of vane figures. The settlers who came to America had been familiar with weather vanes in their native lands, but the traditional cock of Europe, although not forgotten, soon had many rivals for his lofty position in figures that were more timely or appropriate to this country.

The simplest form of weather vane is a piece of cloth used as a wind banner. This sufficed on a farm, for example, until the best whittler in the family shaped a wooden vane during the first winter on the land. These weather vanes were flat pieces of wood cut and shaped in a simple form such as an arrow, a fish, rooster or hen. Some of them were pierced or otherwise decorated to add realism. Since pine was the wood generally used, it is no wonder that so few of these seventeenth- and early eighteenth-century vanes are still in existence. There are some to be seen in museum collections and restorations. One of the most typically American of these wooden profiles is now owned and displayed by the Concord Antiquarian Society in Concord, Massachusetts. This

Copper weather vane, trotter, 19th century, American.

one is in the form of a coiled rattlesnake, which was a symbol of unity, defiance and liberty that became popular here in the years before the Revolution.

Metal gradually superseded wood for weather vanes. Iron was used to a great extent during the eighteenth and early nineteenth centuries, and copper became popular after 1850. Tin, lead and brass also were used, but lead and brass often formed only parts of a vane of other material. The early profile vanes of wood were not large, perhaps two to three feet in length (the coiled rattlesnake at the Concord Antiquarian Society is three feet, one inch long and seven eighths of an inch thick). However, metal vanes of four feet and longer started to become general during the eighteenth century. The size of the vane, of course, depended to some extent on the building to which it was secured.

By 1800, weather vanes were being made chiefly of metal. At first, sheet copper or occasionally sheet brass was fastened to pine so that the figures almost looked molded. However, such vane figures were heavy and swung poorly in the wind. Still, there are many sheet-metal vanes, particularly of sheet iron, without wood backing that were made in the early 1800's. Some of these originally were covered with gold leaf; others were painted in many colors or polychromed.

If a wooden weather vane is found nowadays, it is likely to be a carved rather than a whittled one. This vane, carved in greater detail, served as a pattern for the cast-iron mold in which the long-lasting metal figures were made to put up outdoors. Before 1850 a metal vane was made by soldering together at the edges two convex pieces of metal to form a figure in low relief. After 1850 it became customary to make a cast-iron mold from the detailed wood carving of the figure. The finished figure of copper or other metal, when taken from the mold, was in high relief and displayed more and sharper details than did the metal vane figures of the early nineteenth century. These metal figures were hollow and swung easily in the wind.

Really old weather vanes never had quadrants—that is, arms tipped with initials indicating north, south, east and west. These were not necessary, at least on farms where a weather vane topped the barn, for this building was built with its sides to the cardinal points. The weather vanes topped with large, rounded figures, which became so popular during the nineteenth century, were equipped not only with directional quadrants but also with a gleaming ball.

Iron weather vane, rooster, 19th century, American.

A few of the weather vanes made in America are unique. It is doubtful that anyone in his homeland had the temerity to cut a vane figure of Count Pulaski, the Polish nobleman who joined Washington's army in 1777, yet someone in America did about 1800. The martial figure in uniform, holding sword upraised in one hand, was a tribute in iron to a brave man who died for liberty in America, and the flat surface must have made an excellent vane for the wind to push around. Another sheet-iron vane of the late eighteenth century showed George Washington on horseback. Both parts of this figure were polychromed, and holes in the horse's feet permitted it to be mounted on a horizontal rod. Many other designs that originated in America were repeated again and again.

In Europe the traditional figure for a weather vane was the cock, due to a papal decree in the ninth century. The purpose of the cockerel weather vane was to remind people of Peter's denial of Christ and warn them not to do likewise. As a result, weathercock became a synonym for weather vane. Roosters and hens were a common sight here on farms and in backyards, so they often were models for weather vanes. Roosters are said to have been an especially popular choice in Pennsylvania well into the nineteenth century. Materials, sizes, poses and details varied from place to place and with the skill of the workman. The outstanding collection of weather vanes at the Shelbourne Museum in Vermont includes a varied lot of fowl. There is a rooster, cut in profile from wood and painted red in the late eighteenth century. Another

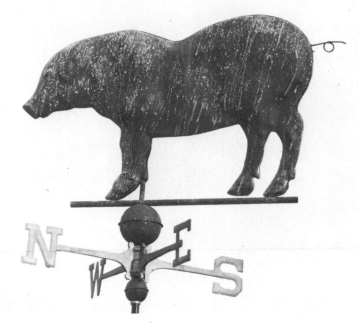

Copper weather vane, pig, 19th century, American.

profile of the nineteenth century in iron portrays a crowing cock, also painted. A plumper rooster, made after 1850, has a body consisting of two hollow castings of iron in the half-round that are bolted together; the tail cut in silhouette was attached with screws. More ingenious is the rooster made in Pennsylvania in the early nineteenth century, for its several sections were carved from pine, glued together, then secured with iron strips and painted. The rounded copper rooster, wherever it was made, could be quite detailed in the arrangement of feathers, tail and comb.

Animals were great favorites everywhere, particularly dogs and horses. On a farm the vane figure might be a cow, pig or even a goose. Nor was the deer overlooked. Along the coast, fish and ships were popular. At least one dolphin weather vane has been

found. This quarter-round creature of copper with attached fins makes an impressive figure although it looks rather more severe than dolphins are reputed to be, perhaps because it had been moved from its own element, water, into the wind. A mermaid seems a natural choice, too, for a building along the coast. A fine example of true folk sculpture is a mermaid, more than four feet long, that was carved from a single piece of pine. This figure had attached arms with one hand holding a mirror, the other a comb.

The peacock, usually of one or more metals, became quite familiar during the nineteenth century, as did the eagle, which became the symbol of the United States when the design for the Great Seal was adopted in 1781. Considering the extent to which eagles were used to decorate buildings and most of their fur-

hopper with glass eyes still surveys the changing scene, although fire and other vicissitudes have knocked it from its perch more than once. Peter Faneuil himself ordered the grasshopper weather vane, but the idea for the figure was not original with him. Rather, his was a copy of the much larger grasshopper weather vane on top of the Royal Exchange in London.

The first person who thought of the angel Gabriel blowing his trumpet for a weather-vane figure had a good idea, since the form is an excellent wind indicator. Who the person was or how many of these figures were pushed about is unknown, at least to me, but an exceptionally handsome example was made in Boston in 1840 for a church in Newburyport, Massachusetts. This full-length figure of Gabriel with wings and robes was six feet, two inches long and was made of sheet copper. The copper trumpet held to its lips is three-dimensional. The complete vane weighed thirty-eight pounds.

Indigenous to America were Indians and the weather vanes for which they unwittingly served as models. An Indian holding his bow and arrow was probably the most popular pose. Sometimes the Indian held a tomahawk instead. The Indian usually wore some kind of feather headdress and he was shown as thin or plump, heroic or ordinary, according to the viewpoint and skill of the designer. Indian weather vanes often were made of sheet iron and polychromed. One distinctive and more complicated vane showed an Indian paddling his canoe. There were several forms of individual Indians, too, such as Massasoit and Chief Tammany.

Copper weather vane, horse and sulky with driver, 19th century, American.

nishings, from furniture to patchwork quilts, during the 1800's, the number of eagle weather vanes seems small. Perhaps this is because the eagle did not lend itself to simple whittling, and carving one was a job for a master woodworker. A good many handsome full-bodied eagles, usually perched on a ball, were manufactured from copper and sometimes gilded.

The grasshopper, although popular here, did not originate in America. The most famous grasshopper vane is the gilded one Peter Faneuil had placed on top of Faneuil Hall when the two-story brick building opened as a market in Boston in 1742. This four-foot, four-inch-long grass-

By 1840, firms were being established to manufacture metal weather vanes. Small and simple ones were still being turned out by country workmen, but the manufacture of vanes helped to make them a popular adornment of property in towns and cities. The vanes became larger and more elaborate in design, in some cases more lifelike. Horses, for example, often were almost recognizable, at least by their pose. In the 1860's when the trotter Dexter was practically the idol of the populace, this horse or his lithographed reproduction was reproduced again and again in metal. A horse attached to a sulky also became a popular design during the nineteenth century. An unusual and perhaps a unique vane in the late nineteenth century consisted of a spirited, if rather simple, horse on which stood a bareback rider; the sheet-copper body of the rider was filled with lead for balance.

Several versions were made of two other copper figures, the Goddess of Liberty and Columbia. Apparel and headdress differed on the two figures. Each one held a flag, recognizable because of its pierced stars and sometimes pierced alternate stripes. The flags usually had thirteen stars, although the figures were made in the 1850's and 1870's. By this time, also, there were locomotive weather vanes to place above railroad stations, a fire engine drawn by two steeds for a firehouse, and a wrought-iron plow for a barn.

No weather vane ever was more suited to the building over which it floated with the winds than the one above a slaughterhouse in New Bedford, Massachusetts. This long, horizontal metal one consisted of a cleaver on whose handle a farmer strode to market holding in one upraised hand a stick and in the other a string tied to the rear leg of a pig, arrested in its march on the blade of the cleaver. The pig is complete to its curled tail and the bearded farmer is dressed in high boots, frock coat and derby. Perhaps also one-of-a-kind is the butterfly vane made in the late nineteenth century. The butterfly was cut in silhouette from sheet copper and pierced and striated to suggest its pattern.

One or more designs of an automobile were made in the early 1900's. At the present time, reproductions of popular nineteenth-century weather vanes rather than the creation of new designs occupy manufacturers. Some reproductions are said to be made from nineteenth-century molds. The carvers and metal workers who produced so many unusual weather vanes remain for the most part anonymous, although some of the important manufacturers of the last century are known.

There may still be some old weather vanes hidden in tumbledown barns and carriage houses and it is often possible to buy a weather vane that was used during the 1800's. Copper figures are likely to be stained and colored with verdigris. It is difficult to say how much cleaning and repairing should be done on an old weather vane of any material. The lucky finder or purchaser may be torn between doing enough so that it can be displayed again outdoors or as a wall decoration indoors and doing little or none so that its value as an antique is not reduced.

21. Pressed Glass

Pressed glass is American in origin and we treasure its many lovely patterns, with their delightfully elaborate names, as much as our grandmothers and great-grandmothers did. But like the ugly duckling pressed glass was at first scorned and unloved, though its story too becomes a happy one. In America of the 1820's, pressed glass found a home only with those who could not afford the more expensive cut glass. For one thing the newcomer didn't have the brilliance or beauty of the bottles and more decorative household objects that were still being made by hand. In contrast to the free-blown and blown-molded methods pressed glass was made by pressing machines, which had just been invented. Molten glass was simply poured into patterned molds, snipped off and then rammed by closely fitted plungers that forced the liquid into every cutting of the pattern. The results were often uneven, flawed and foggy in appearance. Certainly they must have seemed crude in comparison to the smooth, gleaming blown glass. But as so often in our history, Yankee ingenuity came to the rescue. Glassmakers discovered that pressed glass took on a sparkle from light refracted from facets of the pattern, the more facets the better. Gradually the motifs became more elaborate, delicate and imaginative, the workmen more skilled and pressed glass began to be cherished for its own distinctive character.

By 1845 pressed glass was a common household commodity, so common that it was being made in glass factories not only in New England but also throughout the east and midwest. Deming Jarves, one of the men most active in developing the new process, had no monopoly on it and only a small percentage of all the pressed glass made between the 1820's and 1900 came from Sandwich, Massachusetts, where he established the famous Boston and Sandwich Glass Company in 1825. The Sandwich factory was a leader in pressed glass but produced many other beautiful kinds including cut glass.

Although motifs such as strawberry diamond, bull's-eye and fan that were commonly used to dec-

Compote, Brooklyn Flint Glass Co., 1860s.

orate cut glass also were displayed on much of the early pressed glass, it is easy to tell the difference between the two. These motifs on cut glass are deep and sharp to the touch but on pressed glass they are shallow and feel almost smooth. Cut glass always sparkles too. Because pressed glass did not, pieces manufactured during the first years were made with a stippled background. Stippling consists of tiny, slightly raised dots close together that catch the light. Pressed glass with stippled background is known as lacy glass. After 1850 lacy glass was displaced by pattern glass. Stippling was still used in some patterns but only as part of the design. There had been improvements in the process that made the pattern glass attractive. Hundreds of patterns introduced between about 1850 and 1900 are identified by a name. They appeal fully as much to present-day collectors of antiques as they did to housewives who bought this new glass 100 and more years ago.

In the 1840's it was common for households to have four matching pieces of pressed glass known as a table set: a sugar bowl, creamer, covered butter dish and spoonholder These were considered everyday necessities. After 1850 production had increased so greatly that a woman could set a table with her favorite pattern. A complete set consisted of a dozen to two or three dozen different pieces including various serving dishes, tumblers and other kinds of drinking glasses, plates, sauce dishes and the like. Still later a water set could be purchased separately in such patterns as Thousand Eye, Shell and Jewel, Daisy and Button, Crown Jewel and Moon and Star. A large water pitcher, a matching glass tray and water tumblers, lemonade tumblers or goblets and, in some patterns, all three made up a water set.

Special dishes for celery, honey and pickles, egg cups, decanters and glasses for claret and other wines, cordials, goblets and tumblers were available in the half-dozen bull's-eye patterns made just before and after 1850. The large, round concave bull's-eye had long been a motif on cut glass. The first pressed glass pattern that displayed it was a simple one, called Bull's-eye and pro-

Lacy Sandwich glass cup plate, acorn motif, c. 1830-50.

Lacy Sandwich glass cup plate, American eagle motif, 1831.

Lacy Sandwich glass cup plate, octagonal, c. 1830-50.

duced by the New England Glass Company. Later this firm made a pattern combining bull's-eye with small diamond points in tapering panels which they named Bull's-eye with Diamond Point. Other factories, mainly in Pennsylvania and Ohio, offered Bull's-eye with Fleur-de-lis meaning that a five-petaled ornament hangs from each bull's-eye, Bull's-eye and Bar, Pillar and Bull's-eye.

A variant of a pattern displays the main motif but differs in some details so that another name is warranted. When one firm introduced a pattern that quickly became popular, other glassmakers were likely to adapt and change it slightly and offer it under a new name. Thus a pattern made in Ohio and known as Bull's-eye Variant is identical to the original Bull's-eye except that the later one has a small opening above and below each eye. Tulip pattern, which is based on the classic profile outline of this flower, has two variants called Tulip Variant without Sawtooth and Tulip Variant with Smaller Flower. Then there is the quite different Beaded Tulip.

Not variants of each other but easily confused by someone who is learning pressed glass are Dickinson, a late pattern, and Horn of Plenty, an earlier one made of more brilliant glass. A close look shows that Horn of Plenty takes its name from the shape of alternating panels, each combining sawtooth and a clear section with bull's-eye. Dickinson is circled with a curved panel of sawtooth matched to a similarly shaped clear panel with an elongated oval thumbprint.

Crystal is not a correct term to apply to pressed glass in general.

Early patterns based on thumbprint, diamond and other classic motifs copied from cut glass pieces were made only in clear, or white, glass. It was transparent and colorless. In fact all patterns probably were made in clear glass including the many delightful flower and fruit ones that became so popular in the 1870's and 1880's. However many of these also were made in one or more colors. The beautiful shades of yellow, amber, amethyst, light blue, deep blue, apple green or dark green were achieved by adding certain chemicals to the liquid glass. The charming Wildflower pattern for example was made in a clear glass and five colors: dark amber, light amber, yellow, blue and apple green.

When Daisy and Button was introduced, it was made not only in clear glass but also in amethyst, light blue, deep blue, yellow, light amber, dark amber, apple green, dark green and vaseline glass. Vaseline glass is yellow with an underlying blue tint that makes it look for all the world like the salve of that name. Daisy and Button was an adaptation of the well-known cut glass pattern named Russian and the daisy is more of a rosette than a true flower. The basic Daisy and Button pressed glass may show the daisy with a smooth round button or with a button impressed with a star. So popular was this pattern that six variants appeared with descriptive names: Daisy and Button with V Ornament, Daisy and Button with Crossbar, Daisy and Button with Thumbprint, Paneled Daisy and Button, Daisy and Button Single Panel and Daisy and Button with Narcissus. On the other hand the pattern known as Paneled Daisy

has blossoms that look like field daisies and was made only in clear glass. So was Bellflower which was made by many firms for decades; this consistently popular pattern consists of a vine, either single or double, along which are stylized bellflowers and three-part leaves against a ribbed background.

Most of the other flower patterns are delightfully realistic. A woman who enjoys flowers as well as pressed glass will take pleasure from patterns named Beaded Tulip, Bleeding Heart, Clematis, Stippled Forget-me-not and Barred Forget-me-not, Windflower, Fuchsia, Primrose, Thistle and Paneled Thistle. At least four patterns were based on roses. Rose in Snow displays large, open roses with stems, foliage and buds in relief against a stippled background. It was made in yellow, amber and blue as well as clear glass. So was Rose Sprig, sometimes called The Hundred-Leaved Rose pattern. Cabbage Rose does bring to mind its fragrant namesake. Both this pattern and Open Rose, with the sprays of flowers divided by a stem with two leaves and a bud, were made only in clear glass.

Various transparent colors became so popular that manufac-

Celery vase, sawtooth pattern, mid-19th century, American.

Cranberry pitcher, thumbprint pattern, late 19th century, American.

turers introduced still another kind late in the 19th century. These newer patterns had color applied in the proper places on the exterior of the glass. Red and white patterns such as Ruby Thumbprint and Red Block were typical. Applied colors wore off somewhat with constant handling. A mug in Red Block, which was used every day for several years, may have some of the red worn off, but a honey dish in Ruby Thumbprint may be almost as perfect as when it was first purchased. Another pattern, Flying Bird and Strawberry, also called Bluebird, sometimes had berries painted red, leaves green and birds blue. Pieces in this pattern with applied color are scarcer

nowadays than clear ones, which were made in greater quantity.

Appropriate as it might seem for them fruit patterns were not made in colors. Blackberry, strawberry, grapes, cherry, gooseberry, currant and pear each inspired one or more patterns. At least 12 different ones feature grapes. In addition nonedible fruits appear on such patterns as Barberry or Pepperberry, Holly and Beaded Acorn. Willow Oak also includes acorns with leaves. Certainly any piece of Holly pressed glass with its lightly stippled, spiny-tipped leaves and clusters of true to life berries will be brought out for use at Christmas time.

More of the edible fruit patterns than any other type were made not only in clear glass but also in the glass variously known as opaque-white, milk-white or milk glass. This is an opaque white but the old ware is translucent. The white also has a blue tinge, as skim milk does, when a piece of this glass is held up to the light. Pressed milk-white glass was made after 1870. In addition to many miscellaneous dishes, Blackberry, Strawberry, Cherry and Gooseberry patterns were made in sets of milk-white glass.

Fruit and flower patterns prove

that by the 1870's glassmakers no longer derived their ideas for pressed glass patterns from cut glass. Still another departure was the combination of clear and frosted glass. The frosted portions, created by the use of acid, have a matte finish that contrasts strikingly with the clear glass. This group of patterns is headed

Acid-finish cobalt candlestick, Sandwich, 1840s.

by three that are called appropriately Westward Ho, Lion and Three Face. The designs that gave rise to these names stand out against a frosted background: the most coveted pieces are those with covers. These covers have frosted glass knobs; on Westward Ho, for example, the knob is in the form of a crouching Indian.

Other patterns combining frosted and clear glass may not be quite as unusual but they are handsome. Ribbon and its variant Double Ribbon, Frosted Ribbon and Fluted Ribbon each display a different arrangement of clear and frosted panels. Not as well known but worth cherishing are pieces of Roman Key, Frosted Circle and Frosted Stork. Since these last three patterns were also made in clear glass, it may be sheer luck to come across a piece that is both frosted and clear.

Three of the frosted and clear patterns, Westward Ho, Lion and Three Face, are included in the list of ten most popular patterns among present-day collectors. So is opaque-white Blackberry. The pressed glass experts who compiled this list also place on it Bellflower, Wildflower, Rose in Snow, Daisy and Button, Horn of Plenty and Thousand Eye. The tremendous interest now prevalent in pressed glass has probably made it inevitable that some of the 19th century patterns are more sought after than others. However, many other patterns are fun to search for and a joy to own.

After all, the ten patterns made most popular by collectors aren't the only ones worth having. A teen-ager who asked my help in identifying her grandmother's large heavy sugar and creamer was delighted to learn that it was

Victoria pattern and had fun last summer attending country auctions to look for other pieces. She hopes to get enough of this old pressed glass to serve dessert. Then there is the woman who bought a good looking pickle dish in a secondhand store. When she found out it was pressed glass in Kentucky pattern she started searching for small dishes in other patterns named for states. There are many: Indiana, Ohio, Maryland, Michigan, to name a few.

Almost any pattern or piece may spark your interest in pressed glass. One thing is certain: so many were made between the 1820's and 1900 that you don't have to be wealthy to collect this fascinating All-American glass.

Blue opalescent sugar, creamer and tray, hobnail pattern, late 1880s, American.

22. Milk Glass

Milk glass was not originated in America, nor was it brand-new when it attained popularity. There were glassmakers here in the early 1800's who knew how to make milk glass, and during the 1830's and 1840's it was used to some extent to fashion or decorate candlesticks and lamps. By 1870, however, glassmakers in this country were able to produce milk glass in a quality as good as, if not superior to, that produced in England and Europe. American milk glass became noted for its whiteness or clarity of color and its detail.

But it was the technique of pressing, which had been used so successfully to produce clear and colored glass tableware, that introduced milk glass to a wider public in the 1870's. Pressed glass was much less expensive than that produced and decorated by any other method; thus many people made the acquaintance of milk glass through pieces that were given as premiums by storekeepers. At least one condiment, mustard, was sold in small containers of milk glass, too.

The appeal of this different glass must have been strong enough to tempt people into buying pieces to set a table or serve lemonade and cookies as well as small decorative boxes, jars and trays to hold trinkets, toothpicks or soap. Interest was sustained by the production of colored milk glass. But perhaps the most popular of all, then as now, were the pieces that combined a color with white milk glass. Late in the century, such novelties as custard glass, caramel glass and marble glass found buyers as readily as they attract collectors today.

The popular ware, as it became available in more and more forms, was listed in trade catalogues as milk white, white enamel, opaque, opal, opalescent and alabaster. "Milk glass" seems natural to most people, for this glass, like the liquid of that name, has some density. Many pieces, when held up to light, have an underlying tinge of blue that calls to mind skim milk. Actually, milk glass varied in both quality and opacity. Differences in quality can be traced chiefly to the greater care that some glass-

Milk glass punch bowl set, early 20th century, American.

makers took in the purity of ingredients and the mixing and heating of the glass.

According to the late Ruth Webb Lee, glass expert, four different types of white milk glass were made in the nineteenth century. The sort that she designates as milk-white glass is white and so opaque that light does not shine through. "Opaque glass" is not dead white but is partly translucent when a piece is held up to the light. "Opal glass" is still milk-white, but when held up to the light it shows a center of fire like an opal, "Opalescent glass" is thinner and more translucent but less white than opal glass. These differences can still be observed but all four of these basic groups now are usually referred to as milk glass.

The general term "milk-white" was the one preferred by Mrs. Lee, who stated emphatically that "opaque" followed by the color was the correct way of referring to the several colors that were introduced. Thus a black swan would have been called opaque black, an all-blue duck "opaque blue." In recent years, however, it has become customary to refer to opaque colored glass as blue milk glass, black milk glass, et cetera. Collectors as well as antique dealers have fostered acceptance of this modern terminology. By far the greatest amount of milk glass was white. Blue and green, however, were popular colors and some lavender, yellow and black also were made. Appropriate names were chosen for the novelties, for both "custard" and "caramel" aptly sum up the color and appearance of these two sorts. "Clam-broth glass' is a gray-white and "marble glass," often called purple slag, is basically white streaked with color.

The true opal and opalescent glasses in which fire can be seen are easy to recognize in such miscellaneous pieces as toothpick and match holders, tiebacks and vases. More often than not, opalescent glass was combined with another colorful art glass to make the fancy Late Victorian baskets. One of the best known opalescent pieces is the tieback in Petal and Shell pattern that was produced by the Boston and Sandwich Glass Company. Reproductions made in several surprisingly good colors in the 1930's are easy to spot. (To do this, examine good pressed glass, then look at reproductions.) These tiebacks were made in at least three sizes, with the pressed glass disks 2″, 2½″ and 3″ in diameter.

Marble glass or purple slag was also called mosaic, agate and calico glass in the 1800's. It is not an end-of-the-day glass, as some people thought. But it is a novelty opaque glass. Best known is the purple- or rose-and-white marble glass but it also was made with streakings of blue, green and yellow to brown shades. Nearly all slag pieces are rare today and bring high prices.

With its coffee-with-cream tint, caramel glass originally was called chocolate glass. It was introduced at the Buffalo Expositoin in May 1901 and was produced in Greentown, Indiana, between 1900 and 1903. Thin pieces are darker and more uniform in tint while thick pieces tend to be lighter inside and darker outside. Custard glass couldn't be better named because it is a delicate tint of creamy yellow. As a rule, custard glass is decorated quite heavily with gilt or dark green or both. Odd pieces (water pitchers, compotes, trays, mugs, tumblers), not tableware sets, are to be found in caramel and custard glass.

More than thirty patterns of nineteenth-century pressed glass tableware were made in milk glass, usually as an alternate choice to clear glass. All four variations of milk-white glass were represented in the patterns. A few patterns were made in complete sets in opaque colors, of which blue apparently was most popular. Many other patterns had a few pieces made in colored opaque glass but not a complete set. Of course, some designs for plates, platters and pitchers were used only for milk glass.

Probably the earliest pattern to be made in milk glass was Sawtooth. Almost as old is Waffle, which also was made in clear glass

Black milk-glass vase, early 20th century, American.

and milk glass. Best known today is milk-white Blackberry. This is one of the ten most popular patterns among collectors and it also is one of the most expensive to buy now. Other fruit patterns such as Strawberry, Gooseberry, and Grape also were made in milk glass. At the time they were being produced, complete sets could have been bought in such distinctive patterns as Paneled Wheat, Basket Weave, Icicle, and Princess Feather as well as the now lesser known Crossed Fern, Block and Fan, and Barred Hobnail. On the whole, these milk-glass patterns are both white and opaque although Princess Feather is more translucent than most. Opal glass is well represented by Ribbed Opal and Swirled Opal, both of which were made in opalescent and blue opalescent.

One of the most fascinating forms in which milk glass, both white and colored, is found is the dish with an animal cover. Most plentiful of this motley assortment are the dishes with a hen or a rooster sitting on the cover, usually with their heads turned so they are looking to one side. The rooster often had his comb painted red and both hens and roosters were likely to have glass eyes glued in place. Dishes with hen or rooster covers were most common in milk glass and a few were all white except for a blue, amber or amethyst head on the fowl. These dishes, oval, oblong or sometimes round, often were quite plain with a wide, lacy openwork edge. Lacking this edging, the dish was pressed in basket weave, rib or other simple motif.

Some glass factories offered a farmyard assortment of dishes with animal covers that varied in length from 4″ to 10″. One set consisted of a duck, a swan, an eagle and a fish in addition to a hen and a rooster, each one with glass eyes to be glued into place by the storekeeper, who often did not. There were other animal covers in the shape of a cat, lamb, fox, rabbit, horse, cow, turtle, dog, lion or even a camel. One of my favorites has a crouching rabbit surrounded by hens' eggs. It is all white but the farmyard assortment of six different covers is said to have been available in opal, turquoise and green. Both a hen and a cow were made in black milk glass to top a matching dish (when held to the light, black milk glass shows a center spot of purple, amethyst or rosy purple). Lacy-edged dishes of milk glass also came with a hen cover of marble glass streaked with blue, green, yellow or brown. The combination of white and a color, however, must have been popular. Sometimes the dish was blue milk glass and the cover white and just about as often the colors were reversed.

In a smaller number of dishes, the bowl and cover together form the animal. An outstanding example is a duck made all in milk glass. It also was done in all blue milk glass and all amethyst as well as in white with a head of blue or other color. A similar dish took the form of a crouching white rabbit. Then there was a jar about 7″ tall in the form of an owl.

Long before farmyard covered dishes became popular, white and colored milk glass was being used for oil-burning lamps and candlesticks. Low candlesticks with a handle and scrolled decoration are charming. Pairs of tall candlesticks are notable in Swirl, Column, and Loop and

Petal patterns but the two most famous styles are the crucifix and the dolphin. These two were made by most glasshouses from Cape Cod to the Ohio River. Candlesticks in the form of a crucifix were made in several designs and sizes in the 1870's as a response to the religious revival that followed the Civil War.

The candlestick with the dolphin as its standard perhaps differed more from one glasshouse to another. The Boston and Sandwich Glass Company made their dolphin candlesticks with a square, stepped base or a round, scalloped petticoat base. One Pittsburgh firm introduced the hexagonal base as well as the high, round scalloped petticoat base. Sockets, too, varied. Candlesticks entirely of milk glass, particularly the dolphin one, probably are rarer now than those that combine two or more kinds of glass.

Collectors hunt for a pair of matching candlesticks but lamps usually are found singly. Lamps with oil font, standard and base of milk glass usually were pressed in a simple design. Others might combine a milk-glass font with a blue milk-glass standard. Some of the loveliest color combinations occur in lamps: a cranberry glass font with overlay of white milk glass on a white milk-glass standard and base, or a clear glass Honeycomb pattern font on an opalescent standard and base.

Scalloped-edge milk-glass compote, late 19th century, American.

Plates and bowls are prized chiefly for the variety of their openwork edges. Plates in particular have fascinating borders that can be described as heart, heart and anchor, scroll and eye, wicket, block, fleur-de-lis, club and shell, lattice, crown, pinwheel, and many more. With borders such as these, plates need no decoration. Many have plain centers. Some, however, have a pressed design, perhaps commemorative or in tribute to a season or a holiday. Perhaps most treasured now are the milk-glass plates with a hand-painted spray of flowers or a bird in the center. The openwork edges of bowls differ from those on plates and have been given such names as arches, lattice, ball and chain, chain, lacy, crinkled lacy, crinkled chain, chain and petal. Many bowls have scalloped or plain edges and most of them are open. Both bowls and compotes on standards, the latter often with covers, were produced in the patterns made in milk glass.

Sugar bowls, trays, platters and pitchers in all sizes, and syrup jugs were popular milk-glass pieces. Most syrup jugs and pitchers were white milk glass, although blue ones are found occasionally. Pressing was general, perhaps a recognizable pattern such as Rain Drop, Hobnail or Bellflower, then again just a simple motif or two. The small tray in the shape of a shell, clasped hands or a fan and in the conventional shape with a pretty pressed pattern of garlands might have been used for candies, relishes or on a dressing table.

The rather showy custard glass is believed to have been originated by Harry Northwood, who is better known for carnival glass. Some custard glass, like many carnival-glass pieces, is marked on the underside with "Northwood" or "N" in a circle. Probably the most coveted pieces of custard glass nowadays are the creamer and sugar in Argonaut Shell pattern bearing a Northwood mark. The bodies of each piece are ridged and shaped somewhat like a scallop shell and the footed bases are decorated with gold-colored shells, green seaweed and coral.

During the 1870's and 1880's, a quite complete set of marble glass was made for the table. There also were plates with lacy edges and many small odd dishes such as soap dishes, pickle jars, toothpick and match holders, rose bowls and other small vases. Marble glass was made by several firms in the United States and at the height of its popularity a good deal was imported from England.

In the last two decades of the nineteenth century other kinds of milk glass were imported from England and France. To make collecting more complicated, many of the nineteenth-century pieces are being reproduced. One of these, a charming small piece created by the Vallerystahl glassworks in France, consisted of a robin cover for a dish in the form of a nest on a pedestal base of branches and leaves. In recent years, this piece has been reproduced by the Westmoreland Glass Company in Pennsylvania in both white and blue milk glass. Just as with the originals, reproductions of milk glass differ in quality.

Still, I cannot claim that I *always* could differentiate between a compote or candlesticks made in the 1870's and the same pieces reproduced in the 1970's. I often feel, however, that much of the contemporary milk glass is inclined to be less translucent, thicker in appearance and more of a dead white than nineteenth-century pieces. In trying to tell reproductions from antiques, keep in mind the four basic types of milk-white glass that were produced during the 1800's. Serious collectors may be able to avoid errors in buying by finding out which of the many pieces are being reproduced and whether or not they are being made in old molds and from old formulas.

23. Sparkling Cut Glass

Fashions change in glass as in everything else, but nothing ever disappeared more quietly and completely than did cut glass between 1910 and 1920. For about thirty-five years, starting in 1876, a bride could hardly believe that she was properly married unless her presents included sparkling cut glass. A water pitcher, bonbon dishes, candlesticks, a vase or two, sugar and creamer, a knife rest, were gifts for which it was easy to write enthusiastic thank-you notes. A bride and groom could expect to receive additional pieces of cut glass on anniversaries and special occasions, and they usually planned to build up their set in the pattern of their choice as they could afford it.

So many families accumulated sizable collections that the speed with which they were packed in barrels and consigned to attics is still a little surprising. Yet the decline of cut glass might have been anticipated. It had been almost too popular between 1876 and about 1905, and the public demand for it was so great that the quality of workmanship began to deteriorate. Pieces became so overdecorated that they were no longer attractive. They continued to be made until about 1915, and as demand slackened,

Brilliant cut-glass water bottle, 1910-20, American.

Cut-glass cologne bottles from a dresser set, early 20th century, American.

innumerable small cut-glass factories closed and large firms turned to producing other kinds of glass. But make no mistake, the glass that had been cut in the United States between 1876 and 1905 was of fine quality; in fact, it was as fine, if not finer, than the very best produced in any other country at any time. A new appreciation of it has risen slowly in recent years, and people are beginning to realize that its like will never be made again.

The making of cuts on glass in order to form contrasting planes that reflect light is an ancient technique. In this country, glass has been decorated by cutting since the 1760's. It is said to have been done first at the glassworks of the fabulous Henry William Stiegel in Manheim, Pennsylvania. The designs that make each piece glitter and flash were cut by a moving wheel on hand-blown or blown-molded pieces of heavy, transparent glass. Although several substitutes for the expensive cut glass have been offered during the last two hundred years, none, including pressed glass, has suc-

ceeded in displacing it. The two intrinsic characteristics of cut glass are the sharpness and depth of the cuts and the prismatic brilliance. They cannot be imitated. Even a dusty piece of cut glass, if it stands in sunlight, manages to radiate the colors of a rainbow.

Cut glass always was expensive, yet families who could afford the gleaming pieces were ready to buy whatever was available. During the early years of the nineteenth century, the output of domestic glasshouses was supplemented by imports. Glass cutting had been well established in England and Ireland, for example, long before so much as a trickle was being made in America. Ireland's greatest period of glassmaking extended from about 1780 to 1825 and the name Waterford has become a synonym for cut glass produced in that country, although Belfast, Dublin and Cork were other glass centers. The designs cut on Irish glass were relatively simple. Diamond, swag, thumbprint, round lozenge, and sawtooth were favorite motifs which were combined in various ways. The edges of a piece of Waterford glass usually were scalloped and the rims were likely to flare and turn over or have a lip.

Much of the cut glass produced in America between the 1760's and the 1870's also displayed fairly simple decoration. Flute and panel cuttings were widely used as were straight and broken-prism cuts. Motifs on English and Irish glass also were copied here. Flute cuttings are handsome in their simplicity and show off well on such pieces as decanters, compotes and pitchers, which were coveted for the well-appointed dining table. Decanters made between 1830 and the late 1870's, known as the Middle Period in this country, are not difficult to recognize with their flute or panel-cut sides, one to three applied rings around their necks, and steeple or mushrooms stoppers. They are not as scarce as one might expect them to be nowadays.

Production of cut glass fluctuated here during the 1800's. Tariffs enacted by Congress gave impetus to the trade in the 1830's so that, in spite of the introduction of less expensive pressed glass, some firms continued to produce quality cut glass. Of the eighty or more glasshouses operating here according to the 1840 census, a good many included cutting shops. The number had been reduced greatly by 1865, chiefly because of the War between the States. The few glasshouses that continued cutting were in New England and the eastern states. In another twenty years, the boom in cut glass caused factories to flourish not only in these areas but also throughout the Midwest; Seattle and San Francisco on the West Coast each counted a glasshouse among its home industries. Where satisfactory fuel was available and cheap, no town was too small for a cut-glass factory. Two kept busy in my home town of about three thousand five hundred persons in the anthracite region of northeastern Pennsylvania in the early 1900's. Their products helped to satisfy demand, but hardly could have been comparable to those of Christian Dorflinger, one of the most famous glassmen during the second half of the nineteenth century, whose factory was

located about twenty-five miles farther north in White Mill, Pennsylvania.

The tremendous demand, greatest in the history of cut glass, was stimulated by the Centennial Exposition staged in Philadelphia, Pennsylvania, in 1876. Here the handful of glass exhibitors included the Boston and Sandwich Glass Company, the Mount Washington Glass Company, and the New England Glass Company, all from Massachusetts; Christian Dorflinger, and Gillinder and Sons of Pennsylvania; and Hobbs, Brockunier and Company in West Virginia. All continued to be leaders in manufacturing cut as well as other kinds of glass from 1876 to

Cut-glass receptacle for pins from a dresser set, early 20th century, American.

1905, a span of years designated as the Brilliant Period of cut-glass production. Pieces from large and small glass factories of this period were characterized by deep miter cuttings which also were known as brilliant cuttings. These increased refraction and made cut glass more sparkling than it ever had been.

Everyone at some time or other has seen at least a few pieces of glass which were cut during the Brilliant Period. It sparkles not only because of the deep-cut decoration but also because the glass itself was clear and bright. Contributing to these last characteristics was the use of gas heat which could be controlled more accurately than heat from coal. Other techniques related to fusing, annealing, cutting and polishing also helped to make cut glass so beautiful.

Improvement in equipment and techniques also made possible the cutting of many more complicated motifs than flute and panel. In addition to the straight, deep miter cut, an acute-angled or curved cut called a split was introduced. In 1896 when Nautilus pattern was patented, a notched prism cutting was added to the old straight and broken-prism cuts. Fan, bowknot, chair bottom or cane, palm leaf, and a simple rayed star became common and no glass cutter could resist trying the new and different hobstar. The hobstar has so many points that the intersection of their lines forms a central motif resembling a hobnail. Whatever its size, and whether there are six, eight, ten, twelve, eighteen or twenty-four points, a hobstar can be recognized instantly. An elaboration of the hobstar, cut about 1900, was the pinwheel or buzz, a many-pointed star with fan cuts following the direction of the points.

Carried over into the Brilliant Period and combined with the new motifs were such old ones as bull's-eye, block, hobnail which is six-sided and flat-topped, and strawberry diamond. The old English strawberry diamond is a diamond-shaped unit of smaller, deeply cut and equal-sided diamonds. The American version of strawberry diamond with one cross cut into the flat top surface of each small diamond was somewhat coarser but it sparkled fully as brightly. These two slightly different strawberry-diamond motifs, and hatching, which consists of fine crossed or parallel lines, were used to fill in between more important units of the pat-

tern. Minor as they were, they increased the scintillation from the piece of cut glass.

Two or three and sometimes five or six of these many popular motifs were combined to form distinctive patterns during the Brilliant Period. It may seem impossible to identify either a pattern or its component parts, even after comparing a piece of cut glass to pattern photographs. Keep looking at the piece of glass and, sooner or later, individual motifs stand out and can be called by name. Of the hundreds, if not thousands, of named patterns that were cut during the

Cut-glass candy dish or nappy, c. 1920, American.

Brilliant Period, none was better known or more popular than Russian. It was patented in 1882 by the T. G. Hawkes Glass Company in Corning, New York, but probably every glasshouse, large and small, made Russian pattern or a variant of it. Russian pattern, which inspired the pressed-glass pattern Daisy and Button later in the 1880's, displayed an arrangement of stars and hobnails. Plates and some other pieces of Russian have a twenty-four-point hobstar in the middle; the hobstar was added by the Dorflinger factory and later the Hawkes firm included it. According to Dorothy Daniel, an authority on cut glass, the pattern gained its name because, when it was quite new, a complete banquet set was ordered for the Russian Embassy in Washington. Soon afterward, complete sets were ordered to be used for state dinners at the American Embassy in St. Petersburg and at the White House, which is said to have been in use as late as the 1930's.

Every glasshouse also cut its own version of Corinthian pattern, and no two patterns are easier to distinguish between than Russian and Corinthian. A sixteen-point hobstar was dominant in Corinthian pieces. The large sixteen-point hobstar in the center and each of the smaller ones around the side were banded by deep miter cuts or splits. Triangles of crosshatching and strawberry diamond add sparkle.

Strawberry Diamond and Fan was a really handsome pattern that combined only these two motifs with the fans edging each piece of glass. Strawberry Diamond and Star pattern, less widely cut, also included fans but is still easy to recognize. Harvard pattern featuring chair-bottom or cane motif was cut in many variants, which were given other names by different glasshouses.

Neither Chrysanthemum pattern, patented in 1889, nor Bristol Rose, patented in 1893, displayed naturalistic flowers. Chrysanthemum consists of twenty-point stars and small hobstars with deep cuts radiating from the center of each piece to form leaves. Bristol Rose was a fanciful name chosen for thirty-two-point stars with raised rosette centers. An early, realistic flower design that began to appear shortly before 1900 was appropriately named Lily of the Valley. One of the handsomest true floral patterns I have ever seen, cut only by a glasshouse in Honesdale, Pennsylvania, is Poinsettia. It shows off well on tall pieces such as a vase where stems and leaves topped with wide clusters of bracts and flowers extend full length.

The number of patterns was almost equaled by the number of pieces in which most of them were cut, though not every glasshouse made every possible piece in an individual pattern such as Russian or Corinthian. Cut glass was made in sets for the table as well as in all imaginable ornamental pieces. Table sets started with tumblers or perhaps goblets and included glasses for all kinds of beverages and wine. Ice cream sets, consisting of a platter about 7" by 12", plates and small dishes for individual portions, could be purchased separately. A full table set went on to include nappies, which were low, shallow serving dishes, berry bowls, plates, compotes and pitchers. These five important pieces were made in different

sizes. Most families owned sauce-dishes, salt dishes and finger bowls with plates by the half-dozen or dozen, a condiment set, vinegar cruet, salt and pepper shakers, knife rest and toothpick holder. Serving dishes were especially designed for everything from celery to nuts, but were necessarily restricted to things that were not served hot. Heat, hot water, strong cold or any quick change in temperature can damage a piece of cut glass like lightning.

By far the greatest number of pieces and patterns were cut in clear or white glass. Some pieces of Russian pattern were cut in green, ruby, amber, amethyst, blue or yellow; Strawberry Diamond and Fan glistened in red, green or yellow. A much larger quantity was cut in clear glass. Some small amount of color appeared in a few other patterns, and it was not uncommon for any pattern to have wine or cordial glasses either colored and cut, or clear glass combined with red or green and cut. Colored cut glass is considerably harder to find nowadays than clear pieces, particularly glass that is one color all the way through. Somewhat more common is glass flashed with another color. A flashed piece has a thin coating of glass in a contrasting color and, when the design is cut, the two colors show. Another method of adding color, used on cut glass of poorer quality, was application of a metallic luster stain after the piece was finished. All this was true of the Brilliant Period, but long before and even prior to 1830, the Boston and Sandwich Glass Company and a few others were making richly colored and more simply cut perfume bottles, vases,

Barred Forget-Me-Not pattern, c. 1880s, Ohio.

lamps and decanters.

Colored and cut glass made in the United States during the 1800's is an expensive and elusive goal for collectors, not only because it was made in limited quantity but also because twentieth-century reproductions have been imported from Europe. Clear cut glass of the Brilliant Period is irreplaceable, if only because the cost of producing it now would place prohibitive prices on it. Comparatively few pieces bear any marks that are proof of origin, although many patterns were patented and some glass companies registered trademarks. Lack of a mark is no reflection on quality. All nineteenth-century cut glass was good glass, heavy and sparkling; some, of course, was better than others. Weight and sparkle, the heavier and flashier the better, are two indications of quality. Another is sharpness of cutting; a motif such as a hobnail was polished until its sides were smooth, but the edges should feel sharp. Finally, cut glass should ring like a bell when struck lightly with a pencil or the fingers. Not all pieces ring with the same tone and closed pieces such as carafes and decanters sometimes smother the ring.

24. Victorian Art Glass

Victorian Art Glass has come into its own with the return to favor of things Victorian, furniture as well as decorative accessories. Ranging widely in style, sometimes simply but for the most part intricately shaped, occasionally resembling other materials such as china or stone, this ornamental glassware had one dominant charcteristic: color. Whether pale or vivid or a combination of both, color was used with great skill and inventiveness by Victorian designers and craftsmen.

The age was fertile in talented men like Joseph Locke, Nicholas Lutz and Louis C. Tiffany, each of whom created distinctive types of this art. First developed in the 1880s, new varieties appeared in dazzling succession until well into the 20th century. As the sampling of illustations shows, there was something to satisfy every taste, from the simple to the elaborate. For the pleasure of the active collector and the armchair admirer alike, these wares are illustrated here in all their extraordinary diversity: patterns striking or subtle, colors brilliantly clear or meltingly pastel, textures rugged as sandpaper or smooth as the satin after which some of it was named.

Hand-blown cranberry glass vase with gold trim, 1890s, American.

Color is nowhere more strikingly manipulated than in shaded glass, where a piece may start out in red and then blend skillfully into yellow. Amberina, patented by Joseph Locke in 1883, was the first of the shaded wares. It is also the gayest, perhaps because most of it is transparent and the light flashing through heightens its rich tints. Because they are opaque, Peachblow and Burmese seem more like china than glass. Left in their original glossy finish they look like highly glazed porcelain; when acid treatment has given them a velvety mat surface it is easy to mistake them for porcelain in the biscuit, or unglazed, stage. All three of these owe their two-toned effect to an ingredient as romantic as their names: gold. Added to the glass mix, gold makes reheated parts of a finished piece turn rosy red. Another glamor ingredient is the uranium used to give Burmese the yellow base for its lovely talisman rose coloring. Queen Victoria herself was so delighted by a gift of Burmese dishes that she ordered a tea set and some vases in this American ware, and when English manufacturers took out a license to make it she let them call their version "Queen's Burmese."

The main types of Peachblow are: Wheeling, shading rosy red to yellow; Mt. Washington, shell pink to pale blue; New England, called Wild Rose and colored like one. Wheeling is clear, with opaque white lining; the other two are opaque and unlined.

All the versions of Amberina are transparent except for the plated, which has a white lining and looks much like Wheeling Peachblow. Rubina and Rubina Verde are imitations with one color flashed on, that is, added in a second thin coat of glass.

When Burmese first appeared an English critic called this delicately colored ware "the dawn of another day." Only one company made it in North America, but it was turned out in a variety of forms and can be found in tablewares as well as ornamental pieces. Like Peachblow, it may have either a dull or a glossy finish. Decoration may be painted, molded or applied in deftly shaped bits of the same glass as the body, but many prefer the simpler examples that best show off its subtle tints.

Royal Flemish and Crown Milano are usually included in this group of shaded glass, though they are not really two-toned. Crown Milano's pastel tones on a creamy background and the russet shades of Royal Flemish are carefully traced, painted or enameled on. Chintz-like is a very good word for Crown Milano, with its light background and feminine tracery of flowers and leaves in enamel and gilt.

Some types of art glass are frosted; that is, they have an interestingly uneven surface texture. Pomona, the most delicately appealing of these, was blown and then partly etched to contrast clear glass with frosted. Roughest to the touch is Overshot, not surprisingly, since it was made by picking up bits of crushed glass on the hot glass before it was blown. Tree of Life (pressed) and Crackled (blown) got their intricate patterns of wandering lines from molds. All of these are smooth on the inside in contrast to the outer surface.

Pomona is usually decorated with dainty flower and fruit designs done in metallic stains. Most of it has a band of faintly iridescent clear amber at the top. It was imitated in an acid-finished version, but not very successfully. True Pomona was never made in quantity because it was fragile, expensive to produce, and not very popular in its own day. Now it is in great demand.

Its rough surface may be the only trim on an Overshot piece, or it may be just a background for extravagant applied decoration. Tree of Life was used mainly for clear pressed glass table settings. It occasionally turns up in more ornate shapes and in color, and has always been a popular pattern. Most Crackled glass was

Rubina Verde vase, early 20th century, American.

mold-blown, but the effect of cracks appearing on the form could be achieved by plunging the piece into cold water. One firm called its molded wares Craquette, a name not widely used for the type.

Quite a different way to give glass surface interest is to acidize or sand it to a satin finish that makes it a delight to handle. Plush, Velvet Finish, Pearl Satin and Verre de Soie (silk glass) are some of the apt names given to variations on the Pearl Ware theme in patent papers of the 1880s in North America and abroad. Mother of Pearl is the most elaborate in this group, and it was made by a complicated process. At least two layers of glass had to be used because pieces are distinguished by patterns formed by air traps molded in one layer, usually white, and covered with another. Satin Glass, without decoration or molded pattern, is silker to the touch and it shows off the color to better advantage as well. Some makers insisted on further gilding the lily and added additional decoration of one kind or another to this exquisitely lovely glass. It is often lined with a glass of a different color.

Perhaps its suggestion of banked fires seen through mist is what made Opalescent Glass so strongly appealing to the romantic Victorians. Anyway, modern collectors seem to enjoy it every bit as much, and luckly a good deal is still around. It is found in pressed pattern wares as well as blown or mold-blown rarities, and it was used for whole pieces, or as decoration, or as the basis for special types like Onyx. Most Onyx is cream color, with characteristic daisy and leaf pattern in metallic luster, but it also comes in opalescent pink or amber with trim in a deeper tone of the same color. One must be careful in washing Onyx; the luster may wear off.

Glass that combines different colors in a gay, confetti-like effect is called Spatterware; colors may be haphazard, or carefully chosen and arrange so that the finished product looks like tortoise shell or even such a semiprecious stone as agate. If mica or other mineral flakes are dusted over glass to make it sparkle, it is called Spangle. Either of these types is apt to have an outer coat of clear glass or an opaque lining or both.

In Spatter bits of colored glass were picked up in hot glass and

Spanish lace cruet, c. 1860-80, American.

Pink Bristol vase with painted detail, c. 1880, American.

then rolled smooth before it was blown and shaped. It is also known as Splashware and End-of-Day glass, and was made by many firms. Tortoise Shell was made by the same method as more ordinary types of Spatterware, but in tortoise-shell colorings, this was a successful attempt to meet the Victorian demand for glass that looked like almost anything else. It was never cased or lined.

Mica flakes were used to give glitter to most varieties of Spangleware but some types were made with ground-up bits of Aventurine, a brilliantly metallic glass imported in bulk from Italy. Powdered gold was also used but this was of course very rare. Another name given Spangle glass is Vasa Murrhina.

Opaque glass is the kind that looks most like glazed china and it was in fact made in sets that substituted for other types of tableware. White Opaque is the familiar Milk Glass. Some of the colored wares also have names connected with food: Maize, Custard, Caramel (first called Chocolate). Even the Marble Glass mixtures suggest cake! In novelty forms Opaque glass was used for premiums and for containers for groceries. Collecting this can be great fun, but take care. Lots of it is being very well reproduced today, sometimes by the same companies that made it first and from the same molds.

Originally Marble Glass was called Mosaic. Another name for it is Slag, or like Spatterware it

End-of-day Venetian glass vase, c. 1880-1910, American.

may be called End-of-Day. Most of it is purple and white, but it comes in green, brown, blue, and orange.

Venetian Glass has always been very popular. For centuries Venice has been the glassmaking capital of the world, and some of the fanciest Art Glass used Venetian techniques: threads on the outside of a piece or trapped inside in spirals or intricately crossed (latticinio) lacy patterns; applied quilling that looks rather like fins; colored stripes looped in swags. Nicholas Lutz of Sandwich is credited with most American glass of this Venetian type. A great deal of it was imported from Europe.

Similar in some respects to the effects achieved in Venetian Glass are those found in clear form. One of the great charms of the glass of all ages is simply the way it transmits light, and in spite of their passion for making their material look like something quite different, Victorian glassmakers didn't overlook this aspect. They made many pieces that depend for their appeal on shape and glowing color alone, and they also contrived some stunning effects by combining colored glass with colorless. People who believe that a material shoudl speak for itself in any decorative period prize this type highly.

Iridescent glass was first made in a surprisingly successful attempt to copy the soft metallic sheen and shifting rainbow hues of glass that had been buried for centuries. Tiffany's is the first name that comes to mind in this field, with Frederick Carder's a close second and three or four others completing the list. Of course their exquisite, individual-

ly fashioned pieces had to be expensive, but about 1910 a method of giving pressed pattern glass an iridized finish was worked out and in the next decade quantities of these low cost wares were sold. Nowadays collectors call this Carnival glass because it was given away at fairs. It has become such an important collecting category that discussion of the type requires an individual chapter.

Carnival glass fruit bowl, c. 1920-30, American.

Some women probably were lucky enough to obtain a dozen small berry dishes, but the set can be considered complete with six saucedishes and a large bowl. The large berry bowl was somewhat deeper than a fruit dish and its sides sloped up instead of flaring outward.

Berry sets, like fruit dishes, ran the gamut of Carnival Glass patterns. A dozen or more are based on grapes. A pattern almost always is more readily identified on the large pieces and, in fact, its effect may be somewhat different on the small pieces such as saucedishes.

The most important Carnival Glass serving dishes were a matching sugar and creamer, both often with lids, and a four-piece table set. The latter included a covered butter dish and spoonholder or spooner (not available separately) in addition to sugar and creamer. Less common were toothpick holders and salt dishes. Top hats were primarily ornaments, but a few were just the right height to hold wooden matches. Hats were made in great quantity and in many shapes. Carnival Glass also was a natural choice for dishes in

Strawberry pattern carnival glass fruit bowl, 1920-35, American.

Carnival glass goblet, Cosmos pattern, 1920s, American.

Fluted carnival glass vase, 1920-35, American.

which to serve the ice cream sundae, introduced in the early nineteenth century. Sundae dishes could also be used for candy.

Some of the finest workmanship and coloring was lavished on the multitude of vases and baskets that are cherished from the Carnival Glass period. Except for rose bowls made in the early days and slender bud vases, probably from the 1920s, the vases and baskets were decorative in themselves and probably seldom held flowers. Even the flower holders that dressed up the interior of many automobiles were sometimes made of Carnival Glass.

Black amethyst flower holder for automobile, 1920-35, American.

Twisted carnival glass vase, 1920-35, American.

26. The Spell of Paperweights

Paperweights, especially glass ones, have been fascinating people ever since they were first made. No two old ones are exactly alike even though they display the same flower or fruit, for these glass paperweights were handmade. Nor does any glass paperweight look the same from all angles. One reason for this is that the convex surface of clear glass magnifies somewhat the motifs it covers. And always the colors within glow like jewels.

There is a certain satisfaction in owning a paperweight known to have been made seventy-five to one hundred years ago by enterprising glassmakers in the United States. Actually paperweights haven't been made for as long a time as many other pieces of glass, to say nothing of mirrors, clocks and furniture. The first ones were produced in France and Italy in the 1840's. By the 1850's, American glassmakers were experimenting and selling their own paperweights to an eager public. The techniques used by European glassworkers were practiced here and some of the designs they imprisoned within clear glass domes were inspiration at least for skilled workers in this country. It was only natural that paperweights displayed the familiar flowers and fruits and the portraits of heroes in the nation of their origin.

Few glass objects are more decorative and colorful than paperweights yet they weren't merely baubles. The necessity of tackling desk work couldn't help but be momentarily pleasurable if the papers requiring attention were held in place by a gleaming weight. It seems a miracle that the crimson apples and golden pears looking good enough to eat, the pink rose so real that its fragrance is easily imagined or the spirals of brightly colored threads forever twisting within a glass ball were fashioned by men's hands from such common materials as sand and lead or lime for clear glass, plus the metalic oxides that produced the glowing colored parts. Although paperweights never became the principal output of any glass factory, a good number were produced steadily after 1850 by firms from New England to

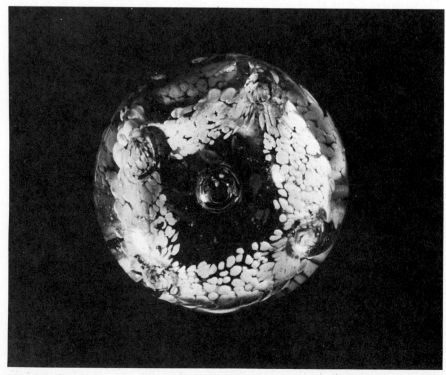

"Candy"-type paperweight, 19th century, American.

the Midwest. Few if any of the old paperweights were signed so it is difficult nowadays to identify their source unless the design or style was typical of a certain glass factory.

The famous Boston and Sandwich Glass Company in Sandwich, Massachusetts certainly made any weight displaying a poinsettia or a group of tiny fruits. The rose, regardless of its color, enclosed in a glass ball that rests on a footed glass base couldn't possibly have been made anywhere but by the Whitall, Tatum Company in Millville, New Jersey. Now known as the Millville or Jersey rose, it is only one of the paperweights originated by proficient glassworkers in this country and produced in multiple. Very different is the flat round weight with a rose design produced by the Mount Washington Glass Company in South Boston, Massachusetts.

Of the many different paperweights produced by this factory in South Boston, the one called Mount Washington rose is excellent quality as well as novel in design. Most important is the frilled pink rose topping a stem with buds and green leaves that is held in a woman's hand. Two butterflies hover over the bloom,

"Candy"-type paperweight, 19th century, American.

whose petals are flecked with gold repeating the color of the ring on the hand. The adept workmen who made these unusual rose paperweights undoubtedly discarded many with imperfections before producing one fine enough to sell. After all, a beautiful paperweight with an attractive design and clear details could not have been easy to make. It has been said that Ralph Barber of the Millville glass factory took six years to achieve the distinctive Millville or Jersey rose weight.

The first Millville rose was a pink, almost full-blown flower nestled against green leaves and encased in a clear glass globe mounted on a clear glass foot. Thereafter similar paperweights

with a red, green, yellow or white rose were made and probably many more pink ones. Details such as petals, which might be opalescent or pointed at the tips, varied according to the workman since at least four men in addition to Ralph Barber were expert enough to produce these rose weights. Nor were the footed glass bases always identical. Collectors consider the finest Millville rose paperweights to be those including a bud and rose leaf as well as the flower. Two other notable flower weights from Millville showed a water lily, either pink or white with green leaves around it, and a pink tulip. The latter is now rare.

Realistic reproductions of flowers and fruits and occasionally vegetables had been made by famous European firms such as Clichy and Baccarat in France since the 1840's. Similar paperweights made later in the United States are distinctive, if only because the flowers are the familiar ones grown in dooryards since the days of the first settlers; roses of course and also pansies, clover, dahlias, bellflowers, fuchsia, lilies of the valley and nasturtiums.

Perhaps the best known paperweights and now among the most prized are the Boston and Sandwich ones depicting the poinsettia, the Christmas flower that Joel R. Poinsett, United States Ambassador to Mexico, had sent back to this country by 1830. The Sandwich poinsettia and the Millville rose, like other individual flowers, set off paperweights three inches or so in diameter. Much smaller weights of clear glass show only a nosegay.

American fruit weights too are quite different from those made

Millefiori paperweight, attributed to Sandwich, 19th century.

in other countries. Two distinct styles were made, and the one with an almost life-sized fruit is particularly luscious even as a glass paperweight. The fruit, usually an apple or a pear, was hand-blown in colors so true to the real thing that one can almost identify the variety of apple or pear. Each colored fruit, tempting in its perfection, was fused to a clear glass base. This paperweight was a specialty of both the Boston and Sandwich Glass Company and the New England Glass Company. The second style, fruit encased in glass, was similar to those that displayed flowers. Many of these show clusters of small apples and pears together or singly, peaches, plums or cherries. Fewer paperweights featured strawberries so the Sandwich one with these fruits and their blossoms and leaves is valuable today. It also is being reproduced. Acorns and walnuts, classed botanically as fruits, decorated other paperweights.

Flowers, fruits and leaves were made separately in appropriately colored glass, often by the workmen in their own homes. In some cases these brightly hued pieces were encased in glass before being arranged in the weight. Many paperweights con-

sist of separate but invisible layers of glass, for parts of a design could be anchored in place by pouring molten glass over them. As a result the colorful motifs seem to float in the clear glass. Still another method was the use of molds to create the design in place; Millville used molds for its water lily weight.

Flowers and fruits made individually in their natural colors were set off by backgrounds that contributed to their beauty. Sometimes these were a color, sometimes latticinio. Latticinio is only one of the glass techniques originated in Europe and duplicated by American glassworkers. It is formed by crossing delicate bands of milk white glass and is most familiar as the flattened, filigree background for many flower and fruit weights made in this country. Sandwich made poinsettia paperweights against blue, milk white and latticinio backgrounds.

Latticinio, here and abroad, was combined sometimes with millefiori. Both techniques had

been originated by the Venetians. Millefiori, which means "thousand flowers," was made from glass rods of various colors arranged so that their ends formed a design. This might be one flower or a bouquet. The rods were fused by heat and then drawn out to any desired length, which left the design the same but reduced it in size. Finally the rods were sliced and the way in which this was done produced different effects. A great many American firms made millefiori paperweights. No two are exactly alike even if they were made by the same glassworker. One sort shows millefiori arranged to form a mushroom cap and depends chiefly on colors for its fascination. Even more charming in my opinion are millefiori florets strung in a garland. It is impossible to tire of a millefiori paperweight, for there is always something new to see in it depending on which way you look at it.

Candy paperweights are always gay because they consist of odds and ends of colored glass apparently arranged haphazardly. Mercury or quicksilver was used by New England and Midwestern factories to decorate paperweights as well as doorknobs and vases. Midwestern glasshouses also became known for paperweights with unusual designs based on arches of colored glass and elongated air bubbles. Colorful and dinstinguished paperweights with cameo portraits became almost as popular here as they were in Europe. The portrait was usually of a noted person such as Benjamin Franklin, George Washington, Robert E. Lee, Abraham Lincoln or Queen Victoria. These cameos under glass were sometimes a ceramic but more often a sulphide with a silvery appearance, actually a combination of fine white china clay with crystal. An occasional cameo portrait was framed in spirals of colored glass. These spirals were not as intricate as latticinio but nonetheless they were effective. Rare and second to none in fascination is the weight through which thin bands of colored glass spiral. One of these bands usually was milk white glass and, if the paperweight was made by the Pairpoint Company in New Bedford, Massachusetts, the other two were almost certain to be cobalt blue and ruby red. Almost as interesting to people today are parperweights displaying coins or tokens.

Irresistible to everyone, young or old, who comes to call on friends of mine is a paperweight on a table in their living room. This one has a little turtle embedded under the round, rather flat, clear glass dome. The turtle was made of bits of real turtle shell and when the paperweight is tilted its feet, head and tail move.

This bewitches youngsters today as much as it did my friend and her brothers when they were children. Other paperweights on this order showed a spider, a lizard or a snake. However a turtle must have been the favorite for large green glass ones were made in this shape. They weren't nearly as captivating as the little shell turtle.

While glassmakers here were experimenting to produce paperweights enclosing realistic flowers and fruits, portraits, millifiori and

the like, they were turning out much simpler weights to satisfy public demand for this new and appealing trinket. Many of the earliest were cubes or ovals of clear or one-color glass. Soon there were lovely angled, geometric paperweights of transparent colored glass with exterior decoration of white enamel. In the late 1800's some overlay paperweights were made. Overlay consists of a coating of transparent colored glass applied to the finished weight and then

Commercial advertising paperweight, early 20th century, American.

cut in facets to show the clear glass underneath. On some paperweights the beauty lies in the faceting and the contrast between clear and colored glass. However on other overlay weights the clear facets permit a motif within to be seen.

Many paperweights are fascinating although they haven't one bit of color inside or out. Faceted weights of clear or white glass, often called crystal, sparkle. Cut glass paperwieghts with the angular cutting called lapidary became popular after 1880; these flash like diamonds in direct light. A lesser number were made in clear pressed glass. One was the round paperweight with a finial made by the Boston and Sandwich Glass Company in their early Star pattern. James Gillinder & Sons in Philadelphia made a crouched lion in frosted pressed glass during the 1870's.

Any kind of paperweight may have been made before 1900 and be quite smooth, for it is a simple matter for a skilled workman to polish away nicks and scars. Old or antique paperweights won't necessarily have a pontil mark on their bases since many good workmen of the 1800's smoothed off the bottom of the weight. Nineteenth century weights never had frosted bases as do many of those now being made. The simplest test to decide whether a glass paperweight was made during the 1800's or recently is to heft it. A millefiori, flower or fruit weight made in the 1850's or 1860's will be much heavier in proportion to its size than reproductions of the 1960's and 1970's.

27. A Galaxy of Bottles

Most people have a few bottles around the house that they can't bear to throw out because of shape or color. A colored bottle is often placed on the crossbar of a window where it catches the light, and when another bottle of different shape or color turns up in a cellar or cupboard, it may be placed in the same window. So it is that many people without realizing it bring together the nucleus of a collection. It may stop with the two bottles, or a different one may be added occasionally, begged from a friend who was about to throw it away,

Medicine bottle, late 19th century, American.

bought at a junk shop or rescued from a refuse basket on the curb. Better yet, anyone who is at all interested in bottles may decide to join a club of collectors and go on digs with them. Bottle collectors' clubs have been increasing in number during the last decade, as more and more people have started to search and dig carefully at old abandoned factories and other sites for the everyday bottles that were manufactured in this country in such quantity and diversity between 1840 and 1900. Of the millions of bottles produced during those sixty years, countless ones were soon broken or thrown away carelessly. Still, many collectors have found the hunting good. On the other hand, a very different sort of collection may be inspired by the dainty perfume bottle with the stopper blown in the shape of a flower, the large square Daisy and Button cologne bottle with a square stopper in the same pressed glass pattern, or the barber bottle in striped opalescent glass.

A few bottles undoubtedly were blown in the first glasshouse in America, which opened in Jamestown, Virginia, in 1608. This venture was short-lived, as were many other attempts to start glasshouses first in the colonies, later in several northeastern states. By the early 1800's, when glassworks were able to survive and flourish, there was a ready market for glass bottles. Pottery bottles for various purposes also were made in some quantity and variety during the nineteenth century. The earliest bottles, made in biblical times, were of animal skins, and other materials such as wood have been tried from time to time. In fact, skin or leather has continued to be used in the Orient, whereas in North America and in many European countries, glass has long been the preferred material for bottles. Whatever the material, a bottle was then, as now, a hollow container with a narrow neck and no handles. The narrow neck facilitated pouring the liquid stored or carried in the bottle. It also made the bottle easier to close. Handsome stoppers of glass or silver were made for decorative bottles that held perfume, cologne and similar liquids, but plain everyday bottles of glass or pottery were more likely to be stopped with a cork or some kind of plug.

For centuries, bottles of all sizes and for all purposes were hand-blown. Most difficult of all to

Hand-blown glass bottle, green, 18th century, English.

fashion by this method was the largest size, known as a carboy. This very large globular bottle had a small neck and was usually green glass. It was made to store vinegar and cider and probably other liquids kept on hand in large quantity. Carboys, technically, should be encased in wickerwork or a wooden box and are still finished that way for transporting corrosive chemicals. Old demijohns, smaller than carboys but holding one to ten gallons, were chiefly green or brown and also were encased.

Smaller bottles were not only free-blown but also blown-molded or pattern-molded by the late eighteenth century. Blown-molding was widely used until well along into the nineteenth century. This method required the workman to blow the metal or molten glass into a small mold of wood or iron which gave it pattern, then to remove the metal and manipulate it by hand until it reached the desired size and shape. The simple pattern of vertical ribbing, swirls or panels was within the glass itself. After about 1812, the blown-three-mold technique made possible arches, baroque scrolls and swirls, and geometric decorations on the bottles that were produced in full-size molds consisting of two or more parts hinged together. Seam marks where sections of the mold met are one clue to blown-three-mold bottles. Some of those made before the 1860's, when iron molds replaced hand-carved wooden ones, also may have "whittle marks" from the mold on the outer surface of the glass.

The 1820's brought pressed glass, a comparatively inexpensive as well as decorative technique that made popular fancy bottles for table and personal use. However many techniques were developed, some utility bottles continued to be hand-blown until about 1860; after the 1860-70 decade, many decorative bottles were handblown and some still are. While blown-molded and blown-three-mold techniques brought pleasing if rather simple decoration to everyday bottles, many other bottles were ornamented in various ways. On them were applied the artists' skills of enameling, painting, etching, engraving, cutting.

Everyday bottles, however they were made, were seldom-colorless or even good clear or white glass. Because these utility bottles had to be inexpensive, the cheapest of essential ingredients went into the formula, resulting in a light green shade that has come to be known as "bottle glass" and is still used today for some soft-drink bottles. Glassmakers' formulas for utility bottles produced shades ranging from aquamarine to olive green, amber to brown. Formulas for cobalt blue, rich green, purple or amethyst, red, and milk-white glass were more expensive, but a good many bottles for different purposes were produced in these colors during the nineteenth century. The demands of food packers and housewives who canned finally brought to market in the 1880's reasonably clear and inexpensive glass containers.

Because of an error in mixing the formula, old glass may change color with long exposure to the sun. Similarly, old bottles that have been buried long enough and deep enough may change, perhaps acquiring a pleasing opalescence or even iridescence, a less attractive milky film, or a

Small hand-blown glass bottle, green, mid-18th century, English.

satiny texture.

It often is difficult to determine when a bottle was made. Color isn't necessarily a clue to age, though shape may be, particularly in a figure or character bottle. Any hand-blown bottle is likely to lack perfect symmetry and no two will be identical. The earliest hand-blown bottles made in America were rough and irregular at the edge of the mouth because the glass was snipped off with shears while still in molten state, leaving no rim or collar. Bottles with this sort of mouth are either slender and somewhat arched or squat and bulbous.

The snuff bottle, commonly found in household cupboards during the eighteenth century, had a distinctive shape. Hand-blown, it was fairly small, either rectangular or square, and sloped gently to a short neck or to a rim without a neck. It was usually colored glass, or, if it was made by Stiegel, of clear glass etched or painted with floral motifs typical of his artisans. The plain styles seem to have lacked stoppers, so probably the large opening was plugged with paper, cork or wood. Smaller and fancier snuff bottles, often vase- or urn-shaped and with appropriate stoppers, may be handsome examples of specialties such as cameo glass.

Perfume bottles, together with smaller vials for scent and smelling salts, are perhaps the prettiest of all. They were hand-blown and molded, pressed and cut, painted and enameled. Some, such as the cut glass ones that became so popular during the last quarter of the nineteenth century, were mostly clear glass; other techniques often relied on true colors for their appeal. The introduction of art glass during the 1870's widened the choice to cameo glass, striped or threaded Lutz glass, painted Mary Gregory, rubina and rubina verde, spangle glass, milk-white and opaque colors. Perfume bottles with sizable decorative glass stoppers, although small compared to bottles made for other liquids, were kept on a dressing table or shelf. Others from 1½" to 3" long were small enough to be carried. The tiniest ones, perhaps in the shape of a seahorse, scallop shell or gourd, could be slipped inside the glove a woman was wearing. Those about 3" long with a stopper, perhaps of silver, that screwed on were carried in a purse or reticule. A pair of glass bottles in one unit was called a gemel. A standing gemel consisted of two separate bottles tapering to points and attached to a footed base.

Cologne or toilet water bottles were considerably larger than perfume bottles and often were made and sold in pairs. These bottles came in square, rectangular, globular or barrel shapes as well as some rather fanciful forms. During the early 1800's many had engraved decoration, while after 1870 cut glass ones became almost as common as pressed glass. Cut glass cologne bottles had faceted stoppers, and a few pressed glass ones such as those in the frosted Lion

Fluted bar bottle, cobalt blue with enameled decoration, 1856, American.

Blown bottle with seal, black, c. 1780, English.

pattern had cut glass stoppers. Among the many cologne and toilet bottles that were imported, perhaps the most distinctive came from Bristol, England, famous for its opaque white and its deep blue glass and, particularly, for dark blue decoration on opaque white.

Cologne bottle, mid-19th century, French.

Cut-glass perfume bottle with silver stopper, early 20th century, American.

Essential to the Victorian gentleman's grooming were the handsome bottles from which hair tonic, shampoo and the like were dispensed in barbershops. Many of these had extremely long, narrow necks into which a sprinkling device was fitted. Every barbershop bottle was colorful. Many were painted or enameled, others were sparkling clear cut glass.

Quite different, but prized by many collectors for their clean, simple lines, are the apothecary bottles that held the ingredients for prescriptions in old-time drugstores. Many of these are clear glass, but amber, cobalt blue or other colored bottles were preferred for some drugs and herbs so they would not be affected by light. Apothecary bottles were square or cylindrical and almost all have shoulders sloping to wide or narrow necks. Originally they all had glass stoppers, most of them ground around the stems.

Glass ink bottles were primarily utilitarian, although a few cut glass and pressed glass ones, often with ornamented metal covers, were made for inkstands. Quantities of ordinary ink bottles must have been manufactured in common green, amber or brown bottle glass. Small and plain as these are, they also are interesting. Not hard to find is the little ink bottle with six sides sloping up to a narrow neck; this style was blown-three-molded before 1860; some examples show whittle marks.

The bottles purchased for pickles, preserves, flavoring, vinegar, patent medicine, hand lotion or any one of a dozen other needs are considered more valuable today, empty, than they ever were by the people who bought them filled. The years from 1820 to 1900 brought bottles in many strikingly individual shapes into homes. This was the period when pickles were bought in green glass cathedral bottles, so called because of an arch on each of the four sides, or in smaller, slenderer bottles with spiral ribbing. In New England, blueberry or huckleberry preserves were sold in good-size bottles with ten plain paneled sides and a round base. After 1860, some kinds of preserves were sold in colored bottles. Essences and flavoring were put up in smaller bottles whose shape often identified the contents. Peppermint bottles usually were tall, slender cylinders; lemon extract for years came in elliptical bottles.

Many kinds of liquids were sold

in quite plain bottles with only the seal or mark of the manufacturer on one side. Later, patents as well as the maker's name were stamped, pressed or molded on the bottom or side of the bottle. Figure bottles were perhaps less common in glass than in pottery. One of the famous glass ones, appropriately known as "Moses striking the rock," held Poland water.

Probably more character bottles, whether of glass or pottery, were imported than made in this country. However, starting about 1850, Toby, or coachman, bottles were produced at potteries in Bennington, Vermont, and elsewhere in the United States. Unlike squat Toby jugs or pitchers, the bottles were in the form of a man, usually full-length, wearing a cloak or caped coat and hat. Coachman bottles came in three sizes with the mottled buff-and-brown Rockingham glaze, the more colorful flint-enamel glaze, or in white graniteware. Much easier to find should be the plain stoneware bottles, usually with a buff or brown glaze, that were used by housewives for bottling ketchup and the like as late as the early 1900's.

Novelty bottles are still being made, and a few of the more unusual ones, including the nineteenth-century Moses bottle, are being reproduced. One great advantage of digging for everyday bottles is the certainty that any finds will be old. However, to identify a glass or pottery bottle made one hundred or more years ago, a person must learn to recognize marks typical of the method of manufacture, glazes of pottery or colors and qualities of glass, and something about the uses for which the bottles were made.

Cologne bottle, Baccarat, late 19th century.

Druggist's bottle, 1870-1900, American.

28. Salt Dishes

Food without salt lacks savor, so man always has believed. Throughout the ages, the economic importance of salt has been equaled by its social and religious implications. Thus a covenant of salt is mentioned in the Bible, the shipment of salt accounts for one of the oldest roads in Italy, and to this day the Persians have a saying "untrue to salt," meaning disloyal or ungrateful. It is no wonder that so many special containers have been devised to hold the fine white grains of so-called common or table salt. These containers range from the priceless salt dish made by the Renaissance goldsmith and sculptor, Benvenuto Cellini, to crudely-made glass ones that sold for pennies during the nineteenth century.

Gold, silver and pewter, pottery and porcelain, all kinds of glass and even wood have been used for salt dishes of various sizes and shapes. These have been known by such names as standing salt, trencher salt, salt dip, salt cup, salt cellar and, latest of all, shaker. The standing salt is perhaps the oldest as well as the largest. It stood 5″ high and occupied an important place on the table, standing in front of the person who sat at the head of the table. Whatever it was made of, the standing salt was a dignified and decorative piece. Not many are to be seen or found nowadays. On the other hand, the trencher salt always was within reach of guests at the table. This was a deep oval, round or octagonal dish that did not have a cover. Small dishes were called salts or salt cellars and averaged perhaps 1¾″ in diameter if they were round, 1½″ if square, and about 1″ high. These were scattered about a table or set one at each place. Salt cups, usually a little larger and mounted on legs, were sometimes used in pairs. Larger salt dishes, 3″ to 3½″ in diameter, were known as salt dips and were used singly, in pairs or at each place on the table. Salt dips, especially glass ones, were common in the United States during the nineteenth century although smaller individual salt cellars replaced them by the 1880's.

Nothing comparable to the Cellini masterpiece has ever been

Sheffield salt with blue glass liner, c. 1890.

made, but smaller and simpler salt dishes of silver, pewter and glass made in this country are interesting if only because of their diversity in shapes and sizes. They attract many collectors because they are small and colorful and a good many examples can be displayed, and enjoyed, in limited space. Without doubt, the greatest quantity were the glass ones of the nineteenth century.

A very few standing salts were made by silversmiths during colonial days. If seen in a museum or restoration, these can be recognized by their height and large spool shape. Silver salt cellars or cups and trenchers were more numerous, but even these were not common, for only families who had silver coins to spare could afford to have silversmiths melt them down and fashion decorative articles for their tables and homes. Salt cellars or cups mounted on applied legs were being produced to order by silversmiths in New York and other cities on the East Coast around 1700. Decoration such as garlands was applied along their sides. The larger salt trenchers also were being made for silver during the 1700's. One by an Albany silversmith, now in the collection of the Metropolitan Museum in New York City, has gadrooned decoration around top and bottom and displays the monogram of the owners on one side. The shape, decoration and style of silver salt dishes changed, as did other pieces from time to time. However, silver containers for salt did not come into fairly general use until after the introduction of silver plate in America in the 1840's, and the prosperous, peaceful years starting about 1870.

Pewter salt dishes were owned far more widely than silver ones in this country. Pewter and its successor, britannia, which is brighter in appearance and more durable, were extremely popular with American housewives until about 1850. Neither pewter nor britannia, which pretty much replaced it after 1825, is as lustrous as silver. Since pewter is said to be highly resistant to salt corrosion, I believe some shakers were made of it for salt. However, open salt dishes were not only more common but also more attractive. Especially so are low open pewter or britannia salt dishes with col-

Pewter footed salt, 18th century, English.

ored glass linings. Some of these had pierced sides so that the ruby-red or cobalt-blue glass glimmered through the silvery metal. Flat, footed, open dishes about 2¼" wide by 3" long and 1¼" high were quite common in American households from about 1800 to 1850. In the previous century, the open pewter salt dish was likely to be cup-shaped and to stand on a pedestal.

Sometimes a pepper shaker with small holes in its top stood beside a trencher or a good-size open salt dish. However, I am inclined to believe that grinders which held peppercorns must have been more common than shakers. On the dinner table in my home, we place between a pair of old red-glass-lined pewter salt dishes the pewter and glass pepper grinder that my great-grandfather brought from Europe in the 1830's. In any case, shakers had domed covers that fastened on containers that were vase or goblet shape and often footed. Actually, pairs of salt and pepper shakers of any material were not common until after 1875.

Salt dishes have been made here of blown and cut glass since the days of Henry William Stiegel, who established his glasshouses in Manheim, Pennsylvania, in 1764-65. "Baron" Stiegel's business failed within a few years, but by the early 1800's several more economically-managed glasshouses had been established in the East. The New England Glass Company, incorporated in Cambridge, Massachusetts, in 1818, produced many distinctive salt dishes. Their first ones were blown-molded, and among the best known of these are oblong ones with straight ribbing along the sides and ribbed "fans" on the ends. These were

Pressed-glass salt, Sawtooth pattern, 19th century, American.

either footed or flat. Octagonal ones displayed ribbing combined with other simple blown-molded patterns.

The development of pressed glass about 1825 brought salt dishes into every home just as it did pretty glass cup plates and glass lamps. Pressed-glass salt dishes could be chosen from an infinite variety. A few had covers, but most of them did not. Some were footed or had pedestal bases, but probably a majority were flat. They were made in round, square, oblong, triangle, boat,

basket, sleigh or sofa shapes. Clear-glass ones can be attractive on the basis of their patterns, but many patterns also were made in one or more colors, including deep blue, rich green or delicate apple green, red, yellow, amber and, more rarely, amethyst. Milk white, opaque colored and opalescent pressed-glass salt dishes were not uncommon after 1850.

Large salt dishes or dips, 3" to 3½" in diameter and at least 1¾" high, were either blown-molded or pressed. These often were placed singly or in pairs on a

Covered salt, hen on nest, camphor glass, early 20th century.

table. They were for the most part rather heavy and plain with the outside molded octagonally or pressed with thumbprints or diamonds. Many of the heavy ones have stars on their bases. An oblong one with canted corners is a change from the many round or octagonal dips.

By far the majority of pressed-glass salt dishes were smaller and daintier than the salt dips. Most are small enough to be used one at each place setting. Among the most treasured are the early, lacy glass ones for which the Boston and Sandwich Glass Company in Sandwich, Massachusetts, became especially noted. Lacy glass is recognized by its allover stippled background which made each piece sparkle. Against this background, patterns were worked out with acanthus leaves, shells, hearts, arches, stars, flowers, leaves, rosettes and scrolls. These are the oldest pressed glass salt dishes, for lacy glass was made chiefly from 1825 to 1840 and to a lesser extent to 1850. Typical are such patterns as Gothic Arch and Heart with a row of arches around the base and a row of hearts under the rim, Cathedral, which has a row of Gothic arches reaching from the flat base to the scalloped rim, and Strawberry Diamond with this cut-glass motif done in lacy pressed glass under its scalloped edge. Lyre is easy to recognize, with the instrument on either side, and scrolled ends.

When pattern glass replaced lacy glass about 1850, tableware sets in most patterns included open salt dishes. Many of these were footed. Some patterns had two sizes: a large salt dish for the table and smaller matching ones to be set at each place. Others such as the popular Sawtooth pattern of the 1860's offered a covered salt dish, a footed salt dish and an open salt with smooth edge. Tulip, made in the same decade, permitted a choice between two footed salts, one with smooth edge, the other with pointed edge making it look more like the flower. Harp, a pattern of the 1850's, was decorated with the lyre motif which had been used earlier on lacy pressed glass. Dewdrop with Star, made between 1860 and the 1880's, had only a round, footed, open salt dish but it has been found in clear, milk white, amber, blue and yellow.

Shakers in pairs for salt and pepper began to appear in pressed-glass patterns introduced after 1875, such as Paneled Daisy, Double Loop, Shell and Tassel with the shaker shell-shaped, and Broken Column. When ever-popular Daisy and Button began to be made in the 1880's, open salt dishes were available in several shapes, including a triangular one. Shakers also were offered in Daisy and Button as well as in variant patterns such as Daisy and Button with Crossbar. Shakers had either pewter or silver-plate tops; the holes in those for salt were slightly larger than in those for pepper shakers.

Whimsical and novelty shapes also became popular after 1875. One of the first was sold at the Centennial Exposition in Philadelphia, Pennsylvania, in 1876, where the local glass firm of Gillinder and Sons displayed salt shakers in the form of the Liberty Bell (open salt dishes also were made in Liberty Bell pattern). During the next twenty years, animals and birds became favorite forms for open and covered salt dishes. The rabbit, squirrel, owl, duck and other selections of glassmakers always were realistically reproduced. Often the poses and resulting dishes were amusing or imaginative. A pressed-glass duck, for example, measures 5″ from tip of bill to tip of tail and shows feathers, bill and every detail clearly. The cavity in its back for salt is 2½″ long and ⅞″ deep. Some duck-shaped salt dishes were formed in the round and a cover consisting of head and back could be lifted off to get at salt within. Another small covered salt dish was a replica of a turtle.

The Centennial Exposition also launched cut glass on its period of greatest popularity in this country. The years from 1876 to 1905 are known as the Brilliant Period, when cut glass was not

Amber glass salt, early 20th century, American.

only of the finest quality but also decorated with deep and intricate patterns. Cut glass, like pressed glass, was made in patterns and sets, and probably every pattern had some kind of salt dish. Open ones might be square, globe or tub-shaped, and occasionally resembled miniature footed tumblers or goblets. Many patterns included both a large table salt and smaller individual ones for each place and, of course, some of these late cut-glass patterns included pairs of salt and pepper shakers with silver-plate or sterling-silver tops. Cut glass sparkles when it is clean, its design feels sharp to the touch and pieces are heavy in proportion to their size.

The quarter-century from 1875 to 1900 was the period when various kinds of colorful art glass were introduced to a ready public. Ornamental pieces rather than serving dishes were the rule, but salt and pepper shakers were made in a few kinds of art glass, notably Burmese, satin glass and amberina. A chubby pair in soft pink satin glass with silver tops is so exquisite that one wonders if the original owners ever filled and used them. In amberina both a large open salt dip and salt and pepper shakers were available.

Neither salt dishes nor shakers were usually part of a set of earthenware or porcelain dishes. Silver or cut-glass salt dishes or pairs of shakers were preferred on tables set with the best china. However, salt shakers had long been made in such earthenwares as Sèvres faïence and Holland Delft. Open salt dips are known to have been made in the English mocha ware and perhaps in other types during the early nineteenth century. Master or standing salts also were made in Royal Copenhagen, the Danish porcelain, and the beloved Meissen Onion porcelain pattern. Early nineteenth-century standing salts made of pottery or porcelain often were 5″ tall and only one was used on a table. By mid-century or a little later,

smaller salt shakers, no more than 3″ tall, became more common. Then when china-painting became a popular hobby among young ladies in the 1890's, hand-decorated salt and pepper shakers often were given as gifts. The designs always were flowers, with arbutus, violets and roses great favorites. They were painted in pastel tints with tops of shakers, for example, covered with gold.

"Take not Salt with a greasie Knife," warned Eleazar Moody, a Boston schoolteacher, in his little book, *The School of Good Manners*, published from 1715 to 1846. He was referring to the custom of dipping into the large salt dip or trencher on the table. Fortunately, before the eighteenth century ended, the range of spoons included tiny ones for open salt dishes. Up until about 1850, these little spoons were made in both silver and pewter. They were 3″ to 3½″ long and had bowls about ¾″ in diameter. In the late 1880's, smaller silver spoons only 2″ long, with bowls almost ½″ in diameter, were made, evidently for individual salt cellars. Little salt spoons also were made of bone and ivory.

29. The Magic of Mirrors

"Looking-glass, Looking-glass, on the wall, Who in this land is the fairest of all?" asked the queen who was Snow-White's stepmother. Two thousand years earlier young ladies could have voiced the same query of a piece of shining metal or glistening ivory, since a mirror can be any polished surface that reflects an image. Glass has been used for mirrors only since the 1500's and, not surprisingly, the

first looking glasses were made in Venice. Not until the 1670's was glass for mirrors made in England, and it was close to 1790 before even a small amount was being produced in the United States.

Nevertheless, even before 1700, some families could boast of owning a mirror. It was called a looking glass here until about 1800, and not one was too small to be a prized possession. Both framed mirrors and pieces of silvered glass for frame makers and cabinetmakers working here were imported from England in some quantity until the 1790's. It is difficult, if not impossible, to tell whether mirrors that hung on walls of eighteenth-century homes were made here or in England. However, it is not only possible but reasonably easy to decide approximately when a mirror was made, because the wood frame that surrounded it changed in size, shape and style when other pieces of furniture did.

The dozen styles originated between 1700 and 1840 were made by both master cabinetmakers and average woodworkers. However, any one of these styles can be recognized either by plain examples or those displaying fine details and rich

decoration. Because looking glass was made in comparatively small sheets and also was scarce and expensive, people had to be content with small pieces. Thus, in order to enhance this accessory, the frame often was fully as important as the looking glass.

The William and Mary period, which extended from 1688 into the early 1700's, established the importance of frames. They were a good 3" to 4" wide and often were topped with an arched piece

Empire-style mirror, 1840s, American.

Opposite page: The many kinds of devices used for lighting comprise one of the most intriguing areas of collecting. Early rushlights and grease and lard-oil burners are very rare today, but lamps burning kerosene or whale oil can still be found in many places. Also widely available are the various types of candleholders—from simple sticks to elaborate brass, iron, tin, or glass chandeliers. Of special interest to the collector are such late 19th-century devices as the brass library lamp illustrated here, and gas fixtures which can be converted easily for use with electricity.

Opposite page. Above (left): An urn from which to serve coffee or hot water for tea need not be merely a utilitarian object but can display highly decorative qualities. From 1860 until the early 1900s, the United States led the world in silver mining, and a great deal of this wealth was spent on the production of articles for the home. Silver tea urns were made earlier in the century of Sheffield plate.

Opposite page: Above (right): Mid- to late-19th century American jewelry is extraordinarily imaginative in design, making use of such semiprecious materials as jet, amber, and garnet. Deep-red garnet crystals (almandine) were often cut *en cabachon* and used as gems or beads. Because of their moderate cost, such stones could be used lavishly, and the resulting display was often brilliant and pleasing. All of the pieces illustrated have silver or gold mounts; very fine iron was also used.

Opposite page. Left: During the 19th century the design of American manufactured silver moved ever so gradually in the direction of increased ornamentation. The basic form of this butter tub or cooler made by Duhme & Co., Cincinnati, c. 1860, is simple, but the classical and rococo revival motifs added to it display an inspired zest for the purely decorative. The handles are formed of sculptured portrait heads of Zeus; similar portraits of Zeus, Athena, and Mercury are within the medallions decorating the sides of the ornate cover.

Antique silver is among the prized possessions sought by almost every collector. The increase in value of coin, sterling, and Sheffield during the past five years has been phenomenal, and, unfortunately, so has been the increase in theft. Particularly valued are handcrafted American pieces such as the waste bowl (B. Gardiner, New York, c. 1830); teapot, sugar bowl, and creamer (J. B. Jones, Boston, c. 1838); and the sugar tongs (marked "I.L.", early 1800s). The sticks and serving tray are Sheffield; the salt and pepper shakers are of late 19th-century Dutch manufacture.

Nineteenth-century brass, pewter, tin, wood, and silver English and American candleholders can be attractively used in any home. Despite the development of more efficient and effective lighting devices during the 19th and 20th centuries, fondness for the soft glow of candlelight lingers on. Candlesticks were sometimes fitted with glass globes, as seen here, or protected with hurricane chimneys. Mounted on the wall is a double tin sconce that may date from the 1700s.

of wood equal to perhaps one-third of the over-all length. The piece attached to the top of a mirror frame is known as the crest. A similar piece across the bottom is the skirt or apron. During this period, frames often were inlaid and crests might be inlaid, perhaps with carved or lighter-colored wood.

By 1750 when Chippendale's styles ruled on both sides of the Atlantic, his fret-carved or scroll-edged frame still was as important as the single piece of looking glass in it. If the glass itself measured only 8″x13″, the frame extended this piece to 13″ by 25½″. This style varied in size and in the intricacy of carving and decoration. Both crest and apron were fret-carved with the crest the deeper of the two pieces. On some of these frames, the crest displayed a carved ornament such as a medallion or a bird; on a few, slender garlands were carved delicately on either side. Ornaments, garlands and moldings next to the glass were covered with gold leaf.

By 1760 a fancy variation called an architectural or Constitution mirror was being made; the latter name is inaccurate though because the mirror predated the American Constitution by several years. Its crest was in the shape of a broken pediment; that is, it swooped into deep curves in the center that were flanked by cyma or S curves. Any number of these crests were scroll-edged too. Surmounting all this was a bird, in England a phoenix, in America an eagle. The bird as well as any other ornament and the molding around the glass were covered with gold leaf, and the cyma curves of the crest and perhaps the outline of the apron were strengthened with gold leaf.

The fretwork mirror introduced by Chippendale probably has achieved the most consistent popularity of all styles. Traditionally, it was made of mahogany and mahogany veneer and, in spite of scrolled edges, remained intact indefinitely. Remnants of one of these old mirrors including the wavy, mottled glass and a dozen or more pieces of the frame were tossed in a basket of miscellaneous items for auction several years ago. The couple who found it bought basket and contents for far less than it cost them to have a cabinetmaker put the mirror together again. This mirror, 11¾″ by 25½″ from tiptop to bottom scroll, now hangs on a wall in their home and the thin lines where veneer and some pieces of fretwork were pieced

and glued can't be detected, even by callers with excellent eyesight who stand only three feet away.

Still another method of framing a looking glass in order to make it important had been started during the Queen Anne period, which began in England in 1702 and reached America by 1725. This was the use of two nar-

Empire-style mirror, 1830s, French.

Convex gilded mirror, mid-19th century, American.

row pieces of looking glass, the top panel about half the length of the lower one. A total length of 36″ or more was not uncommon. A Queen Anne frame always arched softly at the top. Many of these narrow frames were molded and also curved gently on either side of the arch. Probably just as many had a crest of wood, which generally had a scrolled edge and usually was ornamented with gilded shell, medallion or garland of leaves. So popular was this style that it continued to be made into the 1770's, although the new Chippendale fretwork frame also was being made from Boston to Charleston, South Carolina, after 1750.

Chippendale's fretwork frame was still in demand when George Hepplewhite's quite different furniture designs were being copied here in the 1780's. Mirrors in the Hepplewhite style frequently consisted of two pieces of looking glass and, at least in the United States, so did those of his successor, Thomas Sheraton. The two pieces of glass in a Queen Anne frame had overlapped, but in Hepplewhite and Sheraton styles were separated by a strip of wood, an inch or less wide. In the latter, made here between the 1780's and 1820's, it was customary for the upper panel to display a reverse painting on glass. Many of these paintings were no more than folk art, although a few show greater skill. Favorite themes were a landscape, a seascape or rural scene; the frigate Constitution, which won fame in the War of 1812, was most popular of all.

Every detail of a frame in the manner of Hepplewhite contributed to its classical beauty. Typical were some scrolled or fretted carving on crest and apron and, more important, carved draperies, garlands or sprays of flowers and foliage hanging partway down on either side. The crest with its broken pediment sometimes was ornamented with a small medallion and almost always was surmounted with a basket or urn holding a few flowers, leaves or sheaves of wheat on long wirework stems. All decoration as well as the cyma curves gleamed with gold leaf.

A reverse painting on glass was not necessarily a part of a Hepplewhite mirror as it was of a Sheraton. Proof that looking glass had become more abundant here after 1800 is the quantity of authenticated Sheraton-type mirrors that are still hanging on walls. Sheraton's rectilinear frames were copied all over the United States. Two new characteristics that marked his influence were a flat cornice projecting across the top (crests disappeared forever) and the superimposing of pilasters or half-columns on the two long sides, later on all four sides.

The cornice on a Sheraton mirror had a row of small round or oval balls suspended from it. These, like the frame, usually were gilded. The cornice on many narrow mirrors accommodated thirteen balls, which are interpreted by many people as indicative of the thirteen orginal states. However, it does not mean that the frame was made when there were only thirteen states. After all, the first Sheraton mirror frame could hardly have been made here before 1795, when there were fifteen states. Furthermore, many cornices had seventeen to thirty pendent balls.

The pilasters on mirrors made between 1800 and 1840 were often simple half-columns, perhaps burnished with black and metallic paints, or else were reeded spirally or vertically in which case they were covered with gold leaf. After 1815, when four pilasters became general, they touched four wooden corner blocks. These blocks usually had rosettes carved in the centers. Because of the pilasters and cornice, these mirrors were sometimes described as architectural.

A distinct style that owed nothing to Sheraton, although it appeared around 1800, was the round convex mirror with a heavy circular frame. It is often called a Duncan Phyfe mirror although less famous cabinetmakers who worked not in New York City but in many other sec-

Hand mirror, brass, 1890s, American.

Gilded mirror, 19th century, American.

tions of this country made the same style. A better name would be Federal mirror. This convex mirror averaged 24″ in diameter and the circular frame added another 8″ to 10″. This wide heavy-looking frame consisted of concentric circles of molding or beading, or had a ring of balls, reeding or perhaps carving. An authentic Federal mirror has a carved pediment surmounted by a spread eagle and a carved finial of foliage pendent from the base. Every inch of the frame and decoration gleams with gold.

Between 1815 and 1840, the years of massive American Empire furniture, the ornamentation of rectangular mirrors reached its height. A favorite style of this period, which was enriched with pilasters and other elaborate architectural decorations, was appropriately called the tabernacle mirror. It had two pieces of looking glass, but the upper one wasn't always painted. Pilasters were spirally reeded, vase-and-ring or vase-and-cylinder turned, or carved with acanthus leaves. A few tabernacle mirrors were made of mahogany or a native hardwood such as walnut, but the handsomest ones were made of pine covered with gold leaf.

If one is to judge by bidding and prices at auctions, the least appreciated of antique mirrors is the simple American Empire style with a 5″-wide mahogany frame. Yet this is a versatile mirror which was made in many sizes and which can be hung vertically or horizontally if it holds only one small piece of glass. The frame is recognized by its mitered corners and wide cyma molding with flat bands about an inch wide on inner and outer edges.

Although the dressing glass or shaving mirror had been made since the early 1700's, it did not come into general use in this country until after 1800. Placed on a high bureau or chest, this was the right height for a gentleman when shaving. The rather small mirror was attached to uprights on a shallow drawer. A dressing glass or shaving mirror made here between 1790 and the early 1800's shows Hepplewhite's influence in its oval or shield-shaped frame and oval drawer. Thereafter, the frame and drawer followed Sheraton's rectilinear lines.

All except William and Mary and the two American Empire styles are being reproduced, but there are many ways of telling whether a mirror is an antique or a reproduction. Old glass certainly will be cloudy, mottled and blackened in spots. It also will be thin, probably not more than ⅛″ thick, and it certainly will be brittle and, therefore, hazardous to handle. And if it has beveled edges, they will be wavy to touch and narrower than the beveling on modern glass.

Attempting to have antique glass resilvered isn't entirely satisfactory, if only because the chemical process of covering the surface with metallic silver wasn't discovered until about 1840; until then, glass was made reflective, highly so at first, by the application of an amalgam of tin and mercury. However, there is no reason why old looking glass should not be replaced with smooth, clear new glass. If this is done, do have the old glass packed carefully and stored so it can be brought out when and if the mirror is sold or if its authenticity is questioned. Nineteenth-century owners of mirrors made fifty to one hundred years earlier may have substituted glass of better quality when it became obtainable after 1840. In this case, clear glass often replaced the painted panel too.

Other clues to age are construction and wood. Backs of antique mirrors are not closed in neatly as are modern ones. During the eighteenth century and the early years of the nineteenth century, the glass was protected by thin backboards of pine or other softwood, usually unfinished. Veneer frames were common, but if a veneered frame had a crest and skirt, these two parts were cut from thin wood that matched the veneer. Strips of pine glued on the back of crest and skirt were added by the maker, not later on

for support.

Some frames were made of hardwood, but pine was used for those that were to be covered with fine hardwood veneer, paint or gold leaf. Any golden color on antique frames or their decorations was not metallic paint, but gold leaf, which is an extremely thin sheet of real gold. When this wears thin in spots, as it will eventually, it cannot be touched up satisfactorily with gold paint. The application of gold leaf requires an expert's skill.

Brass circus wagon mirror, c. 1870, American.

30. Lamps

The lamps that were made during the 19th century to burn whale oil and, later, kerosene were not only attractive but also provided the best illumination indoors after dark until homes began to be electrified. For centuries some kind of lamp or candle had been used to supplement an open fire for light after the sun set. The fire gave more warmth than light and neither lamps nor candles were entirely safe or adequate.

Lamps had been tried for a longer time than candles to light the interior of a house after dark. But it is no wonder that people who could afford candles preferred them to the lamps that invariably smoked, sputtered and smelled. Handsome fixtures to hold many candles were hung in homes of the wealthy during the 1700's but lamps were still only small pottery or metal containers that held the crudest sort of oil and one or more wicks that gave a feeble light. Then, as now, candles gave a lovely light though a barely adequate one for close work. "Can't see what I'm eating," grumble men nowadays, so what would they say if they still had to read newspapers by candlelight?

The Betty and Phoebe lamps common in Colonial days in

Fluid or oil lamp, brass, mid-19th century, American.

179

Loop kerosene hand lamp, c. 1860, American.

America weren't really an improvement over the lamps that had been used for hundreds of years in other countries. These little lamps can be seen in museums and restorations but no one who comes across one in a pile of discarded utensils is likely to try to fix it up to burn again. Neither of these old styles looks like a lamp to those accustomed to contemporary electric ones or even old-fashioned kerosene lamps. By the time kerosene was available and proved to be an ideal fuel for illumination in the 1860's, men had also found ways to make lamps burn more efficiently.

Many families even in the most up-to-date suburbs keep one kerosene lamp on a shelf for use in an emergency. This is certain to be the plainest one they have ever found, for the attractive and often colorful oil-burning lamps that became so popular during the 1800's can be converted to electricity without damage. Most of the oil-burning lamps had chimneys but many of them did not have shades. In either case many more lamps than shades are found. Lack of a chimney is no problem for similar glass ones are still being made.

Not everyone is as lucky as the friend who phoned excitedly last month to say she had found a shade, two chimneys and two lamps in a cellar cupboard and please come down that evening to see them. The shade is a flaring plain glass one, so thin that it is a miracle that it hasn't been chipped during 95 years of use and storage. This shade is not a milk glass but a cloudy white that is translucent and it rings like a bell when struck lightly. It permits ample light and is just cloudy enough to have cut down the brilliancy of kerosene illumination for people who were not accustomed to so much brightness. The chimneys also are old for they are a slightly different shape than those now being made.

The chimneys can be used on her lamps after they have been electrified, the shade on either one. I would prefer to use the shade for the handsome glass lamp, about 12 inches tall, with a blown glass oil font and pressed glass stem and base which was probably made around 1850. Her second lamp, so carefully wrapped and packed away, is metal and known as a Rayo which was made starting about 1880 to illuminate with kerosene.

Thousands, perhaps millions, of oil-burning glass lamps were made during the 1800's. Most of them are in surprisingly good condition when they are unearthed. All except one style, the peg lamp, can be adapted to illuminate by electricity. The peg lamp, which was made in the early 1800's to burn whale oil, was a small sphere of glass. At its base was a projection or peg so that it could be placed in the socket of a candlestick. The neck was fitted with a metal collar that held one or two wicks.

The development of pressed glass about 1825 made it possible for decorative lamps to be produced comparatively inexpensively. Still, this process didn't do away entirely with the more ex-

Pressed-glass and brass electrified whale oil lamp, 1850-60, American.

pensive techniques such as hand-blown parts and cut or etched decoration. Whatever methods were used, lamps took on an outline recognizable even to those who are too young to have known any but electrical lighting. The standing lamp, placed on a table or wall bracket, averaged 8 to 10 inches high and consisted of a base and a stem or standard supporting an oil font or reservoir. A metal fitting, snugly closing the oil font, equipped the lamp with burner and wicks.

The wicks, wickholder and burner are clues to the kind of oil

Loop pressed-glass whale oil hand lamp, c. 1860, American.

a lamp burned. Round wicks were best for whale oil and were held in slender metal cylinders. If a lamp burned camphene, the wick tubes had to project high above the collar of the burner and if there were two tubes they slanted away from each other for safety. Kerosene-burning lamps, common after 1860, required flat wide-woven wicks. Burners could be changed on many lamps, according to the kind of oil available.

Lamps were made in many pressed glass patterns, both early and late. Argus with its simple but unmistakable design of elongated thumbprints between two bands of connected loops offered a high lamp, lacy Peacock Feather a low footed lamp with a handle. These two patterns are older than Block With Thumbprint. Bellflower and many other popular patterns included one or more sizes of lamps up to and including such patterns as Actress of the 1800's.

Pattern isn't the only distinguishing characteristic between one clear pressed glass lamp and another. Bull's Eye with Fleur de Lis came in two tall lamps, one with a globular font and round base, the other with an oval font and octagonal base. Fonts might

be pear-shaped, urn-shaped, resemble a wine glass or be almost square. Bases seldom matched.

The lamps that combined two or three glassmaking techniques or had one part colored are handsomest of all. It was not unusual 100 years ago to own a lamp with the bowl or font of cut glass, a fairly high stem that had been free-blown and a stepped base that had been pressed. The font was usually the colorful part. A clear or frosted pressed glass font might be supported by an opaque blue stem and base. The cranberry glass font may have been hand-blown, the stem and base of pressed milk glass. Then there were the lamps with overlay fonts, the rich blue or amethyst color cut into designs to show the clear glass underneath. After 1800, when art glass became popular, a shade might be satin glass or an entire lamp of delicate looking Crown Milano glass.

Before the late 1820's, when glass factories began to produce lamps in infinite variety, considerable experimenting had been done to improve the efficiency with which lamps burned. Aimé Argand, a Swiss, had invented the Argand lamp that had a central draft burner in 1784. The value of a glass chimney was discovered accidentally by one of Argand's workmen. He is said to have dropped a bottle so close to the flame of a lamp that the bottom dropped out and, the bottle becoming too hot to hold, the workman let it slip down over the flame. Immediately it was noticeable that the lamp burned with a steadier and brighter flame.

By no means all of the glass lamps were sold with chimneys and shades. However, shades similar to the tall protective hurricane shades used with candles were made for whale oil lamps in the 1820's. Soon afterward decorated shades shaped like a large chimney or a flaring vase became common. These shades often were frosted or etched, had a simple design cut into the glass or displayed a painted garland.

Shades were considered as essential as chimneys after brightly burning kerosene came into general use. This was when flaring half-dome shades appeared. Many of them were the thin cloudy white glass such as my friend found recently. Others were thicker glass, fluted and either green or yellow on the outside.

Both the Solar and the Astral lamps were adaptations of the Argand and became much more popular in this country. The reason was simple. A true Argand lamp required the expensive spermaceti made only from the white wax found in the head of a sperm whale. Astral lamps could burn ordinary whale oil, a Solar lamp whale oil, sperm oil or kerosene. They combined metal and glass in their structure and were equipped with chimneys and shades. The latter might be cut, etched or engraved glass and almost always had prisms dan-gling from them.

Throughout the 19th century almost as many small glass lamps were made as the standard ones placed on a table or wall bracket. Short dumpy lamps with a handle were known as squat lamps. These often were undecorated. Many small lamps used as night lamps were hand-blown or blown-molded with an attached ring handle and perhaps an equally small chimney. Tiny cut glass lamps, only 3 or 4 inches high, became popular for bed-rooms, and lamps of similar size were made after 1880 of art glass such as satin and Tiffany.

One of the oldest styles became known as a sparking lamp. This was so small that it held little fuel and gave minimum light. When the lamp burned out, the young man who had come courting knew that it was time to go home. Many of the sparking lamps, which had neither chimneys nor shades, show the swirls or ribbing that indicates they were blown-molded. Some of them had applied glass handles and many of them were small spheres attached to a stepped base.

Sparking lamps are much older than the miniature lamps, from 4½ to 8 inches high that began to appear in the 1840's. Many of

Pewter and glass time lamp and oil lighting device, 19th century, probably English.

these miniatures undoubtedly were used as sparking lamps and they were practical in sickrooms and nurseries and as night lights. The group includes Fairy, Acorn and true miniatures.

Fairy lamps deserve their name for the daintiness of their coloring and workmanship and diversity of shapes. The name "Fairy Lamp" was patented by an English firm that made candles. Little candle-burning lamps with the Fairy trademark of George and Samuel Clarke are perhaps most valuable in the United States and Europe.

Most Fairy lamps consisted of a cup for the candle and a shade. When the cup or base was ruffled white glass and the shade light blue glass, the name certainly seems appropriate. A shade formed like a flower with rows of glass petals in a pastel tint might also have a metal standard as a stem. Delicate blown glass, clear and colored pressed glass, all kinds of art glass and occasionally porcelain were the chief materials. The Acorn lamp, patented by the famous Hobbs-Brockunier glass firm in West Virginia, was simpler and took its name from the shape of its two parts. The base, often covered with hobnails, resembled a deep sauce dish. Into it fitted a dome of ribbed or swirled glass with a hole in the top.

Miniature lamps were somewhat larger than Fairy and Acorn lamps. Since the miniatures were fitted to burn kerosene, they appeared in quantity after 1860. Some miniature lamps undoubtedly were salesmen's samples, for they were copies of full-sized lamps in popular styles. Some of the loveliest were of satin glass, amberina and other kinds of art glass, painted in the Mary Gregory style, or clear and colored pressed glass. By the 1890's novelty forms such as an animal, a schoolhouse and a Santa Claus became popular.

Miniature lamps are delightful and often amusing to own so few collectors tamper with them to make them burn more safely. The oil-burning table and bracket lamps, tall or squat, lend themselves to present-day use after they have been electrified. A bewildering assortment of converters or adapters is spread out in stores. The number alone should be proof that it takes a little knowledge and skill to select the best kind for an old lamp and install it carefully.

Not every converter can be used on every lamp. Some permit

the use of a chimney and have the three slender metal arms to support a flaring shade. With many, a shade must be clipped to the top of the light bulb. If the lamp is large enough and suitable for hanging from the ceiling, there are fixtures for this purpose.

Pewter whale oil lamp, early 19th century, American.

31. American Clocks

America has added its fair share of illustrious names to the world's great clockmakers. Some were working here in the seventeenth century, and during the eighteenth century every colony had fine craftsmen. They took months to produce a single tall clock, each of its innumerable parts carefully made by hand.

Clocks did not become common in homes until after 1800. However, there are records of tower or turret clocks in Massachusetts settlements as early as 1650. These large clocks on the steeple of a church or on some part of a public building not only showed the time to everyone who passed but also struck the hours. In the town that had a clock, it wasn't necessary to ring a bell or fire a cannon to denote the hour of noon. (A true clock strikes the hours, whereas a timepiece merely tells time.)

The household clock of the seventeenth and eighteenth centuries was a tall one in a hardwood case that stood on the floor without support. In England, where many fine examples were being made during the seventeenth century, they were called long-case clocks. Other names were "tall," "floor" and "hall." In this country, since 1875, when

Henry Clay Work wrote a song called "Grandfather's Clock," they have been better known as grandfather clocks. The long, or tall, case was needed to hide the pendulum and weights and keep out dust. The height varied from five feet to nine feet, with nine feet more common.

A tall clock made by Samuel Bispham of Philadelphia in 1696 is perhaps the oldest American clock still in existence. Similar ones were made earlier in New York, Massachusetts and probably Connecticut. By 1700 skilled clockmakers who had immigrated here had apprentices working with them, many of whom moved on to other towns and colonies when they became full-fledged clockmakers. Philadelphia and Lancaster, Pennsylvania, where a surprising number of fine clockmakers were kept busy, produced many trained apprentices who later became noted for their work. It is doubtful that any clockmakers surpassed David Rittenhouse of Philadelphia, but notable names in other areas include Martin Shreiner of Lancaster, John Wright of New York City, James Jacks of Charleston, South Carolina, B.C. Gilman of Exeter, New Hampshire, and Thomas Harland of Norwich,

Box clock, "Crane's Torsion Pendulum Clock," Year Clock Company, New York, c. 1855.

Connecticut. The four Willard brothers—Benjamin, Aaron, Ephraim and Simon—became perhaps the most famous of the Massachusetts clockmakers between 1760 and the early 1800's.

Making a tall clock was one of the great crafts of the eighteenth century, and the most skilled clockmakers turned out only a few examples each year. During the forty-seven years David Rittenhouse worked at his trade he is believed to have produced no more than one hundred tall clocks. One reason may be that even during the 1700's a tall clock cost several hundred dollars. Ownership of one was a mark of prosperity; the tall clock was displayed as carefully as any family silver and was of equal importance in wills. In city homes, as a rule, the tall clock stood in the parlor or hall, but in farmhouses it was placed in the large kitchen, which was the center of daily living.

The finest hardwoods were chosen for the cases of tall clocks. Walnut and mahogany were preferred and cherry was also used to some extent in America. Satinwood and other exotic hardwoods were used for inlay when this decoration became popular. The style of these cases changed as did other pieces of furniture. Early tall cases had square tops, and around 1700 the arched top became common. The broken-arch pediment, which was common in the first half of the century, was carved with the two S scrolls terminating in rosettes or accented with three finials carved in flame, urn or steeple form. When the Chippendale style became popular about 1750, carved wood fretwork often surmounted the arched top and the three ball

or steeple finials were likely to be brass. Some of the finest cabinet-makers of the eighteenth century produced beautiful cases for tall clocks. Those with a carved block and shell can be traced to the originators of these motifs, John Goddard and Job Townsend of Newport, Rhode Island. David Rittenhouse may have collaborated with his contemporaries Benjamin Randolph and William Savery, who were masters of the American Chippendale style in Philadelphia. Later in the century the Willards had fine cabinet-makers of the Federal period to work with in their neighborhood. Much plainer, of course, were cases of walnut or cherry made in rural areas.

Dials were as fascinating as the cases were handsome. The earliest dials were square and the metal used for them was often brass with the numerals engraved on a silver ring. After 1770 painted or enameled dials became general. The spandrels, or the four pie-shaped pieces that filled the corners, were decorated with floral sprays, figures or ornamental metalwork. Throughout most of the eighteenth century, cases had arched tops that left room for a semicircular cartouche above the dial. At first the clockmaker

Steeple Clock, Atkins Clock Company, Bristol, Conn., c. 1859.

signed his name and perhaps the town where he worked on the cartouche instead of the face of the clock. Then about 1720 moving figures were introduced into the cartouche to make these tall clocks more fascinating than ever before. Here was placed a ship that rocked on the ocean, a deer that pranced, Father Time with his scythe, or some other animated figure. Soon afterward a moon wheel was added to the clock's mechanism and the monthly phases could be noted by looking at the relative positions of the two hemispheres and the moon, usually with a man-in-the-moon face, in the cartouche. Some of these cartouches also had a painted sky and gold stars. The moon wheel had to be set independently of the clock, but it was quite accurate and some owners found it as useful as the time-telling of the clock. A variation, incorporated successfully by Rittenhouse but rarely attempted by other clockmakers, was the orrery, which showed the movement of several planets. The orrery in one Rittenhouse clock included the planet Uranus, which was discovered in 1781.

The making of tall clocks continued in Pennsylvania until close to 1850 but tapered off before this in New England, where many clockmakers were experimenting with styles that would be smaller and cheaper. A dwarf, miniature or small tall clock, later nicknamed the grandmother clock, was made to some extent in the early years of the nineteenth century. It was a duplicate of the tall clock except for its height, which never exceeded four feet and sometimes was less than that.

Wall clocks began to be made in some quantity and diversity in the late eighteenth century. As appealing today as it ever was is the type known as the wag-on-wall clock. The earliest form, made before 1800, was basically a tall-clock movement without the protecting case. In the nineteenth century smaller wag-on-wall clocks were made, some of them with milk-glass or china faces.

Far more original was the banjo clock, patented by Simon Willard in 1802 and promptly copied by many other clockmakers. The first banjo clocks were only timepieces to hang on the wall, but later ones struck the hours and a few had an alarm mechanism. The clock's resemblance to a banjo is obvious. The simple, clear, round dial at the top was surmounted by an eagle or a simpler finial such as an acorn. The tapering case, whose length was needed to house the pendulum, ended in a rectangular box. Banjo clocks, which averaged about three feet in length, were both plain and fancy. Many had simple hardwood cases, and an early one might be fully enclosed with the wood. Soon the waist and rectangular box were faced with glass panels decorated with reverse paintings of a scene, an eagle or a geometric design. Banjo clocks with painted glass panels had cases of hardwood or of softwood, such as pine, covered with gold leaf.

Undoubtedly the banjo clock was the inspiration for two other distinct styles of wall clock that first appeared in or near Boston. One was the appropriately named lyre clock. This also had a clear dial framed in a simple case and surmounted with an eagle or a finial. The center section was carved and decorated in the form of a lyre. The glass covering it was frequently embellished with sprays of foliage or flowers. The rectangular box at the base usually had a pendent bracket, and if it had a glass panel, this was painted in reverse with a scene or an involved geometric design.

Although it is uncertain who designed the lyre clock, it was produced by such outstanding clockmakers as Aaron Willard Jr. and Lemuel Curtis. Curtis, who worked in Concord, Massachusetts, and Burlington, Vermont, made banjo clocks too, but his special contribution to the gallery of American clocks was the truly magnificent girandole. This clock, about forty-five inches long, had a pendulum box of the same shape and design as the gilded convex mirrors that were popular in the early 1800's. The pendulum box had the wide circular frame studded with balls and a pendant of acanthus leaves, but did not have sockets for candles, as did the girandole mirror. The frame around the face of the clock was similar to that of the pendulum box and was surmounted by an eagle with either folded or outspread wings. Both the center section, flanked with brass sidearms, and the pendulum box displayed reverse paintings on glass. A mythological or patriotic scene usually adorned the convex glass of the pendulum box, while the center section was likely to be decorated with an eagle and shield, flowers, oak leaves and acorns, or scrolls. Occasionally the long center section held a working thermometer framed by delicate painting.

Cabinet (or parlor walnut) clock, "Patti" model, E.N. Welch Manufacturing Co., Bristol, Conn., c. 1887.

Three brothers of Lemuel Curtis helped with his girandole clocks: Samuel, the eldest, painted the dials; Benjamin and Charles did many of the fine reverse paintings on glass. Curtis probably made no more than fifty of his stunning girandole clocks, for this skilled clockmaker lavished such care and detail on them that he was working against the trend to smaller and less expensive shelf clocks.

Shelf clocks, particularly the handsome bracket type, had been made in England since the early seventeenth century. Bracket clocks were virtually ignored by American clockmakers, and shelf clocks did not begin to come into their own until after the Revolution. The size and shape of a shelf clock permitted it to stand on a shelf, bracket, mantel, table or the like. Incidentally, the first clock with an alarm is said to have been a pine shelf clock, twenty-nine inches high and twelve inches wide, produced by Levi Hutchins in Concord, New Hampshire, in 1787. Rarest of American-designed shelf clocks is the sizable and well-named lighthouse clock, designed and patented by Simon Willard a few years after his banjo clock. The lighthouse clock can be classed as

an oddity, for Willard himself made only a few and other clockmakers did not copy it. On the other hand, the pillar-and-scroll shelf clock, introduced by Eli Terry of Connecticut about 1818, became immensely popular and later was made by many New England clockmakers. This clock also takes it name from the case, which has pillars on either side and scrolled woodwork on top and bottom. The top scroll often was surmounted with three finials, as was the pediment of a tall clock.

In the 1820's the shelf clock with ogee case appeared and was manufactured in at least six different sizes until after 1900. It was named for the ogee molding applied on the four front sides of the case. The steeple clock, designed by Elias Ingraham of Bristol, Connecticut, came along about 1840 and the beehive clock not long after. By this time Connecticut clockmakers were dominating the industry, and their shelf clocks, in a variety of cases, were purchased by rich and poor during the nineteenth century.

Eli Terry, as inventive as the finest clockmakers of the eighteenth century, accomplished a great deal more than designing the classic pillar-and-scroll shelf clock. To him goes credit for converting clockmaking from craft to an industry, since he worked out assembly-line methods of factory production and proved that mass-produced clocks could be sold. By the time an economic depression struck the United States in 1837, another Connecticut Yankee, Chauncey Jerome, had implemented other ideas that kept the clock industry thriving. Jerome had figured out the advantages of brass over wooden parts. He knew that dampness could halt wooden works, that the teeth of gears broke easily and that skilled hands were needed to put wooden movements together. If pieces were brass, so Jerome reasoned, they could be made by machine and assembled more easily; parts would be interchangeable from one clock to another. Terry's assembly-line methods had produced a shelf clock that could be sold for as little as forty dollars. Jerome's changes brought the price of similar clocks down to about twelve dollars. The Yankee peddlers who invaded all parts of the United States were glad to add the comparatively small and inexpensive Connecticut shelf clocks with foolproof brass parts to their stock in trade.

Nineteenth-century shelf clocks can still be found all over the United States. They are the most plentiful of all the old clocks. Three things add to their value and authenticity: the maker's paper pasted inside the case, the original tablet or reverse painting on the glass door and the original movement in the original case. Older styles of wall and tall clocks come on the market occasionally, but authentica-

Cabinet (or kitchen oak) clock, E. Ingraham & Co., Bristol, Conn., c. 1895.

tion should be demanded since some fakes are known to have been made. Many a clock that is one hundred to two hundred years old still ticks off the minutes and strikes the hours. If not, cleaning and repair should be done carefully, for some old clocks have not benefited from work done by repairmen or even later clockmakers. Reproduction of several old styles are being made, but when their movements are powered by electricity and the clocks tell time silently, they always seem to me to have lost their voice along with their tick.

Iron and enameled wood mantel clock, Wm. L. Gilbert Clock Co., Winsted, Conn., c. 1900.

32. Wooden Boxes

Boxes have a longer history than most pieces of furniture, for these simple receptacles always have been treasured for storing personal possessions and household goods. Their origin is lost in time but, large or small, boxes have been made for centuries of so many materials that both rich and poor owned them. The earliest ones known to have been made in America were of wood. Boxes for various purposes also were made of silver, pewter and other metals, china, glass or papier-mâché. But the wooden ones, ranging from those which were small enough to hold a toothpick and which were carried in a pocket to the painted ones which held a bride's finery, were

not only well made but often ingenious in their construction and attractive both inside and outside.

However utilitarian and however old the box, it was seldom unadorned. The very care with which it was mortised and joined adds to the attractiveness after accumulated dust and grime have been removed. Interiors were finished smoothly, sometimes fitted for specific storage and frequently lined with colored papers or fabrics. Carving, incising and moldings added pattern to the covers and sometimes to the sides of the box as well. Painting was not uncommon on wooden boxes. Many early nineteenth-century ones were decorated charmingly

with floral sprays, birds and occasionally a rural scene and later ones often displayed a stenciled design. Perhaps the most distinctive painting was that done on boxes made by the Pennsylvania Germans. Their favorite motifs were colorful tulips, hearts, doves and peacocks, angels, unicorns and occasionally a knight and his lady.

More often than not, these hundred to two-hundred year old boxes can be used proudly at the present time although probably not for the purpose for which they were made. Three wooden boxes given to the first owners between 1860 and 1880 for an entirely different function now hold jewelry on the bureaus of three sisters who live in widely separated states. These women cherish the boxes that their great-aunts in New Hampshire gave them and plan to hand them on to their daughters. Originally one was a writing box, popular with Victorian ladies, another may have been either a sewing, trinket or cosmetic box because of the mirror attached to the inside of the lid and the third was simply a beautifully finished wooden box with a lock and key.

All three boxes are mahogany, each one approximately 11″ long

Carved, chipped sailor's game box, c. 1800, probably American.

by 8″ wide and 3″ to 4″ deep. The exterior of the writing box is banded with a stenciled design in gold leaf and black. The interior has been fitted with a narrow trough along the front to hold penholders and pencils with a compartment just the right size for an inkwell at one end and a slanting felt-covered lid over the rest of the box where stationery can be kept. An inner cover cleverly attached inside the lid of the box is so unnoticeable that it makes a safe place to keep letters.

The box with the mirror under its lid is fitted with a shallow tray divided into eight compartments. One of these was made into a velvet pincushion. The tray, the interior of the box and its hinged cover are lined with green and white wallpaper, as good as the day it was put on. On top, the cover has been incised with a floral spray. The third box has a beautifully carved lid which compensates for its lack of interior fittings and lining.

By far the oldest wooden boxes, so old that they are seldom seen now except in museums or restorations, are Bible boxes. Some of these were brought by the colonists from England, Holland and Germany and others were made here during the 1600's of native hardwoods. This imposing box in which the family Bible was stored was deep and rectangular with a hinged lid and was one of the most important furnishings in most homes. The heavy wooden box was decorated with paneling, molding and carving in the fashion of the time. In the Pennsylvania German area, Bible boxes were painted with the typical motifs used on all furniture made there.

Desk boxes also were made during the 1600's. These were mahogany or rosewood, the exterior sometimes displaying inlay of other woods or even silver. Desk boxes were hinged so they could be closed and put away when not in use. When opened out flat, they averaged 19″ in length and provided a slanting surface, often covered with velvet, on which to write. Across the top were compartments for an inkwell, a shaker or small box that held sand or pounce (ground cuttlefish bone) to sprinkle on the writing

Carved Bible box with iron lock, 18th century, English or American.

to dry the ink, penholders and pens cut from quills. By about 1700, desks as we recognize them were beginning to be made in some quantity but the desk box continued to be a gentleman's accessory into the early 1800's.

As typically Pennsylvania German as the painted Bible box was the bride's box. This was likely to be oval and of a quite good size, 18″ or so in length. Often this gaily painted box intended for ribbons, laces and other personal items was given to the bride by her husband-to-be. Similar but smaller boxes were known in New England and other parts of the country as trinket boxes. They weren't always oval. At least one, made in New England in the late 1700's, was shaped like a small trunk and decorated tastefully with painted flowers and birds.

In direct contrast were the simple, well-made and utterly plain boxes for which the Shakers became noted. They turned them out during the 1800's in their colonies established in Kentucky, Ohio, New York, Massachusetts, Connecticut and New Hampshire. For their oval, round or rectangular boxes made in graduated sizes, the Shakers preferred the thin strips of wood known as splint which were overlapped and riveted together.

Pine wood generally was used for the handy boxes seen in kitchens. Salt and sugar boxes were most common and made in all parts of the country. The plain wooden salt box with a high back to hang it on a wall is a very old convenience that was made until the early 1900's. Salt boxes are recognized by slanting covers similar to the steep roofs of salt box houses.

Boxes for other purposes also were made to hang on walls of kitchens, pantries and also barns. Many of these have quite different proportions from the salt box. A wall box found in upper New York state several years ago has a back 12″ high and a shallow, uncovered box 4″ by 5″ by 11″. This pine box bears scars and cracks and the underside of the back shows traces of red-brown paint. The whole box may have been painted that color when it was new. Old-fashioned square nails, probably hand forged, hold it together. The proportions indicate that it may have been used to store candles, although candleboxes usually had sliding lids. Or it may have been hung on the wall above a washstand to hold a comb and brush (common between 1860 and 1900).

The knife box, also of pine, was almost as common on a table or counter and as plain as the salt box hanging on the wall. The de-

Walnut candlebox, 19th century, American.

Painted two-tier candle box, 19th century, American.

sign for wooden knife boxes was so practical that similar ones are still being made of plastic. The shallow, rectangular kitchen knife box was divided lengthwise into two or more compartments. The partition in a two-compartment box was high enough to be carved into a carrying handle. At the other end of the scale were the handsome mahogany knife boxes made to stand on a sideboard when this piece of furniture was new in the 1780's. These were rectangular with slanting covers or were urn-shaped; comparatively few were made in America, perhaps because only a skilled cabinetmaker dared attempt them.

Excellent workmanship as well as fine woods were expended on spice boxes, which remained popular long after exotic spices were no longer scarce or high-priced. Plain oak spice boxes were brought from England and innumerable ones were made from cherry, maple and walnut in Pennsylvania and other eastern states. Since housewives demanded spice boxes until the late 1800's, they show as many changes in detail as did furniture during the eighteenth and nineteenth centuries. Spice boxes are seldom labeled as such and a person who finds one can only guess at its purpose because of the size of the box and the number of small drawers. A small one only 5″ or 6″ high is certain to have six drawers while larger ones, 20″ or so high, will have nine to a dozen or more little drawers, each one to hold a different spice. A 33″-high spice chest made in Philadelphia in the late 1700's looks somewhat like a Chippendale highboy and smaller ones might be more accurately described as spice

chests or cupboards. These in fact are sometimes mistaken for toy or miniature furniture. It is easier to recognize the stacked round or oval spice boxes.

Spice boxes, it has been said, were kept not in the kitchen but in the dining or living room. Many of them had keys. These two characteristics are equally true of teaboxes, which became fashionable to own during the late eighteenth century and the early years of the nineteenth century in both England and America. The teabox was an elegant one of mahogany or rosewood with lines following those of furniture of the period. Each box was divided into two to ten or twelve compartments for different kinds of tea and had a special compartment for the glass which was used to mix the teas to a person's taste. The box and its compartments were lined with lead. Each compartment had it own cover to seal off the special aroma of the tea, often with a knob of wood like that of the box. An old teabox when opened still exudes a faint fragrance of tea even though it may not have been used to store it for more than a hundred years.

Sewing boxes like spice boxes and teaboxes were often works of

Decorated deed box, 19th century, American.

Children's game box, découpage decoration, early 20th century, American.

art, yet their owners referred to them as workboxes. Since sewing was such an essential accomplishment, it is no wonder that both boxes and accessories were attractive. The Shakers made plain sewing baskets on the order of their splint boxes. The handsomest sewing box I have ever seen is the one a bride from New Haven, Connecticut took to her new home in Virginia in the late 1700's. The box itself was mahogany with inlay trim and was lined with velvet. Like many old sewing boxes, it was fitted with a shallow tray for accessories. The tray in this box was indented to hold large cutting shears, an emery bag in the shape of a red strawberry, a pincushion and spools hand carved from apple wood. Underneath, fabric and the like could be stored, which is probably why the bride is said to have called this her patchwork sewing box.

Decidedly clever were many of the boxes to hold spools of thread which came into general use during the 1800's. One of the simplest is a small wooden tub with handles and a tight cover. Needlebooks with flannel leaves often had wooden covers. Accessories of this sort were given little girls to encourage them while they were learning to make fine stitches.

Many small boxes for various purposes, often in odd shapes, were made in this country and were also imported. American ones sometimes were made of two kinds of wood in contrasting colors instead of being decorated with inlay or veneer. Plain and fancy examples which have been found and treasured include wooden snuffboxes shaped like a shoe complete with pearl buttons and another like a small bellows. A fan-shaped toothpick case was meant to be carried by a lady. Some wooden inkwells had glass liners, although one realistically cut and decorated to look like a drum did not. Pounce boxes, small desk accessories, had perforated tops so the sand or ground cuttlefish bone in them could be shaken on the writing paper to dry the ink. Pounce boxes, snuffboxes, toothpick cases and ladies' patchboxes which held the beauty spots popular in the seventeenth and eighteenth centuries were made of many materials in addition to wood.

Not as personal, but fascinat-

Mahogany tea caddy, bombé style, late 18th century, English.

ing because people have become accustomed to shopping for food that comes in plastic bags and sealed packages, are wooden boxes made for shipping and displaying products in stores during the 1800's. Some of these boxes were splint but most of them were pine, maple or even oak. Anyone whose grandfather or great-uncle was the proprietor of a general store has a good chance of finding some of these boxes gathering cobwebs in an attic, cellar or closets of an old house or in the barn. A thorough dusting is likely to show a soundly constructed box that may be enlivened with a label lithographed in color. A cylindrical splint box with a tight-fitting cover and, on the side, a large two-color label of a nineteenth-century wholesaler of spices in New York City was found recently in an attic in northeastern Pennsylvania. Over the original label had been placed a small white sticker on which had been written in spidery script "Black Pieces." This split box must have been appropriated by the wife of the storekeeper in the

1890's and now her granddaughter is using it to keep her mending out of sight.

A carefully made box with brass hinges, a brass catch and brass support to keep the cover in place when raised was rescued from the cellar of an old Ohio house and, after a little cleaning of the wood and waxing, makes a fine button box. It is 11½″ by 6½″ by 3¾″ deep. The colored lithograph of garden carnations with lettering above and below including the name "D.M. Ferry & Co." is in as good condition as it was the day it was pasted inside the cover, and it also provided the clue to learning that this had been a display box for packets of seed sent to stores in the early 1880's.

Boxes of all shapes and sizes in which tea, coffee, grains, cereal and the like were shipped or displayed years ago are other possibilities to be dug out of a clutter of discards. If their advertising or identifying lithographed labels are still intact, they add authenticity and a fillip to finding a present day use for the boxes.

33. Antique Picture Frames

Large and important antiques aren't always the easiest ones to work into present-day homes. The young suburban couple who have no dining room and inherited a Federal sideboard are far less happy than the couple who quietly gathered up close to forty picture frames, first used during the nineteenth century, from the old homes of two grandmothers —or perhaps it was their great-grandmothers. The young people may never be able to use all these frames and may eventually discard the last few that have sat around for years, but the stack is there to be drawn on for one purpose or another as long as they are interested.

Their hoard includes frames in a range of sizes, shapes, woods, finishes and decoration, each one typical of the nineteenth century. Starting with the Federal period, which already was well advanced by 1800, pictures became increasingly popular and were seen in more and more homes, rich as well as poor. At first frames were needed for oil paintings and watercolors, now referred to as American Primitive paintings, and for small silhouette portraits. Considerably later, as the Victorian period progressed, paintings were still favored by those who could afford them, and prints of all kinds, wood and steel engravings, lithographs and, finally, photographs became comon everywhere. Frames for these various types of pictures were made sometimes from fine hardwoods, such as mahogany and walnut, or of pine that was painted, gilded or covered with gold leaf.

Large, wide frames were typical of the years between 1800 and 1840, when itinerant painters made it possible for so many families to own pictures. A frame in good condition from this period is certain to be different from and probably more valuable than most Victorian frames. These were the days when a portrait,

Crisscross frame, 19th century, American.

unless it was a silhouette or miniature, fitted a frame in the neighborhood of 25" x 21". Such a frame was likely to be gilded. A large scenic painting done between about 1820 and 1840 might have a 2"- to 3"-wide frame of mahogany or walnut with shallow blocks attached to each corner or a dark hardwood frame with mitered corners. Still another type of frame for a large picture was wood with narrow carving on either side, the carved borders covered with gold leaf or gilding and the rest of the frame painted black. Later, these large frames combined molding that added depth and gilded edges, perhaps spirally turned or bead-

Pine frame, 19th century, American.

Cast-iron frame with brass finish, 1860-80, American.

ed. All these early nineteenth-century types are so obviously frames that it is difficult to use them for any other purpose, although mirrors also had wide frames with mitered corners and narrower ones with shallow blocks on each corner.

After 1840 smaller frames (often approximately 11½″ x 13½″) became as common as the large ones. Some of the most attractive ones, well worth finding and keeping, are oval. One of the earliest, probably in the 1850's, was an oval frame of pine, usually painted black. Its chief distinction is its decoration—four units spaced around the frame in raised relief in the form of fruits and foliage, flowers and foliage, or perhaps acorns and oak leaves. Both the raised decorations and the raised line of beading, sawtooth or other small design around the glass are gilded. A later Victorian oval frame of gleaming mahogany or walnut is recognized by its several moldings varying in height to 2¼″. The lowest molding around the inside is covered with gold leaf or gilded, and although this now is usually somewhat faded or worn, it still accents the hardwood.

Oval hardwood frames in a range of sizes reached their height of fashion in the 1880's and were commonly used to display photographs. A paper mat set off each photograph and helped it to conform to the shape of the frame. Neither the handsome frame nor the well-cut mat softened the grim expressions assumed by most people in the early days of photography. As a result, the photographs are likely nowadays to be removed. The obvious next step is converting the frame into a mirror, which can be hung on the wall or given an easel back to stand on a table.

There are bound to be some crisscross frames in a collection of nineteenth-century ones, if only because they are so easy to find. Although more dated-looking than some of the other styles, they are interesting. They are made of natural dark wood, usually walnut, and are shallowly carved or incised. The really distinguishing feature is that the four sidepieces appear to crisscross so that about an inch of wood extends beyond the four corners of the frame. This was accomplished by mortising the two long pieces into the crosspieces, or vice versa. The wood pieces that make the frame average about 1″ in width and about ½″ thick. Slender wood easels that folded flat when not in use are attached to the backs of small sizes, implying that these frames were

Cast-iron frame with brass finish, 1860-80, American.

Standing picture frame, silver plate, 1880s, American.

used for photographs. The large ones, of course, hung on the wall.

A pile of these crisscross frames may seem, at first, to have no two alike. Actually countless numbers were produced in each style in which these frames were decorated, but your grandmother may have owned several different ones. Neat and dignified is the frame that has its pieces of crisscrossing wood reeded in two widths. On each corner where the sides intersect is a white china button ringed with brass. Quite attractive is a larger frame (4″ x 6″ around the opening) that is incised to resemble bark and has a three-lobed leaf cut out and fastened on each corner. Sometimes a person is lucky enough to obtain a matching pair of large frames, and I know of one woman who is searching patiently for a fourth so that she can at long last hang up her set of Currier and Ives' prints, *The Four Seasons.*

Rococo frames also are typical of the Victorian years. The rococo frame consists of an elaborate openwork arrangement of scrolls and leaves or plumes colored gold. On small oval ones, the frame itself was often almost as wide as the opening. Rectangular frames of this sort, however, had much larger openings in proportion to the frame. These modest-size frames with easels on the backs were cast of a gold-colored metal. Good-size frames of scrollwork 2″ to 3″ wide were cut from pine wood and gilded or covered with gold leaf.

Originally, the large rococo frames held rather sentimental art prints, but they also make handsome mirrors now. The wide but more solid gold-colored frames of late Victorian years may be more valuable than the oil paintings within, which often were done by amateurs. The painting, engraving, lithograph, print or portrait in a good, old frame may not be to your liking, but it is advisable to find out whether it has any value from an art or a collector's standpoint. Mats are seldom usable or worth saving because of soil, spotting or fading. There are so many nineteenth-century frames in good condition that it is pointless to bother with those that are too soiled to get clean, are falling apart, have pieces of scrollwork broken off or relief decoration badly damaged.

34. Dolls 'Round the World

Dolls have existed almost as long as men, in all parts of the world. The doll's progress reflects the development of our human whimsey, sophistication and ingenuity. Over the centuries, as skills evolved in woodcrafts, ceramics, sculpture and needlework to name just a few, we have applied them to doll making. The doll has appeared in myriad versions: hard and soft, rigid and

Minerva doll, composition head, cloth body, wooden legs, 1860-90.

mechanical, silent and vocal, bland and personable, fragile and indestructible; and, thanks to dedicated collectors, we have well-preserved examples of many of them. The liveliest period in the doll chronicle occurred in the 1800's, during the Industrial Revolution, with the growth of the doll-making industry. The charm, beauty, and fascinating variety of models produced is convincing proof that the doll is truly a thing immortal.

The word *fashion* has become almost synonymous with French dolls of the late 1800s because the Paris touch gave such charm and style to dolls and costumes that they won world-wide approval. A toymaker named Jumeau introduced a doll in Paris in the 1860s that revolutionized doll making. The Jumeau dolls have bisque heads with lifelike faces, set-in glass eyes, and elaborate wigs. They are so exquisite and their clothes so minutely perfect that they became known as French fashion dolls although there is no evidence that they were ever intended as anything other than toys for children.

Just as elegant as the Jumeau creations are Parian dolls. The very word *Parian* suggests beauty, and, when the first doll heads

made of this fine white china clay appeared, they created a sensation. Their resemblance to the white marble from the Greek island of Paros led to the name Parian. Blonde, with pale or softly tinted complexions and delicate features, they were molded throughout Germany from the 1850's to the 1870's. The hardness of the paste made it possible to mold the heads in great detail, and the modelers delighted in

Émile Jumeau "closed mouth" bisque doll, 1878.

Clocks of the type used in schoolhouses, churches, and other public places during the late 1800s and early 20th century are widely sought by collectors. So great is the interest in these models, in fact, that reproductions abound. There is nothing, however, like the real thing, and the price may not be much greater than the well-made imitation. This calendar clock, not a true "regulator" despite the message on the glass tablet, was made by the E. Ingraham Co. of Bristol, Connecticut, around 1904. It sold at that time for $5.85. The octagonal frame and case are made of press-molded oak; the brass movement is of the 8-day variety.

Opposite page: Clocks made in America during the 19th century are found throughout the world. The inventiveness of the New England clockmaker displayed in the use of brass mechanisms and in the adoption of assembly-line techniques of manufacture guaranteed him a market wherever accurate time was kept. The oldest of the clocks shown here is the tall-case or grandfather clock from Lancaster, Pennsylvania; the youngest are the tambour models seen in the foreground. Other distinctive forms are the banjo clock on the wall, a timepiece first patented by Simon Willard in 1802, and the steeple or sharp Gothic clock directly in front of the tall-case.

Small wooden boxes, often unassuming in appearance, may be very valuable antique objects. Used in the past for storing money, jewelry, or other special items such as a family Bible, these containers were usually handmade either at home or by skilled cabinetmakers. Many of the boxes are miniature chests; the veneered French jewelry box at left dates from the early 19th century and is in the form of a casket. Behind it is an American miniature chest of the 19th century also used for jewelry. Even work or sewing boxes were sometimes finely crafted, as is the example illustrated at right with the American flag pincushion. Much simpler in form are the pine candle boxes (on the wall and to the right) used to store what was once an expensive commodity.

the color fired up best and the dolls were almost all blue-eyed, supposedly in tribute to Queen Victorian. China dolls made up with calico bodies and china limbs were available, but quantities of heads were sold separately to be completed at home; in those days, dolls were a luxury and little girls, like today's collectors, regarded them as treasures.

An important variation of the china doll is that of bisque. When clay comes from the kiln it is in a hard form known as "biscuit" or bisque. This can be glazed to produce glossy china but it can also be left in the unglazed, bisque state. It is out of bisque proper that some of the most beautiful dolls' heads in the world have been made. Especially notable are the creations of the Jumeau family whose dolls, as noted before, set a standard of beauty and excellence which has never been surpassed. The Jumeaus gave their bisque dolls lustrous glass eyes, modish wigs of mohair or human hair and sensitive, realistic features. In the 1860s the first swivel heads, an invention of Monsieur Jumeau's son, appeared on the company's bisque dolls and supplanted the stationary ones known in collectors' language as shoulder heads. Other famous makers of bisque include the French firm Bru, which later merged with Jumeau, and several in Germany, among them Armand Marseille and Kestner.

There are many dolls, known broadly as specialty dolls, which defy rigid classification. This group includes some of the most intriguing and ingenious figures ever made. Some, like the half-dolls or realistic celluloid and Schoenhut dolls, were made in this century. Others, such as the

Wooden doll, 18th century, probably English.

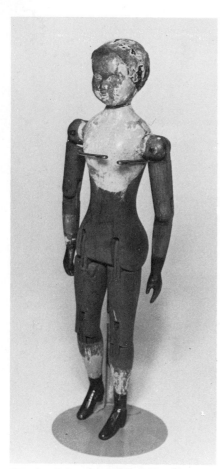

Wooden doll with pressed and painted features, metal hands and feet, Joel Ellis, 1873.

wooden dolls that were set in church niches, and the mechanical dolls that perform feats ranging from smoking to swimming, go back to the 1700's. Of course, innumerable specialty dolls were created in the 19th century too; among the most charming are those representing peddler women carrying miniature wares. Half-dolls first became popular in the late Victorian era and were sometimes used to top pincushions and lamps.

Wooden and rag dolls come in every variety. A catalogue of wooden dolls might begin with the Egyptians and carry on to every country on the globe. Fathers whittled them for their children and wood was the staple material of doll making until the 19th century when wax and other new materials were introduced. Early American "Pennywoods" or "Peg Dolls" are prized collectors' items today. American dollmakers who endowed the wooden dolls with flexibility and charm were Joel Ellis, whose creations were usually prim-faced, and the Schoenhut family, famous for baby dolls, circus characters, and animals. Rag dolls are truly one-of-a-kind creations. From the most inexpensive of materials, a charming fig-

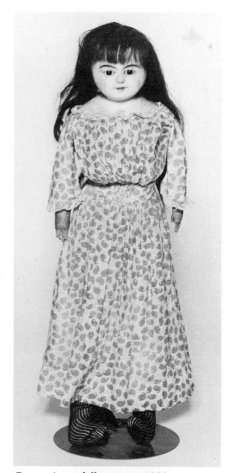

Queen Anne doll, wax, c. 1830.

ure was formed by a loving parent. In the 20th century, of course, most of these dolls have been created outside the home in craft workshops, if not a factory. Rag dolls by makers in the American South can be very appealing and collectible.

A strong, comparatively recent trend in doll collecting is toward costume dolls, representative in physiognomy and clothing, of the nations of the world. Returning U.S. servicemen often brought these home to their daughters in the 1940's and '50's and tourists frequently purchase these dolls as souvenirs of their foreign travels. Purists who scorn the plentiful modern versions need not despair. It is still possible to collect geographic dolls made in the 19th century. Among them are some with German bisque heads or wax molded over composition dating from 1870 to 1900, and they are dressed in their original, intricately detailed native costumes.

Rag doll, 1900, American.

35. The Romance of Fans

Fans, those decorative trifles that have been called a woman's most romantic weapon, disappeared with the widespread installation of air conditioning in this country. Less than one hundred years ago, a fan was as much a necessity and as common in warm weather as was a shawl in winter. During the nineteenth century, it was a perfect gift for a woman of any age. Small fans were made for little girls and tiny ones for dolls.

Beautiful fans of feathers and silk, and utilitarian ones of straw and paper, are still being made and used in many countries, chiefly in the Far East. In the United States as recently as the 1920's, feather fans were an important accessory with evening dress, and simple paper, cardboard or palm-leaf fans were kept close at hand on hot summer afternoons. Fans such as these, as well as a good many older ones, are packed away in many an attic or trunk, just as is the one my grandmother carried to church on summer Sundays in the early 1920's. This one is black Chantilly lace mounted on carved black wooden sticks with a few shining silver sequins twinkling on the lace and inset in the sticks.

The chief purpose of a fan was to create a current of air to cool one's face in hot weather, and when one was sitting near an open fire in the winter. (Some of the Victorians claimed that a fan protected a lady's complexion from the sun, but this does seem a little farfetched.) And, of course, a fan was important in a sickroom to make a person with fever more comfortable. The practical purposes of a fan often were only an excuse for carrying it as an attractive accessory to a costume. It has been written that a clever woman who knew how to flutter her fan could express any emotion with

Feather fan, pressed metal decoration with beads, Chinese, 1920.

it. This delightful instrument could be agitated so as to signify anger, modesty, timidity, mirth and all the stages of a flirtation. Sometimes called flirting fans, but more precisely known as quizzing fans, are those designed with large peepholes which were covered with a transparent material that made them almost unnoticeable. There were popular by the mid-1700's in England and Europe, and enabled the owner to look innocent yet miss nothing of the risqué play of the period. The same purpose was served by small mirrors which were sometimes attached to the guards.

Then as now, fans were thought of a as a woman's prerogative. However, for centuries men also carried fans. In England in the early 1600's, a man of any consequence owned at least two fans; one was to use when walking through the streets, the other for social occasions calling for full dress. These fans usually were of ostrich or peacock feathers attached to a handsomely decorated handle. Men still carried fans when exquisite folding ones were made in Paris in the 1700's, but before that century ended the custom died. As if in compensation, more and more women took up the tradition.

The origin of fans is lost in legends. The first fans were flat screen fans which did not fold. The Chinese invented these useful and beautiful articles, and there is good reason to believe that the Japanese introduced the folding fan, which is so familiar to us today, between 600 and 700 A.D. In ancient Egypt, the fan was a royal emblem of authority, happiness and repose, and in Mexico before the Spaniards came a fan was a symbol of authority. Fans also had religious significance, which was represented in the ostrich-feather fans of Assyria and Egypt, in the myrtle and acacia fans of Greece, and in the flabellum, a disk of silver or silver-gilt mounted on a long handle, of the early Christian church.

From a symbol of royalty, fans gradually became an accessory of the wealthy and an indispensable part of a costume. Fans were in general use in China and Europe by the end of the sixteenth century, and during the eighteenth century Paris became the center for manufacture of the finest folding fans. By the late 1700's, fans were so popular that not only costly ones of decorated parchment, vellum and silk were being made, but also less expensive ones of gauze and paper.

Undoubtedly one of the first fans was a palm leaf, and many other materials for fans were shaped in the same outline. Some palm-leaf fans were fluted or pleated. This may have inspired the screen fan which consists of a rigid mount attached to a handle; the earliest feather fans were of this style, and straw, cane, bamboo and grasses were woven into hand screens. Parchment, silk and linen could also be framed

Organdy fan with sequins, c. 1900.

and decorated as screen fans. This type soon progressed from its original leaf shape to round, square, octagonal, elliptical or pear shapes.

The folding fan is more familiar, for it became the dominant type in Europe and America. It consists of sticks and a mount. The sticks are a number of slender blades, with the two end ones slightly wider to form a guard. All sticks are fastened together at the handle end with a pin or rivet. The mount, also known as the leaf, is pleated and stretched over the sticks and covers from about one-half to two-thirds of their length. The folding fan varied in shape. In the sixteenth century it opened to about one-third of a circle, by about 1700 to a semicircle, and after 1760 to a slightly larger spread.

The folding fan was introduced to Europe primarily through Portuguese trade with India and the Far East in the late 1500's, and spread quickly from Italy and Spain to France and England. Its popularity by the 1700's was well deserved because of the fine workmanship and elaborate decoration lavished on it. Ivory and mother-of-pearl, delicately and intricately carved, were preferred

for the sticks. Lacquer, tortoise shell, horn, bone and fine woods also were used. It was not uncommon for these carved sticks to be embellished with gold, silver, enamels or even jewels. The favorite mount was vellum, particularly the sort made from the skin of newly-born lambs or kids; fanmakers called it chicken skin because of its thinness, strength and lack of grain. The earliest vellum mounts made in Europe and England were cut in fine openwork patterns which, like ivory fans, were sometimes combined with gold or silver lace.

When France took over leadership in fan production during the 1700's, the decoration became *gouache* painting. The themes varied from time to time, but rural and classical scenes, portraits and, much later, flowers predominated. The vellum or chicken-skin mounts sometimes had different paintings on each side with the more elaborate one done on the front of the fan. Leading artists and calligraphers decorated many fans and occasionally signed their names under their work.

Silk, lace, and paper perforated in imitation of lace also were used for mounts. Silk or lace might be decorated with painting, or embroidery and bits of mica, or perhaps tiny jewels might be added for sparkle. Colored spangles as part of the basic decoration became popular in the late 1700's. By this time too, less expensive fans of gauze or paper, the latter with printed decoration, made it possible for the average woman to own one. Some of these first printed fans were illustrated with current events or directions for dance figures. Printed fans also could be safely scented with perfume, which had not been practical for the more expensive fans with *gouache* painting. Heretofore, the only way to add fragrance had been to insert a tiny vinaigrette or scent box in the handle of a fan.

A variation of the folding fan, known as the brisé, became popular in the 1700's in both France and England and in America too. The brisé had no mount or leaf but was composed of a number of thin flexible blades which were fastened at the handle end by a rivet, and which became wider toward the top where they were strung together with narrow ribbon. Some brisé fans had overlapping blades on which a painting was executed. A small ivory one, for example, displays a narrow band of birds and flowering treetops against blue sky and clouds. Better known probably are the perforated brisé fans, either richly carved ivory ones from China or equally fine carved sandalwood ones from India. Many a perforated and carved sandalwood fan was brought by clippership captains to their ladies in the United States.

Whether used for a brisé fan or only for sticks, sandalwood is unmistakable both for its light tan, almost yellow color and its fragrance. Incidentally, one sign of good quality in a fan is sticks for which only one material is used for the full length; and if sticks are carved over the full length, then the fan indeed shows excellent workmanship.

Still another variation of the folding fan is the cockade or rosette which has a circular pleated mount which may be folded flat and which is supported by a handle. This style must have been the forerunner of the mechanical fan whose round mount can be folded and pulled down into an extension of the handle by moving a lever.

In the early 1800's in France, attempts were made to copy in smaller sizes many of the gorgeous fans made a century earlier. The Victorian years, 1837-1901, brought fans into ever wider use. A Victorian woman was as proud

Silk fan, Victorian fishing scene, painted grain on wood, c. 1880.

of her fans as she was of her jewels, and she took equally good care of both. Fans of silk, satin, gauze, lace, feathers, ivory and sandalwood, paper, parchment and, occasionally, leather ranged from dainty to impressive in their designs and proportions. Painted decoration was often charming although neither as skillful nor as elaborate as in previous centuries. During this era too, sticks of fine wood, ivory or bone were likely to have been pierced instead of carved, or perhaps carved only on one side; after 1859, pseudo-carving was done by machine for

Paper fan, Japanese design, c. 1900.

inexpensive fans. However, on costly fans of fine materials and workmanship, sticks often were inlaid with mother-of-pearl, silver or gold.

Dainty, small fans of painted or pierced ivory, of delicately tinted feathers or of silk were considered appropriate for young ladies. More elaborate white ones were customary for brides until about 1900. Often a bride's fan was made entirely of ivory with lace-like carving, perhaps of florals and birds; or it might have been silk painted with roses and forget-me-nots mounted on carved ivory sticks. Mourning fans, mostly black and gray, had appeared in the 1700's and Victorians continued the custom with rich, deep-black ones. However, a fan made of sheer black material embroidered with gold thread and starry gold sequins and mounted on tortoise-shell sticks was not a mourning fan; this, like the fragile black lace fans glittering with spangles, was for older women or to complement a ball gown.

The style always carried by Jenny Lind, the concert singer, became very popular in this country in the 1850's. Hers was a small fan that consisted of separate oval leaves of silk embroidered with sequins and mounted on carved sticks. It was made in colors and in black. Paper fans with colored lithographs also became common during the Victorian years. They were gay and inexpensive, although colors often were harsh and designs almost crude. Then came the paper or cardboard fans displaying advertising. No town was too small and no city too large to be included in the free distribution, a custom that extended well into the 1900's. Both screen and folding styles were imprinted with a message about some commodity such as coffee, or some place of business such as the corner drugstore. Some were novelties such as a cardboard fan with three wide blades secured to a cardboard holder. Hotels, stores and resorts were leaders in giving away advertising fans.

In the 1890's, it became a fad for young women to decorate their own fans. These were heavy black paper or perhaps black leather and on the folds the owners pasted cutouts of college pennants, printed headings clipped from stationery of schools, hotels and resorts, and similar mementos of parties, balls and travels. The more thickly the black fan was covered with clippings, the greater the belle who decorated it. The social life recorded is bound to fascinate anyone who finds one of these fans nowadays.

Many a nineteenth-century fan that was not high priced seems charming by modern standards. It is difficult, if not impossible, to date a fan accurately, unless it is a distinct style such as a Jenny Lind, or an advertising fan whose product or firm can be traced. Artists of the eighteenth century often signed the paintings they created on fans, but this isn't necessarily a clue to the actual fanmaker. An approximation of age may be possible if a fan is a family heirloom or if the owner can offer documentary proof of where and when it was made or purchased, and when it was first used. A valued or treasured fan should be displayed in an open position in a glass case or frame. This is important, since opening and closing an old fan causes wear along the folds. Old fans should be protected against ex-

cessive heat or cold, both of which can cause discoloration and separation of the parts.

Anyone who starts collecting or saving old fans is likely to come across accessories designed especially for them. For example, the boxes in which fans were purchased and stored by the owners are long and narrow and often are made of handsome material. Brocade and leather boxes, padded inside to the shape of the fan, were common even in the nineteenth century. Boxes covered with velvet, satin or plush probably are in good condition still, whereas a paper box may be falling apart. When they were new, many fans had a short length of silk cord in a harmonious color attached to the ring at the end of the handle. Longer cords or chains also were made so that a fan could be worn on the person. Some were finely-wrought chains of silver, othere were of woven or braided straw or narrow ribbon, and perhaps you'll be lucky enough to find one of these accessories packed away with the fan itself.

36. Sewing Accessories

The women who helped settle America had to practice many household skills, none of them more important than needlework. Many found time not only to make clothes for their families but also to embroider their own petticoats, handkerchiefs and "best" aprons. They produced their own household linens, quilts and coverlets for the beds, hangings to keep out the cold, chair coverings, cushions and carpets. By the early nineteenth century, as day-to-day living became easier, at least in cities and towns, women turned to needlework chiefly to decorate their homes, but learning to sew neatly and to do all kinds of needlework continued to be an important part of every girl's education. She was frequently encouraged in this by being given some of the small accessories that were helpful in sewing by hand. Really nice ones were often handed on from mother to daughter.

A needlewoman prized her thimble most of all, and many women undoubtedly brought their thimbles with them when they immigrated to America. It also was possible to buy silver and gold thimbles in the colonies during the seventeenth century, for they were one of the small articles

Sterling silver thimbles, c. 1920, American.

that apprentices invariably were taught to make by master silversmiths. Thimbles, of course, had been known and used for centuries before America began to be settled. No one seems to know exactly where or when they originated, although China, Egypt and Holland have been credited at one time or another with making the first ones. The oldest thimble I have seen or heard of is an Etruscan one of bronze used about 300 B.C. It resembled a ring with a flat side against which the needle could be pushed—

more like the sailmaker's thimble, which was worn on the thumb, than the thimble a lady slipped over the tip of a finger.

The thimble worn as a cap on a finger was known as early as the twelfth century, when crude ones of bone, metal or leather were being made in Holland. In the fourteenth century iron thimbles were used in Spain. Thimbles have been made of many materials: embroidered cloth in China, porcelain in France, bone of various kinds in many countries, ivory, onyx and several metals.

Unquestionably the most durable as well as some of the prettiest thimbles have been silver, silver gilt or vermeil (silver that has been gilded) and gold.

Silver and silver-gilt thimbles were being made in England in the early sixteenth century. The first ones had a cone-shaped top above a rim that often was engraved with a motto or a line of verse. Throughout the sixteenth century English thimbles were made of two parts, invisible after joining. The domed upper third was hand-raised or -cast and covered with indentations that were punched by hand; the lower section, or band, was shaped from the plate and seamed vertically. Until about 1750 all identations were hand-punched and consequently showed some irregularities. Symmetrical indentations impressed by a machine are typical of thimbles made after the mid-eighteenth century. Well before 1800 thimbles were being produced in England in a single piece by spinning. The lower band varied not only in width but also in decoration. In the early 1700's it was commonly chased or engraved with scrolls, a wreath of flowers and leaves, or displayed a cartouche enclosing a tiny crest. By the end of the century, filigree

work of fine wire was soldered to the band, but engraved decoration did not disappear. Some thimbles were enhanced with small semiprecious stones or paste. Enamel or some kind of pottery, such as faience or delft, added color and distinction to the bands of many thimbles made in Europe.

Thimbles were seldom marked by the silversmiths. However, a number of gold and silver thimbles, authenticated as having been made in America in the seventeenth and eighteenth centuries, are to be seen in museums and displays of historical societies. The silver thimble that Paul Revere made for his wife disappeared, but the gold one he made for his youngest daughter is owned by Boston's Museum of Fine Arts. This thimble is 1¼" long and has an indented top above a molded edge. On the body is inscribed "Maria Revere Balistier." Many thimbles made here during the seventeenth and eighteenth centuries were round cups no more than ¾" high.

During the eighteenth century in America, some thimbles were made from single pieces of silver, following a method used in Europe during the sixteenth and seventeenth centuries. Early in

Sewing bird, brass, 1853, American.

Fold-out sewing case, English, late 19th century.

the nineteenth century, patents were being granted here for producing thimbles mechanically and for rimming them without solder. Still, decoration such as flat chasing, engraving, bright cut and the like was done by hand. After 1850 some silversmiths kept busy producing only thimbles of silver and gold. The gold thimble became immensely popular here during Victorian years. A woman who owned one was justifiably proud of it, although I can't help wondering whether she saved her gold thimble for sewing bees and used a silver or bone one at home. A few thimbles were made in two shades of gold, and around 1880 silver thimbles with gold bands were introduced.

By mid-nineteenth century, thimbles were pretty much the shape and size they are now. They averaged ⅞" in length and, because fit was important, were made in different sizes. Both the top and upper two thirds of the sides were covered with tiny symmetrical indentations. The band, from ¼" to ⅜" in width, commonly was decorated with scrolls or foliage and flowers and, especially on a gold thimble, often had a narrow decorative edging. Above this on the plain surface was engraved the first name or monogram of the owner. More rarely, gold thimbles were banded with small moonstones, sapphires or other gems. As a general rule, thimbles, like other silverware, were simpler in America than in England. Some English thimbles made during the Victorian years were engraved, in the manner of souvenirs, to show a landmark such as London Bridge, The Tower or Saint Paul's Cathedral. Souvenir thimbles may have been made in America, but I have not run across any and certainly they never became as popular as spoons.

Not as essential as a thimble but adding a little fun to humdrum stitching was a sewing bird. This is a decorative but still useful variation on the sewing clamp used in saddlery to hold leather while it was being stitched. During the 1800's in America many women owned either a sewing bird or a fairly simple clamp that could be screwed to a tabletop or similar surface to hold fabric while it was being hemmed or stitched. Just as embroidery scissors in the form of a stork became popular in the late nineteenth century, so also did the sewing clamp in the form of a bird. The bird, about 3″ long, was made of brass, iron that was sometimes lacquered or painted gold color, silver or a white metal. The beak of the bird could be opened to insert the material by pressing a lever in the tail. The back of the bird often supported a tiny velvet-covered pincushion. Some of these decorative sewing clamps are said to have been made in the form of a dog rather than a bird.

Needle books or needle cases always have been important, for a needle was precious and easily lost. A needle book had leaves of

Pattern maker, German silver, early 1900s.

flannel in which to insert the needles. The covers may have been wood, probably whittled by a father, brother or sweetheart, or of a finer material such as mother-of-pearl. Needle cases with hinged tops also were common during the eighteenth century and perhaps earlier. A needle case took many forms and was made of many different materials. An eighteenth-century one of porcelain was molded and colored to represent a stalk of asparagus and was hinged to open near the tip. Of the same period are enamel needle cases tipped with a flower such as a tulip. By the nineteenth century needle cases were being made of silver and in odd shapes, such as a 3″-long banjo complete with strings.

Whether these little sewing accessories were pretty or only practical, it was natural that some convenient way of storing and carrying them developed. Earliest was the etui, a small container that hung from a ring attached to the wait. Etuis, common during the seventeenth and eighteenth centuries, were made of silver and jeweled, of enamel with a design of flowers, or of leather trimmed with silver. An etui could hold an assortment of small articles or, if desired, a small pair of scissors plus other sewing accessories.

Holding more accessories and easy to carry to wherever a person wished to sit and sew was the box, usually called a workbox, that appeared during the eighteenth century. The one a bride brought from her home in Connecticut when she married a Virginian in the 1790's is still cherished by her descendants. They call it "Anne's patchwork sewing box," for the shallow tray that fits in the top can be lifted out to get at patches and other things kept underneath. The shallow tray was indented to hold without slipping her cutting scissors, her emery bag like a fat red strawberry, a folded tape measure, spools of thread and an attached velvet-covered pincushion. There are no patches stored under the tray now, but there are the bride's needle book with carved mother-of-pearl covers and green flannel leaves, little mother-of-pearl boxes for spools of thread, and a couple of little paper packets of thread from England. Thread in these 1″-square paper envelopes was not easy to handle so it was taken out and wound on spools. These homemade spools were carved in the shape of a cross from applewood. Since they were made by young men, the number of spools a girl collected was one measure of her popularity.

Wooden lace medallion makers, c. 1890.

Although there is no darning ball or darning egg in this box, there was room for a simple one. This might have been merely a piece of wood whittled to the shape and size of a hen's egg or a small ball. Glass or china eggs also were used to slip inside an article to be darned in order to draw it smooth. Darning balls are said to have been made of ivory too. A darning ball with a handle, hand-blown of colorful glass, was too large to store safely in a workbox. These bright glass darning balls were made in the United States in sufficient number to be fairly common during Victorian years.

A sewing box is so relatively easy to come across now that it must have been considered indispensable during the nineteenth century. Its size averages 11" long, 8" wide and from 3½" to 4" high. The shallow tray is more often divided into compartments than indented to hold specific tools. One compartment was always stuffed and covered to serve as a pincushion, and one or two others sometimes had wooden pegs on which to slip spools of thread. The interior was lined with paper, usually wallpaper, or fabric and often had a looking glass inside the lid. In keeping with her mother-of-pearl accessories, Anne's patchwork sewing box was mahogany with inlay. Sewing boxes, or workboxes, were made chiefly of fine hardwoods such as walnut, cherry, maple or oak. The exteriors of the handsomest ones were decorated with figured veneers, with an inlay of wood in contrasting color or of mother-of-pearl. A few had light carving, perhaps of a flower spray, on the cover, or stencil decoration, usually in metallic

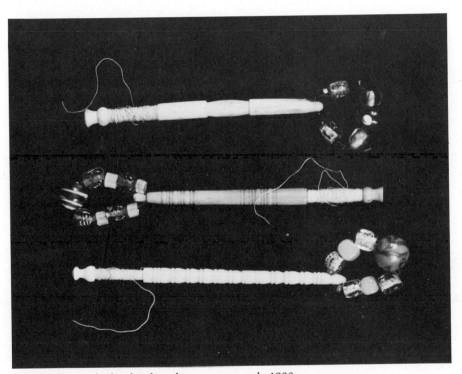

Lace bobbins with glass beads and ivory stems, early 1900s.

Cloth pincushion, early 1900s, American.

Wooden needle container, early 1900s.

colors. The plainest box of maple or oak was likely to have attached to the outside of the lid a small silver plate on which the initials of the owner were engraved in script. None of the many wood sewing boxes I have seen have been exactly alike, but each one had a tiny lock and key. Easier to carry, plain but beautifully made of overlapping splints, with a splint handle, were the Shakers' open sewing baskets.

When spools of thread such as are bought today became available, any number of different boxes were designed to hold a family's supply. A small wooden box for this purpose was exactly the shape of the common washtub with a little handle sticking up on either side and a tight-fitting cover. A larger and cleverly designed holder of about 1850 held twenty spools of thread in two shallow cupboards topping a shallow drawer. Each cupboard has a wooden knob at one side and is pierced with two alternating rows of five holes each. Thread from each spool was slipped through a hole so it hung outside without becoming tangled or snarled.

Although the workbox was certain to be equipped with a simple pincushion, most women

made
them
selec
roun
steel
per s
and
were
or en
lio a
Weal
wore
cloth
migh
fram
or ce
pearl
In
mad
Unit
prese
tons
visit
of tv
valu
ette's
W
their
othe
tons
that
ered
woo
ceal
the
wom
ing
man
mad
rivet
chea
look
Woi
kinc
and
chu
part
whe
gray
N
clot

owned one or more separate pin-cushions too. During Victorian years, plump pincushions in various sizes and shapes adorned every bureau and were a wonderful excuse for doing fancywork. The favorite sort had a needlework top with a floral, conventional or whimsical design worked in needlepoint, cross-stitch or other embroidery stitches. Pincushions with beadwork tops were a fad at one time and usually displayed a heavy all-over pattern worked out in beads of different shapes and colors. All kinds of fabric from linen to wool were used. Nowadays perhaps the most appealing of all the Victorian pincushions are the sterling-silver or silver-plated containers in shapes such as an oval or a heart, stuffed and covered with velvet or velveteen in some fashionable color.

Cardboard pin holder, 1860-80, American.

a pebbly surface. Many were painted or enameled, incised with gold, decorated with silver or bronze, or inlaid.

Victorians loved glass buttons if we are to judge by the many charming ones in cranberry, red, cobalt blue and other colors. Opaque blue and milk white buttons are as attractive as china ones made during the 1700's and early 1800's. Some glass buttons were painted in the style Mary Gregory used on pressed glass, others resembled minuscule paperweights enclosing flowers or millefiori just as large paperweights for desks did. Victorian gentlemen wore on their waistcoats "jeweled" buttons with glass centers and metal rims, but probably women preferred the glass-centered ones with glass rims in the dewdrop motif of pressed glass.

Equally fascinating to present-day collectors are the little transfer-printed china buttons called calicoes. Great-grandmothers would frown if they knew that these plentiful buttons that they bought on cards by the dozen to sew on their house dresses, their husbands' shirts and the children's clothes sell now for a dollar or more apiece. Calicoes, with holes in the center instead of a shank for sewing them on, are decorated with spotted or figured patterns typical of calico cloth in various colors.

More unusual china buttons also were transfer printed, which was the common method of decorating Staffordshire tableware. Like the tableware, buttons might display commemorative designs or a set of four to six each have a similar scene such as the four seasons or six of Aesop's fables. More expensive china buttons, made in the 18th and 19th centuries, included exquisite examples of decorated porcelain from the Coalport factory in England, from Meissen and other potteries in and near Dresden, Germany. Blue jasperware buttons with white cameo decoration in relief were worn first by men in the late 1700's and weren't necessarily made by Josiah Wedgwood, the Englishman who invented the process of making this type of stoneware. Buttons of Delft, the tin-glazed ware with blue decoration against a milky white background, probably were made in Holland, and Satsuma buttons have been imported from Japan since the 1800's.

Glazed pottery buttons with a brown, green or cream mottled coloring were produced during the 1800's at potteries in Benning-

Black glass buttons, late 19th and early 20th century, American.

Painted cera

ton, Vermont, Waterbury and Norwalk, Connecticut, and various other towns in this country. Then in the 1890's, when china painting was a fashionable pastime, young ladies wore hand-painted china studs down the fronts of their white shirtwaists. Favorite motifs for studs, which were inserted through button-holes, were flowers, Gibson Girl profiles and classic heads.

New England, and particularly Connecticut, became a center of manufacture for brass buttons, too. Waterbury factories must have turned out thousands of buttons for uniforms worn by all branches of the Army and Navy during the Civil War. Buttons worn by Union troops are fairly plentiful, much more so than those of the Confederate Army. Collecting military buttons of the United States can become a lifetime obsession because of the several branches of the armed services and the many wars.

Also of metal, chiefly brass, are buttons issued during Presidential campaigns or commemorating Presidential inaugurations. The custom started with George Washington's inaugural in 1789. For this, one copper button had a "GW" in the center with "Long Live the President" around the upper edge. Another had a linked border with the initials of the 13 original states. Other buttons with appropriate designs honored, among other Presidents, Rutherford B. Hayes, Zachary Taylor, Abraham Lincoln and James Garfield. Perhaps the greatest variety centered on William Henry Harrison, for buttons were produced in several sizes and with several insignia linked to his campaign: his portrait, a log cabin, a cider barrel, etc.

Painted ceramic buttons, late 19th century, American.

Only within recent years have synthetics begun to displace natural materials for buttons. The list is unbelievably diversified. Silver and copper were popular metals during the 18th century when a lesser number of buttons also were made of Sheffield plated silver and gold. Pewter was widely used in the United States during the 1800's, and brass and gold-plated brass were more popular 100 years ago than at present. Sometimes combined with a metal were minerals such as quartz, agate, jet and goldstone. Semiprecious stones, paste and flashing bits of glass in imitation of precious gems lent importance to many old buttons. In addition to the many kinds of glass and ceramics, mosaic, papier-mâché, enamels and cloisonné were not uncommon. Bone, horn, wood, leather, ivory and vegetable ivory were used generally for decades. Vegetable ivory buttons, long a European specialty but also made in the United States after 1859, were made from the nuts of the corozo palm in South America, which were first used as ballast for sailing vessels.

Many countries have produced pearl and mother-of-pearl buttons from various kinds of shells. Cheaper grades were cut from river shells. Mother-of-pearl buttons haven't always been as simple as those generally used today and no kind of button is more exquisite than some of the antique mother-of-pearl ones that were beautifully decorated with carving, piercing or engraving.

All kinds of decoration employed in various crafts, such as cabinetmaking, metalworking, pottery, glassmaking, printing and the like, were applied to buttons. They were enhanced by painting, enameling, embossing, chasing, engraving, carving, molding, piercing, cutting, transfer-printing and inlay. Silk and metal threads such as were used in lacemaking and embroidery ornamented buttons of the 17th and 18th centuries.

Material or decoration are as obvious classifications as military, campaign and commemorative buttons for collectors who decide to specialize. Others search for buttons with designs of flowers, insects or animals; a sport such as hunting, tennis, auto racing or sailing; or transportation such as bicycles, railroads or automobiles. Railroad buttons might depict a train or engine or come from a trainman's coat, and automobile buttons certainly should include one or more of the large metal ones sewn on the loose coats called dusters that were worn when riding in automobiles during the early 1900's.

The recognition and momentum that button collecting gained during the depression years of the 1930's should be proof that it need not be an expensive hobby. People will spend ten dollars without a qualm for a different kind of button or one that is needed to complete a set and, admittedly, much higher prices have been paid for a single button. The demand for one kind or another sets the current market price, but a great many buttons have little monetary value and probably never will. Most people collect buttons for fun, not as an investment.

A collection usually starts with an old button bag or box found in a sewing machine or much older sewing table. Occasionally a person is lucky enough to find a charm string, a fad that started among teen-agers back in the 1860's. Each one aimed to get 1,000 buttons to put on her string including an extra large, very fancy one called a "touch" button, and the girl who succeeded was certain to meet and marry her Prince Charming! At first glance, a charm string may look dingy and the buttons dumped out of a box or bag only a dusty pile. But spread out some of these buttons and start looking at them and fingering one here and there. Suddenly, eyes may light up at the sight of a calico button, a colorful or odd glass one or a charming small metal button with a cutout leaf silhouetted against its round cup. Their lure is hard to resist and the quest for more will never be boring.

Bracelet made of antique buttons.

Index

Adams family (potters), 53, 54, 56
Agate glass. *See* Marble glass
Agateware, 18-19, 29
Alabaster glass. *See* Milk glass
Amberina glass, 143, 144, 167
Andirons, 92
Anglo-American ware. *See* Old blue Staffordshire
Apostle pitchers, 24
Apostle spoons, 65, 72
Argand, Aimé, 182
Argyles, 75
Art glass, 143-47, 160, 167, 182, 183, 185. *See also* individual types
Augustus the Strong, 11

Banks, china, 16
Barber, Ralph, 153
Basalt, black, 15, 19, 30, 61
Basins, 82, 83
Bassett, Frederick, 81
Basting spoons, 72, 80
Battersea Enamelworks, 61
Beakers, 82
Bed warmers, 93
Belleek porcelain, 46
Bell pulls, 49
Bells: 94, 95-100; animal, 97-98; carillons, 96; change-ringing, 97; church, 95-97; crinoline, 99; crotal, 97, 98, 99; door, 100; figure, 99; hand, 99; sleigh, 97, 98; table, 99
Bell woman, the, 15
Bennington potteries, 13, 16, 24, 162, 228-29
Berry bowls, 149-50
Berry spoons, 73
Bible boxes, 194

Biedermeier baldpates, 204
Bispham, Samuel, 186
Bisque dolls, 209
Bisque figures, 12
Blue and white china. *See* Old blue Staffordshire
Boardman brothers (pewterers), 81
Bobèche, 106
Bonbon spoons, 73
Bone china, 29, 46, 61
Boston and Sandwich Glass Company, 107, 126, 133, 135, 139, 141, 153, 154, 156
Böttger, Johann Friedrich, 11, 18, 28, 51
"Bottle glass," 159
Bottles: 157-62; apothecary, 161, 162; barbershop, 161; cologne, 160, 161, 162; figure, 162; ink, 161; perfume, 160, 161; snuff, 159-60; stoneware, 162
Bouillotte, 110
Bow pottery, 12, 30, 32, 62
Boxes, wooden, 193-98
Brass, 89-94, 106, 107, 229
Brides' boxes, 195
Brisé fans, 215
Bristol pottery, 42
Britannia metal, 74, 75, 80-81, 164
Brooklyn Flint Glass Co., 126
Brooks, John, 61
Bru, 209
Bulb pots, 49
Burmese glass, 143, 144, 167
Buttons, 226-31

Caddy spoons, 69, 70
Cake baskets, 77
Calico buttons, 228, 231
Calico glass. *See* Marble glass

Candelabra, 91, 109, 110
Candle boxes, 89, 91, 195, 196
Candles: 105-106; spermaceti, 105-106, 108; tallow-dip, 105
Candlesticks: 16, 32, 42, 82, 89, 90-91, 106-108, 132, 134-35; crucifix, 135; dolphin, 107, 135; pricket, 106; tobacco, 108. *See also* Chambersticks
Cantonware, 52, 55
Caramel glass, 133, 146
Carboys, 158
Carder, Frederick, 147
Carnival glass, 27, 136, 147, 148-51
Castleford pottery, 18
Cat figures, 12
Caudle cups, 41
Caughley porcelain factory, 52, 63
Cauliflower ware, 19, 28, 30
Cellars. *See* Salt dishes
Cellini, Benvenuto, 163
Centennial Exhibition, 139, 166, 167
Chafing dishes, 75
Chalkware, 15
Chambersticks, 82, 90, 108
Chandeliers, 109
Chantilly porcelain, 12
Charm strings, 231
Cheese scoops, 71
Chelsea pottery, 12, 29, 30, 31, 62
China, origin of term, 51
China-head dolls, 204, 209
China painting, 167, 229
Chinese Canton, 18
Chinese export porcelain, 18
Chinoiserie, 12, 43, 44, 51, 53, 63
Chippendale, Thomas, 28, 173, 174
Chocolate glass. *See* Caramel glass
Clam-broth glass, 133
Clarke, George and Samuel, 184